Jomon Potteries in Idojiri ①
Tounai Ruins

Compiled by
Idojiri Archaeological Museum

Translated by
Norio Yokogoshi, Takeo Fukazawa, Freddy Bellouard

Texnai

Idojiri Archaeological Museum

In the southwest foot of Yatsugatake mountains, many Jomon ruins have been excavated and those tell us the culture and life of those days(about 8,000-2,300 years ago).

In the museum are chronologically exhibited more than 2,000 potteries and stone tools that are excavated in Fujimi town area and through which we can learn about the transition and use.

In conjunction with them, many other materials such as dwelling houses, foods and personal ornaments are also exhibited, and these are placed to be understood at first glance. In addition, the view on religion or the world view and mythology of that period have been revealed by the studies of those potteries and clay figures, but these theories are also unveiled enthusiastically with those exhibits.

Outside of the exhibition hall can be seen some more materials such as a couple of stone monuments, farm fields and a rock garden that contains stone tool materials in the 5,300 square meters site, and these contribute the studies of foods life and farm tools of those period. Also, at the archaeological site of Idojiri, we are able to soak in the Jomon world for while beside a restored dwelling, listening to the sounds of spring water that will never dry up. Next to the Archaeological Museum is situated the Museum of History and Folklore that is collecting folklore materials of this region.

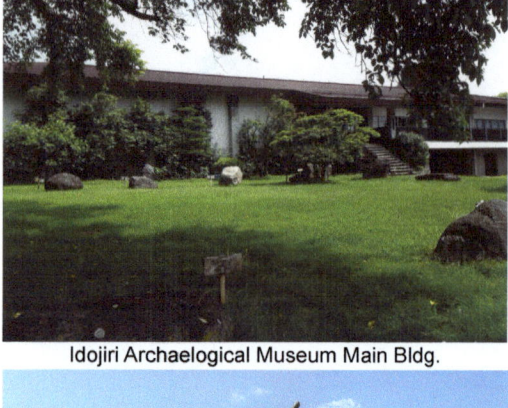
Idojiri Archaelogical Museum Main Bldg.

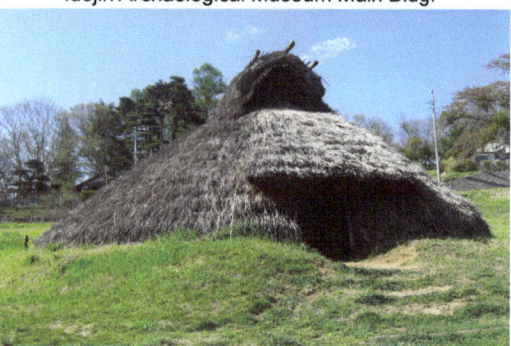
A Jomon dwelling restored at the Idojiri site

- Location: 7053 Sakai, Fujimi-cho, Suwa-gun, Nagano prefecture 399-0101
- Access by train: 15 minutes walk from Shinano-sakai station of JR Chuo Line
- Access by car: 6km for Shinanosakai from Kobuchizawa IC of Chuo Expressway or 2km for Shinanosakai from Kamitsutaki traffic light of National Highway 20.
- Opening hours: 9:00-17:00
- Closed days: Mondays, the day following National Holiday, Year-end and New Year season
- Entrance fee: ¥300.- (Adults), ¥150.-(Children)

Tel: 0266(64)2044
Fax: 0266(64)2787
e-mail: idojiri@town.fujimi.lg.jp
http://userweb.alles.or.jp/fujimi/idojiri.html

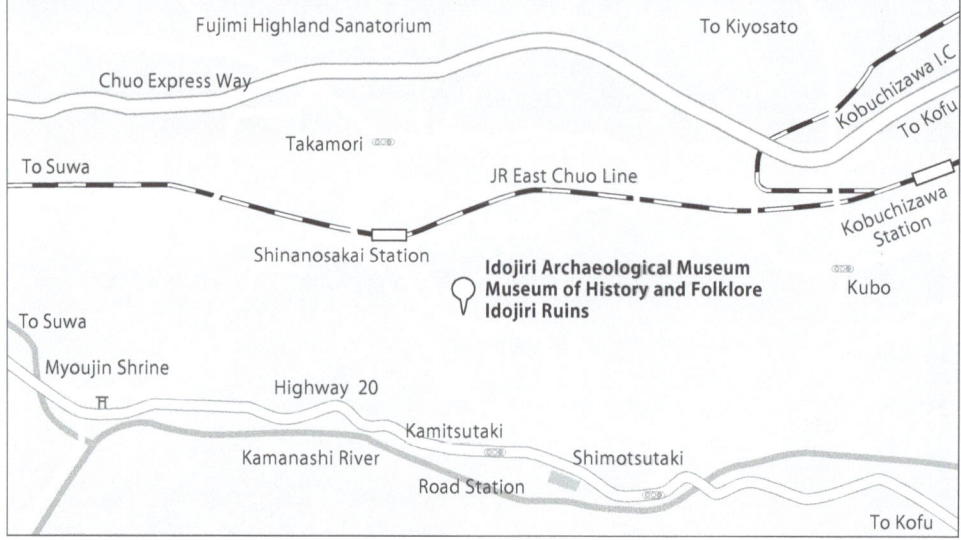

Jomon Potteries in Idojiri Vol.1 Tounai Ruins   Color Edition

Compiled by Fujimi-cho Board of Education Idojiri Archaeological Museum
Translated by Norio Yokogoshi, Takeo Fukazawa, Freddy Bellouard
1st Edition: Published on 15 October, 2015
Printed by CreateSpace, An Amazon.com Company
Published by Texnai, Inc.
        2-1 Udagawa-cho, Shibuya-ku, Tokyo, Japan Tel: 81-3-3464-6927   Fax: 81-3-3476-2372
        e-mail:texnai @ texnai.co.jp   http://www.texnai.co.jp/POD/
© Fujimi-cho Board of Education, Norio Yokogoshi, Takeo Fukazawa, Freddy Bellouard, 2015
ISBN 978-4-907162-96-2

Cover designed by Takeo Fukazawa

Forword:
Jomon Potteries in Idojiri and the Excavations

In the Japanese Islands, earthenwares and polished stone tools began to be produced approximately 13,000 years ago, but it was an American zoologist Edward Sylvester Morse who started to excavate and investigate the ruins of that period scientifically.

Invited by the University of Tokyo, Edward S. Morse arrived in Japan on 18th June, 1877. On his way to Shinbashi from Yokohama port on 20th June, he unexpectedly saw layers of shell exposed on the left cliff of the railroad near Omori station through the train window. Later he found a lot of archaeological remains such as potteries, bone tools and animal bones there, and started a full-scale excavation and investigation under the permission of Japanese government. It was the discovery of "The Shell Mounds of Omori", which was the opening of archaeology in Japan.

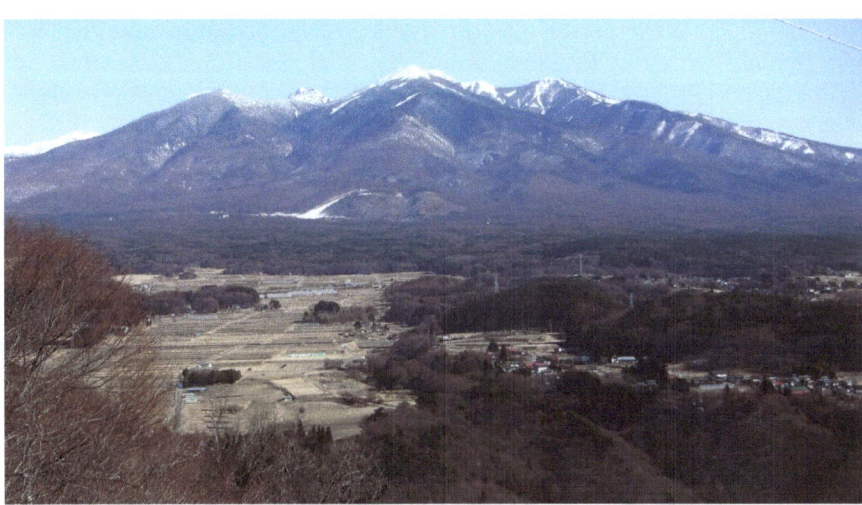

The southwest foot of Yatsugatake mountains. Many Jomon ruins can be seen in this area.

Many potteries were excavated from the Shell Mounds of Omori, and as some potteries had 'rope-pattern', he named them "Cord Marked Pottery" on his report.

Later it was translated into Japanese as "Jomon" and became the origin of "Jomon Pottery". Discussed in academic conferences, the period of Jomon potteries became known as the "Jomon Period", and the culture "Jomon Culture".

In the Japanese archipelago, Jomon culture lasted for ten thousand years and spread from Kuril Islands in the north to Kagoshima and Okinawa Islands in the south until a group of people who had the technique of wet-rice cultivation came to Northern Kyusyu from the continent in the 3rd century BC (or 10th century BC according to a theory).

Investigating the potteries of Jomon culture, the styles are so various according to the periods and locations, and quite a few of the potteries have high evaluations more as art than just vessels.

The Jomon potteries from Fujimi town in Nagano prefecture introduced in this catalog are also ones of them created in the middle Jomon period (approximately 4500~5500 years ago) and excavated in the southwest of Yatsugatake mountains located almost at the center of the Japanese Islands.

Even comparing to the potteries of other regions in the same period, the mysterious and powerful molding have already been well recognized both at home and abroad.

In Fujimi town more than 160 Jomon ruins have been found such as the Idojiri ruins, the Sori ruins and the Tounai ruins. It was since about 1893 when this area has been developed into the field from the wilderness. "When I was plowing the field, I found some very strange remains and got scared. To avoid a divine punishment I buried them back into the field carefully, and made a rice field on them" says an old man's story.

According to the report 'Idojiri (1965)' that was edited later by Eiichi Fujimori, an archaeologist of this area, the archaeological investigations in Fujimi town had proceeded as follows:

It was in 1915 that the first archaeological investigation was executed in Fujimi town for the first time and it was at a Dolmen-similar site by an ethnologist Dr. Ryuzo Torii of the University of Tokyo.

This investigation was reported in "The History of Suwa vol.1" that was compiled by Ryuzo Torii and it was the first publication on the Stone Age ruin of this area. Most of the ruins we know today in this area had been already found, but they had not been investigated academically yet. People had just found and picked up many remains of Jomon period unexpectedly when they were plowing the fields.

The first archaeological excavation and investigation in Fujimi town were executed during the war period in April 1943 by Fusakazu Miyasaka and Yukio Hoshina who had already excavated neighboring Togariishi ruins.

With the participation of Eiichi Fujimori and a researcher of this area Yuroku Muto, the excavation became more active, and the Jomon ruins known today such as Sori, Tatsuzawa and Kyubeione were investigated in succession.

From this period the local residents grew aware of the archaeology. The Idojiri Ruins Preservation Society was organized by the people in 1958 based on their experience of those excavations, and some students from the research club on Geography and History of Suwa Seiryo high school

Forword: Jomon Potteries in Idojiri and the Excavations

also started to join the excavation.

It was 'Idojiri (1965)' that was compiled by Eiichi Fujimori and published as a report on the excavations from 1949 to 1961. In this report was proposed "The Theory of Pottery Chronology" that determines the chronology by the potteries and established "The Chronology of Idojiri" based on the potteries uncovered in the ruins of Fujimi-cho. In addition, "The Jomon Farming Theory" was proposed here and it began to lead the researches of the Jomon Culture in Japan.

However, the more they excavate, the more number of archaeological remains they had, the safekeeping of those artifacts became a problem.

It is also noted in 'Idojiri (1965)' that "Gradually the former village office had become like an archaeological museum and the numbers of visitors increased." It was at that time that the construction project of a public archaeological museum was proposed.

For this proposal of the public museum construction, it is written in "Sori", the report published by the Fujimi-cho Committee of Education as follows.

"By the first and second investigations, Sori has proved to be a very important ruin which represents the middle Jomon period in the southern foot of Yatsugatake mountains.

However, just a few years later spread a rumor that says someone might purchase the whole area of Sori ruins and start developing a grape vineyard to produce wine. Hearing this rumor, the opinions of residents was divided by two.

One thought was if a large company comes to their village, it will be a good chance to develop this area. The others who participated in the excavations and recognized the importance of the ruins found it impossible to accept them and maintained that they should never let the people from Tokyo destroy the legacy which our ancestors left for them. It was quite a bit of simple insistence that was based on their local patriotism of those days, but the voices of residents on the preservation became a motivational force to move the municipal authorities with the assistance of the Idojiri Ruins Preservation Society which already had a considerable power as a preservation society.

At that time, as the municipal authorities was worried about the choice of a construction site of the institution that stocks and exhibits those materials they had excavated until then, they suddenly decided to purchase the land for constructing the institution for it within reasonable conditions. The institution that was constructed at the Sori site this way was the Idojiri Archeological Museum of Fujimi town.

In 1970, after the third excavation, the storage house was constructed first, and in 1973, after the fourth and fifth excavation, the main building was constructed.

Afterwards, the research on the ruins in Fujimi town were executed principally by the Idojiri Archaeological Museum and the Board of Education of Fujimi town.

Especially among those, some figuratively very unique potteries and clay dolls such as "Cylindrical Vessel with a statue of God" were unearthed from Tounai ruin in 1984 and 1988, and the 199 artifacts were registered as National Important Cultural Properties of Japan. "

And till today the research has been continued to ascertain the view of the world of those days based on the study of Jomon Farming and Earthenware Iconography.

At the Idojiri Archaeological Museum, we have been creating an image database of those potteries since 1996. And, at this time, we decided to publish a series of catalog for each ruins in the manner of Publishing On Demand toward the world. This catalog is the Vol.1 and contains 24 masterpieces of Jomon potteries excavated in Tounai ruins and registered as National Important Cultural Properties. The commentaries on each potteries and excavation sites were written and compiled based on the report "Tounai, the center of prehistoric philosophy" that was published in 2011. As for the photos, we selected at least three photos for each pottery from the multi-view photos that were shot for creating the image database and laid out one photo by one page.

Idojiri Archaeological Museum

Here are the authors and other contributors.

1. Authors of commentaries: Kimiaki Kobayashi, Seishi Higuchi, Takashi Komatsu
2. Drawing:
   Potteries: Akiko Oguchi, Atsuko Koike, Yuko Sato, Motoi Tanaka, Seishi Higuchi, Eriko Yamanaka
   Remains: Michiko Kobayashi
3. Multi-view photos: Hiroaki Seki, Norie Hiraide, Satoshi Torii, Takeo Fukazawa / Texnai Inc.
4. Legend:
    1) A direction of compass indicates magnetic north.
    2) A level string indicates the height(m) above sea level.
    3) A broken line indicates a part of buried remain.
    4) On the illustrations of potteries, a part of mesh indicates an exfoliation or loss of the surface.
       An index line on a rim indicates the front and back side that face each other, and an index line on a body indicates the right and left sides.
    5) An ID number of the last line of pottery data is the ID number of the image database.
5. Translator: Norio Yokogoshi, Takeo Fukazawa, Frederic Bellouard
6. Production: Takeo Fukazawa, Norie Hirado, Satoshi Torii, Shin Hamazaki/Texnai,Inc.

Contents

Forword: Jomon Potteries in Idojiri and the Excavations --------- 5

Discovery and Excavations of Tounai Ruins --------- 5

Catalog

    Cylindrical vessel with a statue of God --------- 20

    Bowl with a frog pattern --------- 28

    Big bowl with eyes on four sides --------- 34

    Cylindrical vessel with compartment patterns --------- 38

    Cylindrical vessel with cross pattern --------- 42

    Deep bowl with a statue of one-eyed God --------- 46

    Cylindrical deep bowl with oval compartment patterns --------- 52

    Deep bowl with non-decorative rim --------- 58

    Deep bowl with dual eyes and snake pattern --------- 62

    Deep bowl with deformed Mizuchi patterns --------- 68

    Steamer type deep bowl with snake pattern --------- 74

    Liquor pot with snake pattern --------- 78

    Both ears bowl --------- 82

    God statue type deep bowl --------- 86

    Diamond shaped deep bowl with frog patterns --------- 90

    God statue type deep bowl with a frog pattern --------- 94

    Deep bowl with compartment pattern of vertical stripes --------- 100

    Five-stage deep bowl with dual eyes --------- 104

    Clay figure with a snake on the head --------- 108

    Large bowl with breast-shaped rim --------- 112

    Deep bowl with dual eyes --------- 116

    Perforated flanged earthenware with half-man half-frog pattern --------- 120

    Deep bowl with Mizuchi pattern --------- 124

    Diamond shaped frog pattern type large bowl --------- 128

    Deep bowl --------- 132

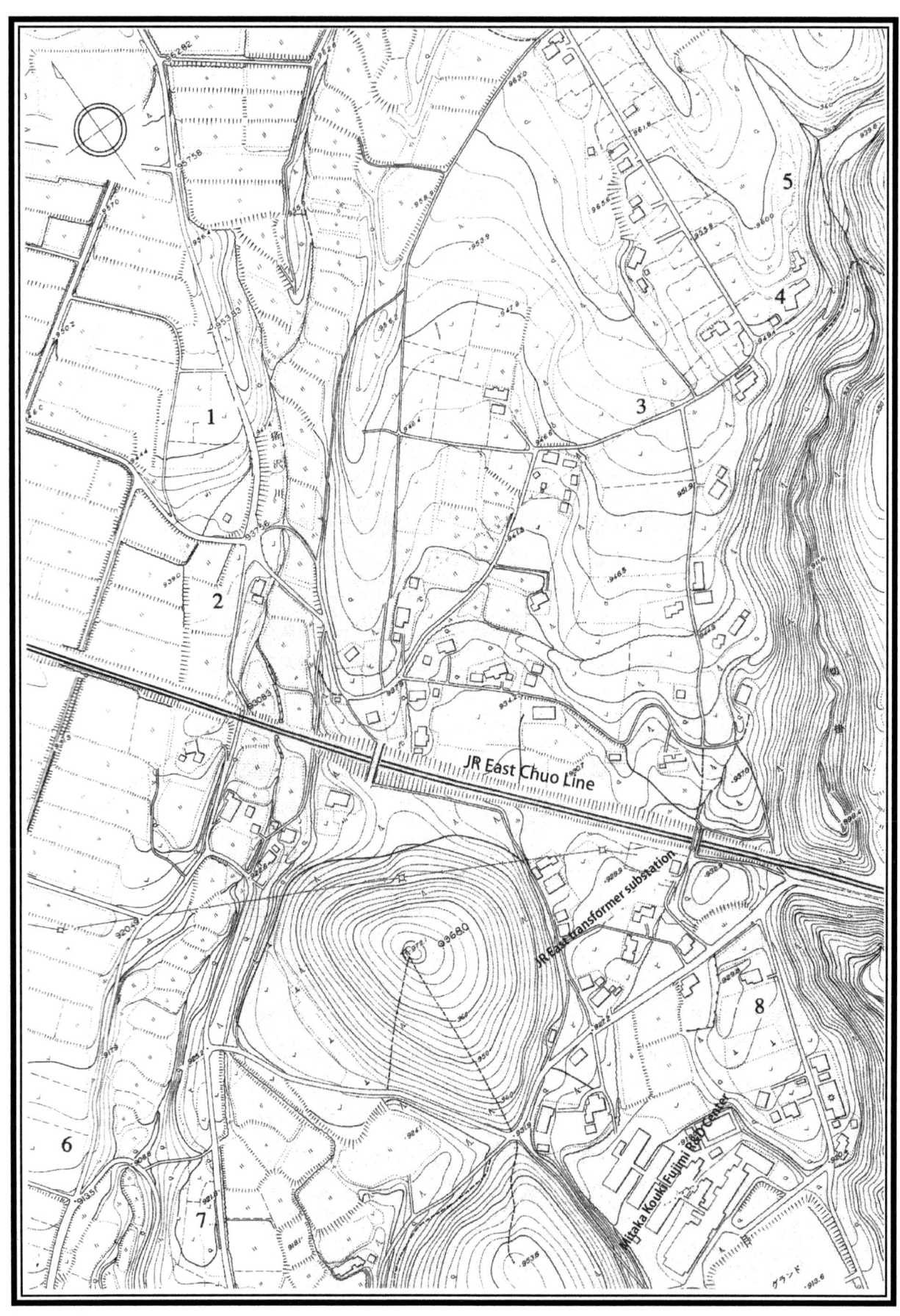

Topographic map of Tounai area (1:5000 , 1975)
1. Kyubeione 2. Mujinazawa 3. Tounai 4. Aramichi 5. Kagobata 6. Toudonomiya 7. Idaira 8. Moridaira

Discovery and Excavations of Tounai Ruins

From the Report of Excavations 'Tounai'(2011)

1. Environment of ruins

Tounai ruins are located in Eboshi district that is 600 meters away to the northwest from Shinanosakai station of JR East Chuo Line. Yatsugatake mountains seen from this area is accompanied by Mt.Amigasa at the center that is located in the southernmost of the volcanic belt and Mt.Nishidake and Mt.Mitsugashira on the right and left side at the same height and distance. The appearance is so tender and symmetric, it looks like an eagle trying to fly away.

Between the hillside and skirts of Mount Amigasa(2,524m) can be seen a double-headed rise(1,423m) like a nostril called Hanadoya. It is a lava cone appeared about 200,000-150,000 years ago, and the leva cone of Mt.Amigasa seems to be made 150,000-100,000 years ago afterwards. Miraculously thanks to the existence of Hanadoya, Mt.Amigasa has its frontality, and the line connecting the summit of Amigasa and Hanadoya makes it a central axis of the volcanic edifice and the foothills. This is the ridge line seen from both Suwa and Koufu basins and it indicates the direction of East and West. And, the right bank of Mujinazawa river in Eboshi district is located on that extension.

It might be because of that kind of geographic conditions, but, many ruins from Early to Mid Jomon period are crowded along the ridge and it forms the west group of the Idojiri ruins that are divided by Kikkake river. Those are the ruins such as Kyubeione, Mujinazawa, Tounai, Aramichi, Kagobata, Toudonomiya, Idaira and the others (see Topographical map of Tounai area[1].

Among them, three ruins of Kyubeione, Tounai and Aramichi which belong to the former half of mid Jomon period are located in a line at elevation of 950 meters. Although only one dwelling has been found in Aramichi, but it is located 150 meters away to the east from Tounai on the end of a gentle slope of a narrow ridge. Kyubeione is located in 350m west at the right bank of Mujinazawa River. It is a dwelling site from Early to Mid Jomon period. As Tounai is a dwelling site settled in the Mid period, some relationship with the preceding ruins of Kyubeione can be assumed obviously.

It is a rather slow ridge for this neighborhood with the width of 120 meters from East to West, and 230 meters from North to South is assumed to be the ruins area. At the period of development after the war, it is said that the upper part of bypath through Takamori district today was a pine forest, and the lower part was a forest of mountain cutting. There

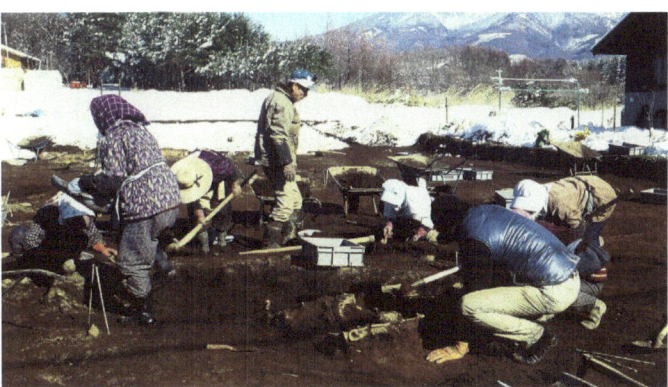

Excavation by Fujimi-cho Board of Education, 1984

were three springs and one of them is still welling just below the intersection of the west end of ridge and the bypath. Another one is located 100 meters away to the west and only one rice-field was cultivated those days. Although the other one was located at a field near a longitudinal road for the development of Takamori of the east side, the water flow seems to have changed because of a road improvement in Heisei period and the spring is said to have dried up[2]. Probably several thousand years ago, people who lived around here would use these springs.

2. History

(1) Discovery of ruins

After the war in 1947, this area began to be developed by the Development Agency of Farmland to increase food production, and 5 households were settled. One of them was Mr.Tatsuo Kodaira. He was from Chino City, and his parents' house was close to Mr.Husakazu Miyasaka's house. As his father was also a teacher, from the period of elementary school to senior elementary school, he was forced to help the excavations of Togariishi ruins during spring, summer and autumn vacations and is said to have become interested in potteries and stone tools eventually.

The reclamation work was like this: about 4 six-ton tractors like tanks that were being used in the military came to the place and by bounding 5 or 6 scrubs and pines, uprooted them with a thick steel wire of 5 centimeters in diameter. After that they put large ploughs on the tractors to plow, and at the end they developed the land by hand about 33 m² a day with reclamation shovels and all-purpose shovels with three teeth. By this kind of reclamation works, the ruins of Stone Age came up to the surface of the ground.

---

1 As for Kyubeione,Mujinazawa and Aramichi ruins, they are reported in 'Idojiri' edited by Eiichi Fujimori(1965).
Kagobata ruins are reported in 'Investigation of Kagobata ruins in Fujimi town'by Yuroku Muto(1968).
Toudomiya and Idaira ruins are reported in 'Toudonomiya'(1988)
Idaira ruins are also reported in "Idojiri".

2 According to the story by Tatsuo Kodaira, Hisakazu Nakamura and Kazunori Kobayashi.

His wife Kazuko he got married with before long was also interested in history, and the couple became to collect the potteries and stone tools at intervals of their hard labors. At that time, as his father Kesao Kodaira showed Miyasaka a grip of a pottery with whorl pattern, the first excavation started. In November 1953, the excavations were executed at Tatsuo Kodaira's field and in March following 1954, at Takao Fujimori's field, and the dwelling site 1&2 and 3 to 8 were found there. For these excavations, Tatsuo Kodaira, Ken Masuzawa and a student team of the Geography and History Club of Suwa Seiryou highschool and Okaya-Higashi high school partipated[3].

For your information, by a curious coincidence in the same summer 1953 the dwelling site #1 was also excavated in the neighboring Aramichi district by Suwa Archaeological Institute of Eiichi Fujimori[4].

(2) Former excavations

Much later in autumn 1961, a construction of water pipes was carried out running obliquely through the ruins. In a construction ditch of 70cm in width and 1.3 m in depth that was made only by hand drilling, about 7 spots of cross sections of dwelling sites were exposed. Tatsuo Kodaira and Kunimitsu Fujimori took charge of the works. In the easternmost dwelling site a coal seam of 15cm in thickness was piled up and it was assumed as a dwelling site caught in a fire.

Motivated by this construction, in March and June following 1962, new excavations were started by the Idojiri Preservation Society. The Preservation Society that was organized after an epoch-making result of an excavation at Idojiri ruins in spring 1958 had been investigating notable ruins every spring. It was the fourth year's excavation and the student team of Geography and History Club of Suwa Seiryou Highschool participated after a while from the excavation in Idojiri. In March in an area of 11m in longitude and 12m in latitude were found like a festival site or a grave and it was named "special remain'. They excavated the dwelling site #9 in June.

Also, from summer to winter in the same year, Tatsuo Kodaira discovered many relics at several spots and confirmed the existence of each dwelling site. #10, 11, 14 and 15 correspond to it. The discovery was thanks to their farm work and the labors of pulling up remaining roots of pines.

In July 1965, the official report 'Idojiri' was compiled by Eiichi Fujimori and published from a publisher of arts.

---

[3] Annual report of Japanese archaeology 6 in 1963 'Tounai ruins in Suwa, Nagano Prefecture(first)' by Husakazu Miyasaka
Annual report of Japanese archaeology 7 in 1958 'Tounai ruins in Suwa, Nagano Prefecture(second)' by Husakazu Miyasaka

[4] 'Potteries of mid Jomon in Aramichi, Suwa District, Nagano Prefecture' Archaeological notebook 1 in 1958 by Tsugio Matsuzawa
'Ruins in Aramichi, Suwa District, Nagano Prefecture's Annual report of Japanese archaeology 6 in 1963 by Eiichi Fujimori

The records of excavations in Tounai ruins until then were described in the report.

(3) Investigations in accampany with housing land developments, — Excavations of Dwelling site #32

When almost 20 years had passed since then, the world had been changed drastically. In spring of 1984, a part of the ruins was sold as a villa site($394m^2$). For this unexpected news, suddenly a person in charge of cultural assets of the town made contact with the new owner. However, due to a reason that the ground might be in danger of sinking, the pre-excavation could not be accepted. However, the investigation at a trench and an excavation at an entrance of the water main in the presence of the owner were accepted.

The excavation was executed from the 8th to the 27th of May and three spots of dwelling sites could be confirmed. One of them on the east side was a buried layer. Kodaira examined it and judged it to be the second dwelling site that was excavated in 1963 according to the location in the whole.

Late in autumn, the town got news from the landowner that they are scheduled to sell a neighboring land ($732m^2$) as a villa site. This time, they agreed to excavate in advance and started an urgent investigation. They began the work on the 22th of November and barely finished digging up before the 24th of December and buried it back with heavy machines on the 29th. Total 11 dwelling sites including #32, lots of small pits like tombs and a part of a so-called Central Square of an annular village were unearthed. It was also at that time that the 'Cylindrical Pottery with a Statue of God' was found from the dwelling site #32.

(4) Exposure of stones by deep plowing

One year later, in the end of 1985, some large-sized tractors came into a field to plant corn for animal consumption and a deep plowing was executed. Due to this deep plowing, lots of stones in shallow ground came up to the surface. Although many fragments of potteries and stone tools were scattering in the field, any entire lump of pottery was fortunately not found. The deep plowing continued until the winter of 1988 and the neighboring field was also plowed deeply. Next, a field under a byway crossing the ruins from the east to the west was also plowed as well and many stones exposed. Unavoidably on all such occasions, they executed plane-table surveying and stored them in the Archaeological Museum after the numbering.

The number of stones excavated from two lands above the byway was approximately 130. They vary in length over 60cm to fist size, and the shapes were also various like flat, pillar, round rice-cake and polished hand mill. Most of them were andesites and some were dolerites or greywackes. Also, in the north side of a field, six dwelling sites were confirmed. The site was circular and blackish, and fragments of potteries could be found here and there.

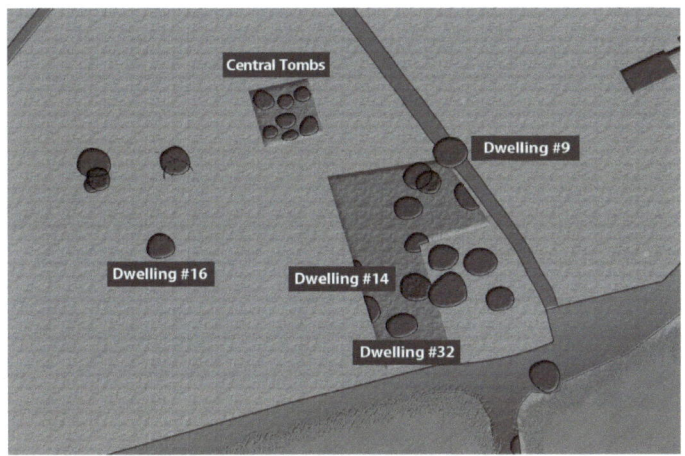

Dwelling sites of Tounai

Meanwhile, the number of stones excavated from a field under the byway was over 30. Half the number was pebbles of andesites bigger than 40-50 cm in diameter. Some of them exceeded 70cm.

(5) Investigations due to road improvements

In 1988, some road improvements for widening started on a road in Takamori in the eastside and a road in Tounai district. In accordance with this, a latitudinal road to Takamori district and an eastern longitudinal road of the ruins became targets for the excavations.

Then, the excavations were executed in the latitudinal road area from the 16th November to the 1st December and in the longitudinal road area from the 26th of March to the 27th of April in the next year. Subsequently, from the 13th of September to the 29th of November in 1988, the longitudinal road area was excavated. 1 dwelling site and about 100 small pits were found in the latitudinal area of 1600m^2. 9 dwelling sites and 60 small pits were investigated in the longitudinal area of 750m^2.

With these, the urgent investigations for 6 years completed the first stage.

Much later in 2008, an outdoor branch office of a radio system for disaster prevention was to be established in a field, they investigated that area from the 9th to the 21st of September. The area was 10 m^2 and no remains were recognized.

(6) Protection of ruins

In the spring of 1990 when the excavations associated with the road improvements were finished, a part of the field neighboring with north side of the previous area for a villa site was also being sold as a housing site. If this area becomes a housing site, the eastern half of the central part of the circular village will get lost. So, all they could do was to purchase the relevant lands. The reason why the mayor decided it mostly depended on the existence of the 'Cylindrical Vessel with a Statue of God' that was excavated 1984.

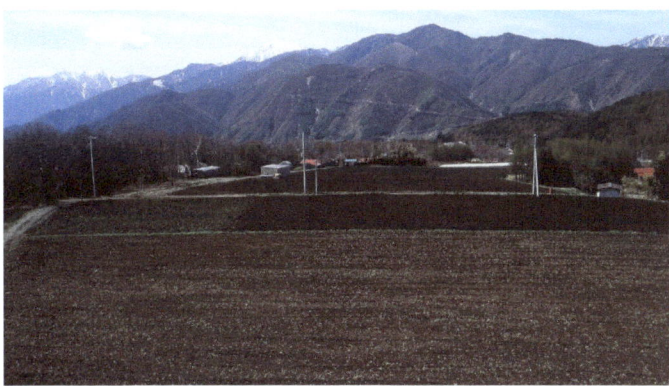

Tounai ruins in spring, 1983

After many complicated negotiations with the land owner, in April of 1991, the town finally could purchase two lands of 656m^2. Furthermore, 1,630m^2 that belongs to the former owner was also purchased in December, and remaining 772m^2 and 325m^2 in a forest were bought in October of 1993. In total, 5 lands of 3,382m^2 became owned by Fujimi town.

However, after 1994, the finance of the town became hard, and interruption of more purchases got unavoidable. Later in March of 2006, the Board of Education assigned the municipal lands and neighboring Mitsutomo Fujimori's field (1245m^2) as the historic sites of Fujimi town.

Meanwhile, in June of 2002, 199 artifacts excavated from Tounai ruins were assigned as National Important Cultural Properties of Japan. Those were 47 potteries and 151 stone tools that were excavated in the special remains and the dwelling sites #9 and #32, and 1 clay figure excavated from the dwelling site #16.

One of the municipal property's 'Clay figure with a snake on the head' was donated to the Board of Education of Fujimi town by the three co-discoverers Tatsuo Kodaira, Yutaka Kobayashi and Yuroku Muto in November of 2001[5]. On that occasion, the clay figure was named 'Shrine maiden with a snake' at the suggestion of another discoverer Kazuko Kodaira.

(Kimiaki Kobayashi)

---

5 Incidentally, a commemorative exhibition for assignment of artifacts from Tounai ruins to cultural properties 'Reviving Jomon Kingdom in the plateau' was held.
Illustrated book of commemorative exhibition 'Tounai' Board of Education of Fujimi Town 2002.
Lecture texts 'Reviving Jomon Kingdom in the plateau' Board of Education of Fujimi Town 2003.
'Reviving Jomon Kingdom in the plateau' Gensousya publishing 2004

Discovery and excavations of Tounai ruins

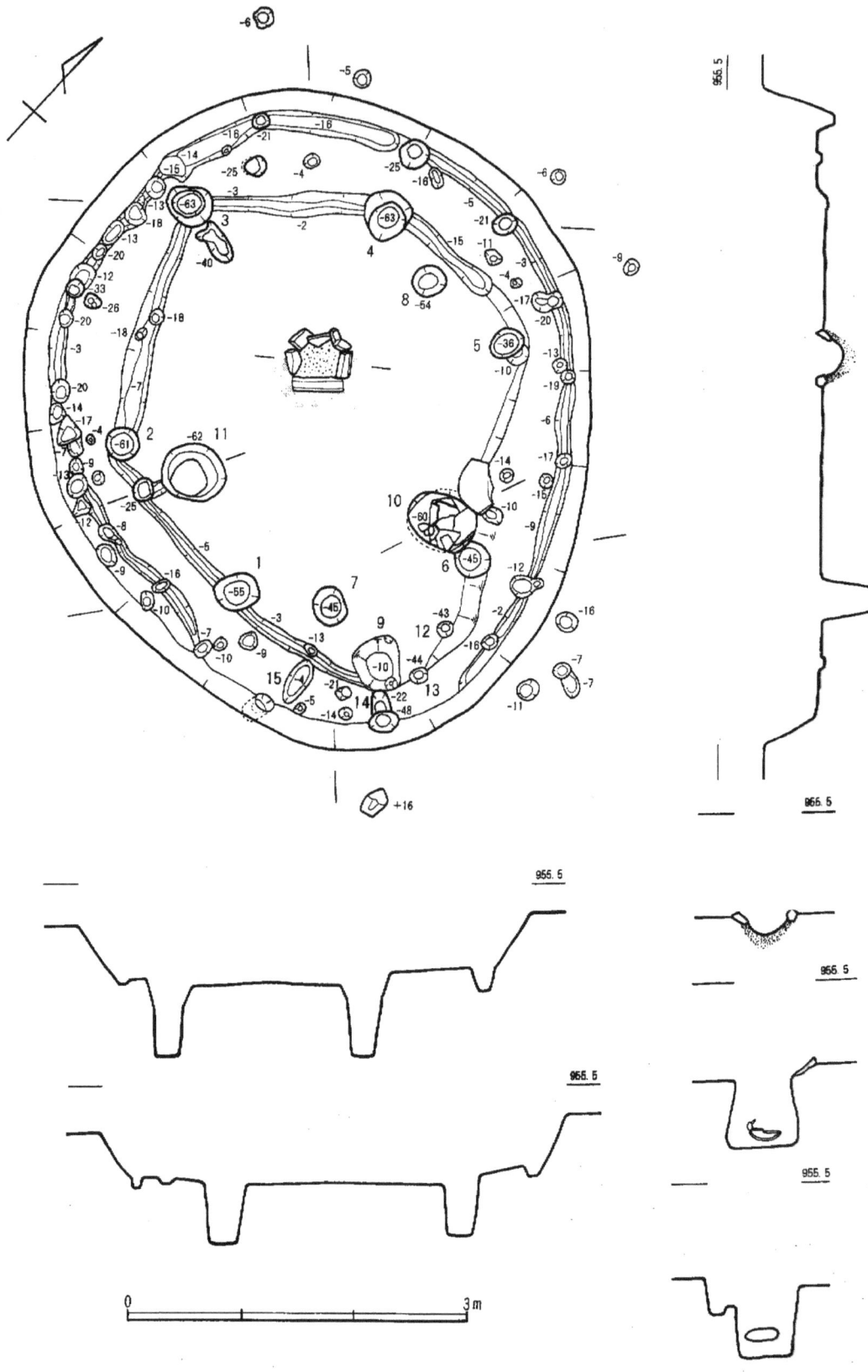

Fig.1　Dwelling sites #32　(1 : 60)

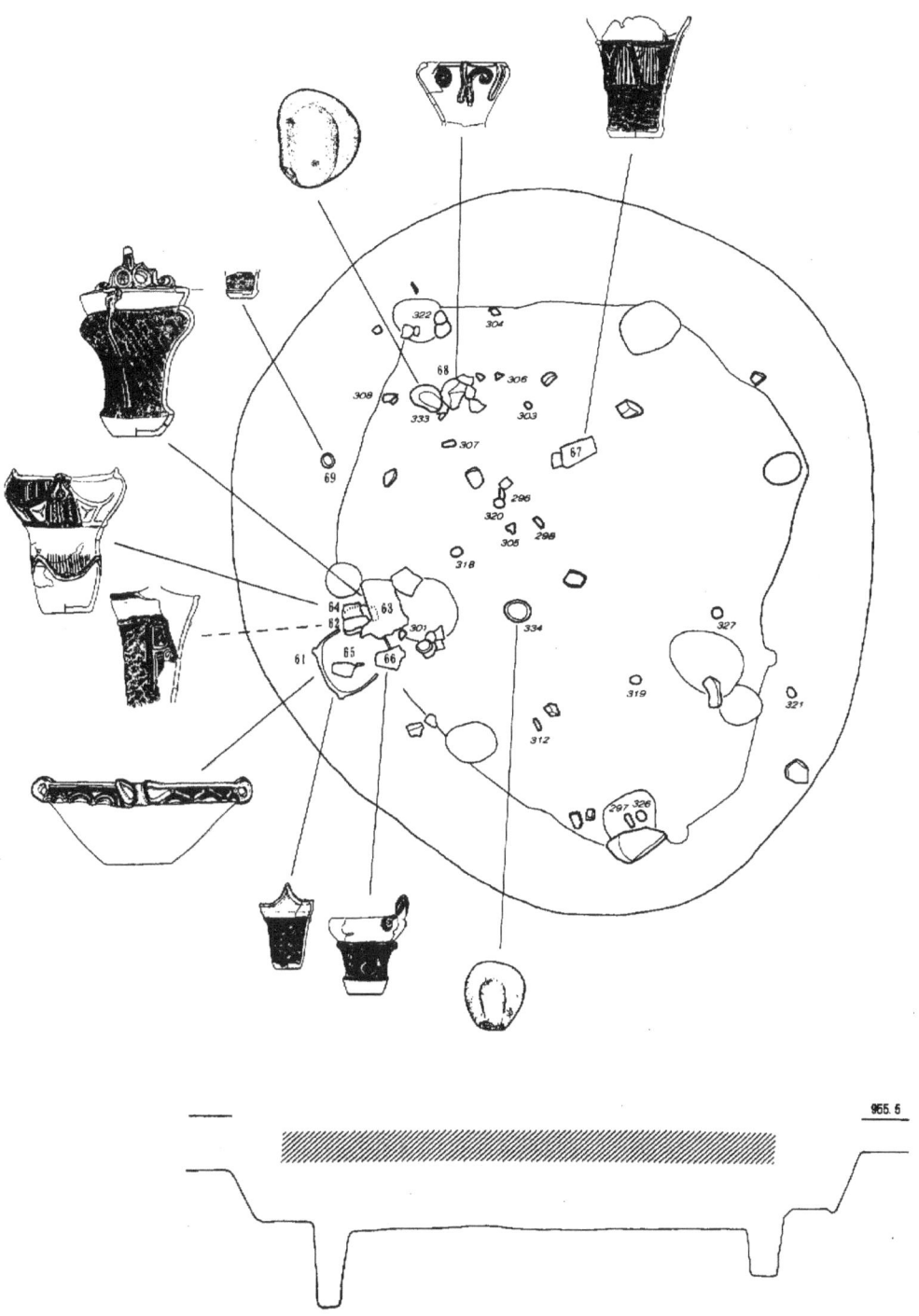

Fig.2 Potteries uncovered at the dwelling sites #32, upper layer (1 : 60)

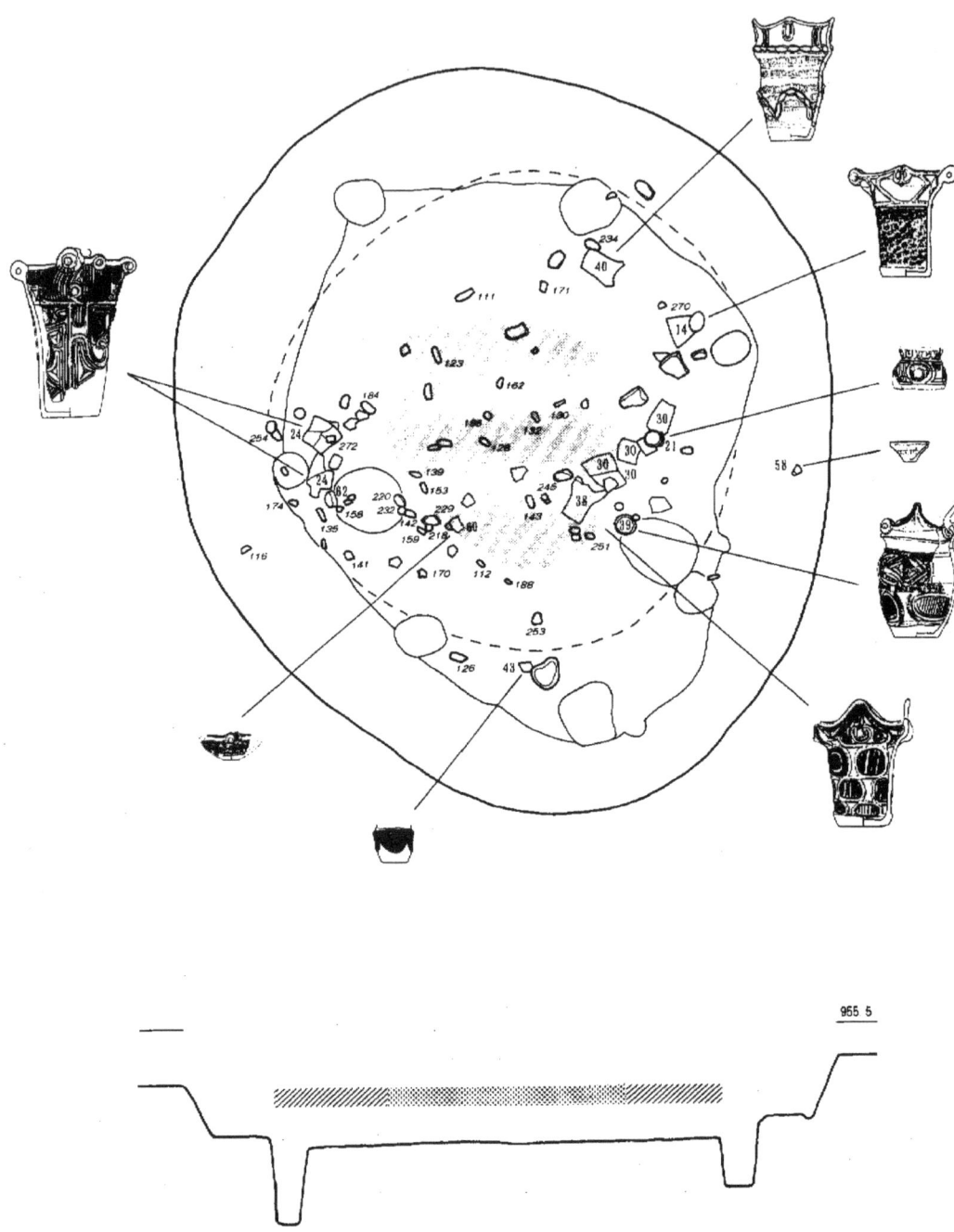

Fig.3　Potteries uncovered at the dwelling sites #32, upper layer（1：60）

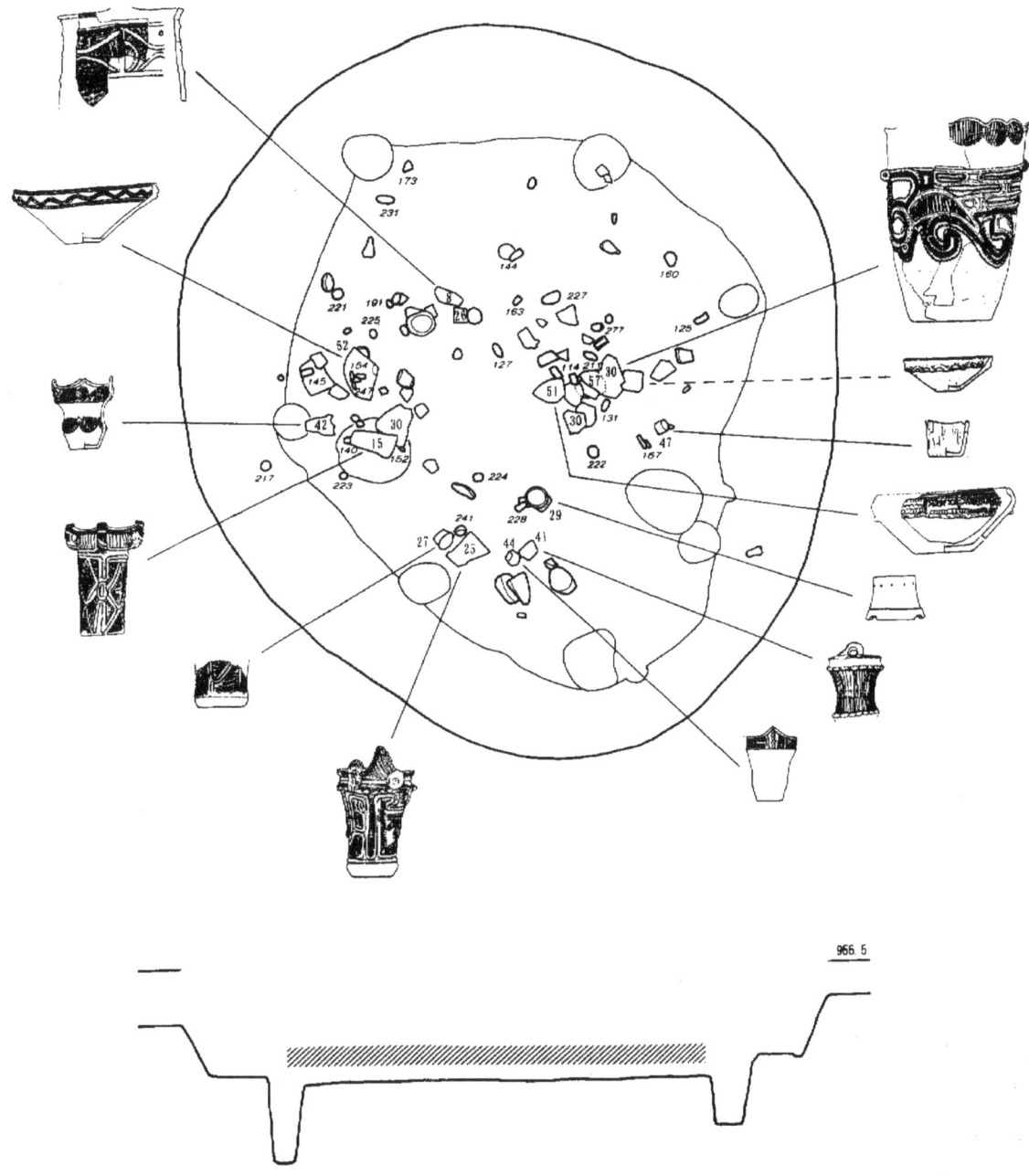

Fig.4　Potteries uncovered at the dwelling sites #32, middle layer（1∶60）

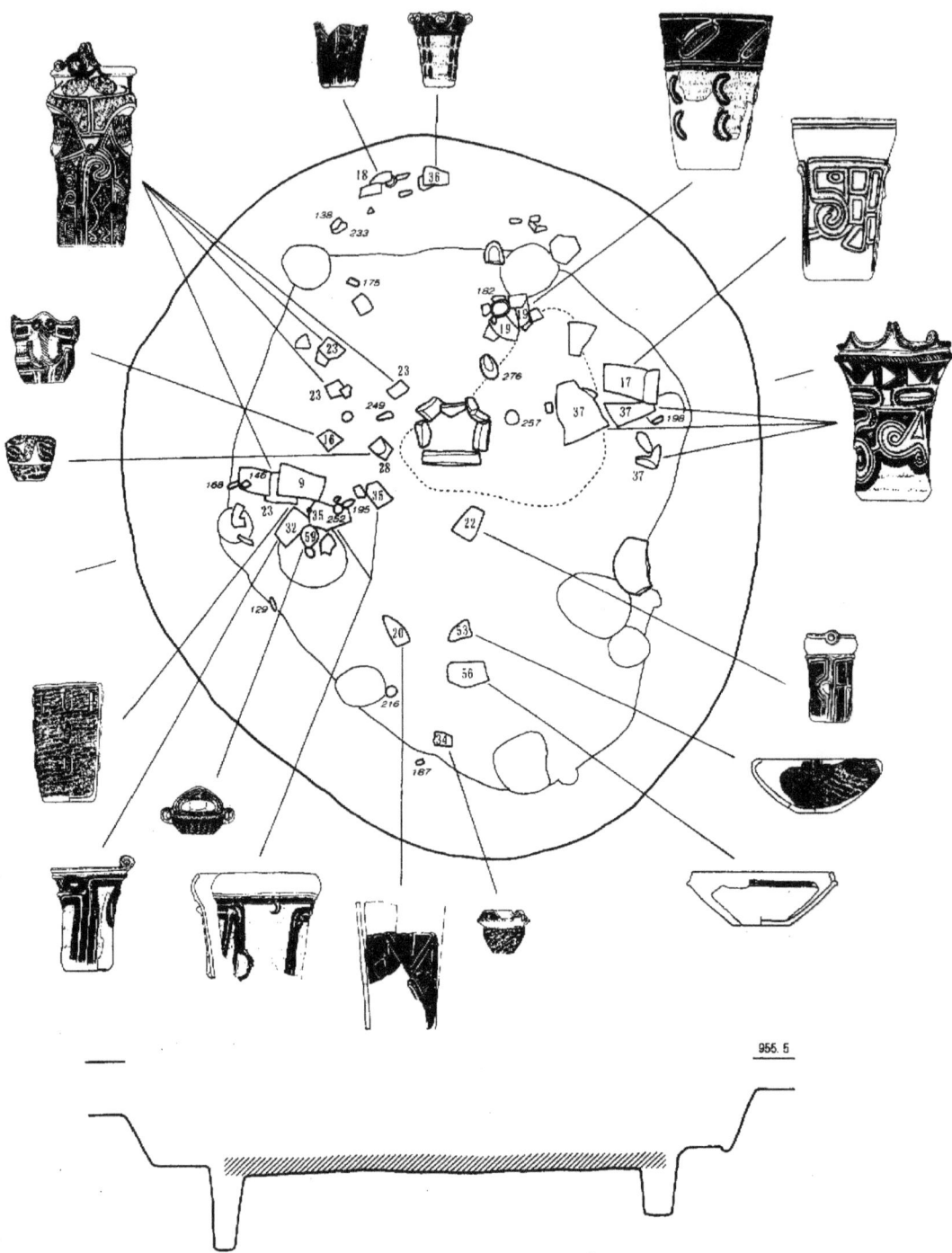

Fig.5 Potteries uncovered at the dwelling sites #32, bottom (1:60)

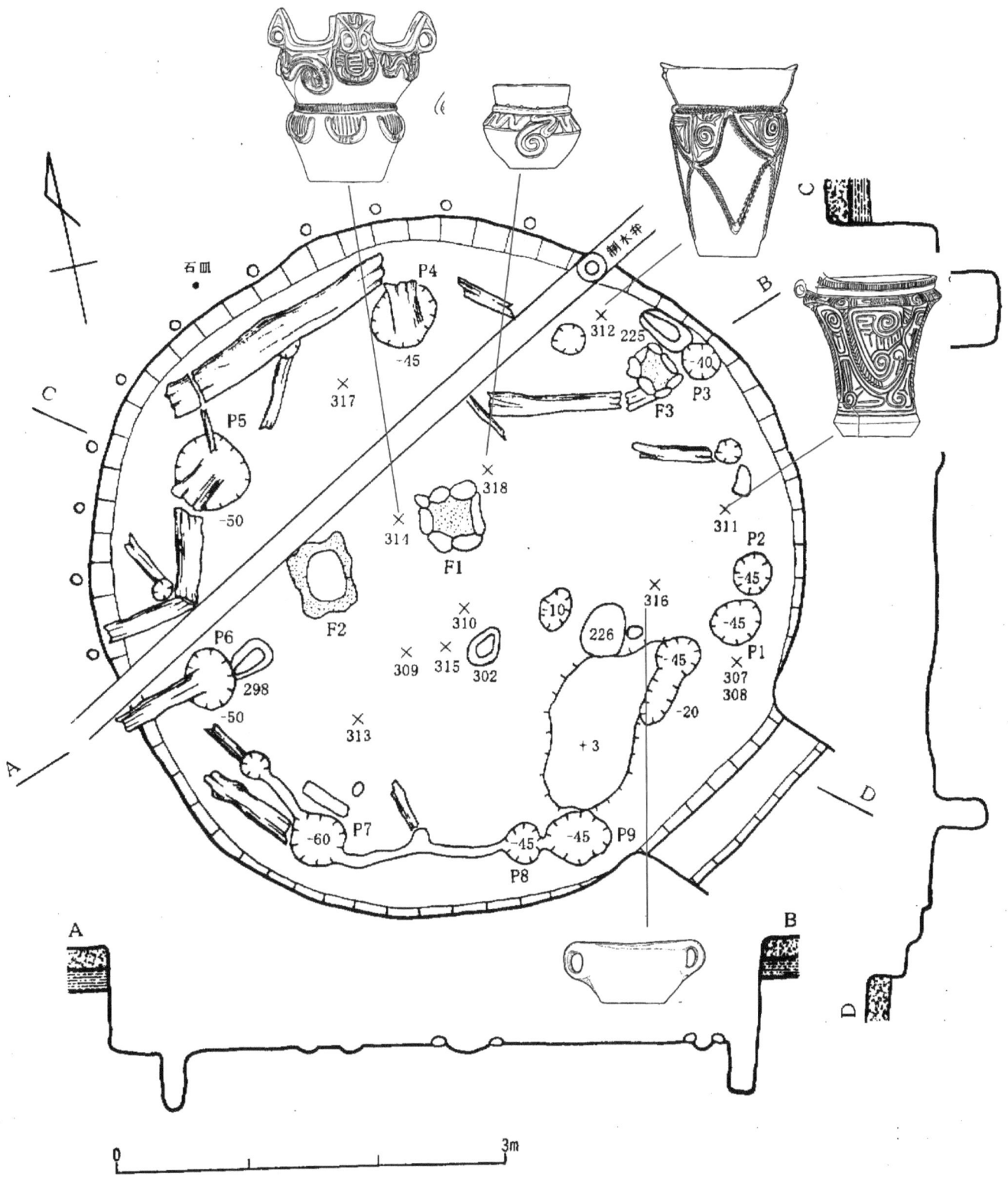

Fig.6 Potteries uncovered at the dwelling sites #9 (1:60), remain number based on "Idojiri"

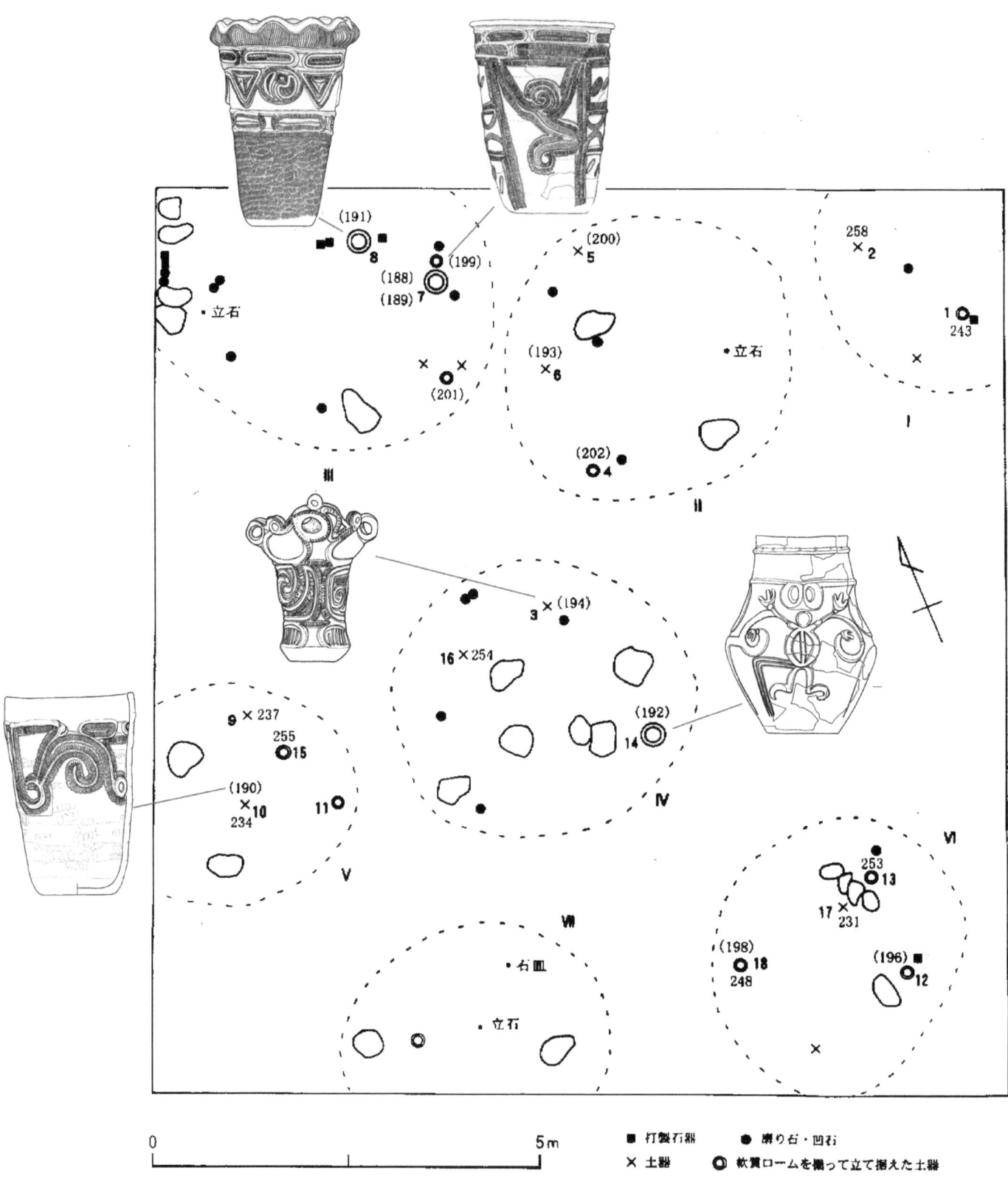

Fig.7 Potteries uncovered at the special remains (1:100), remain number based on "Idojiri"

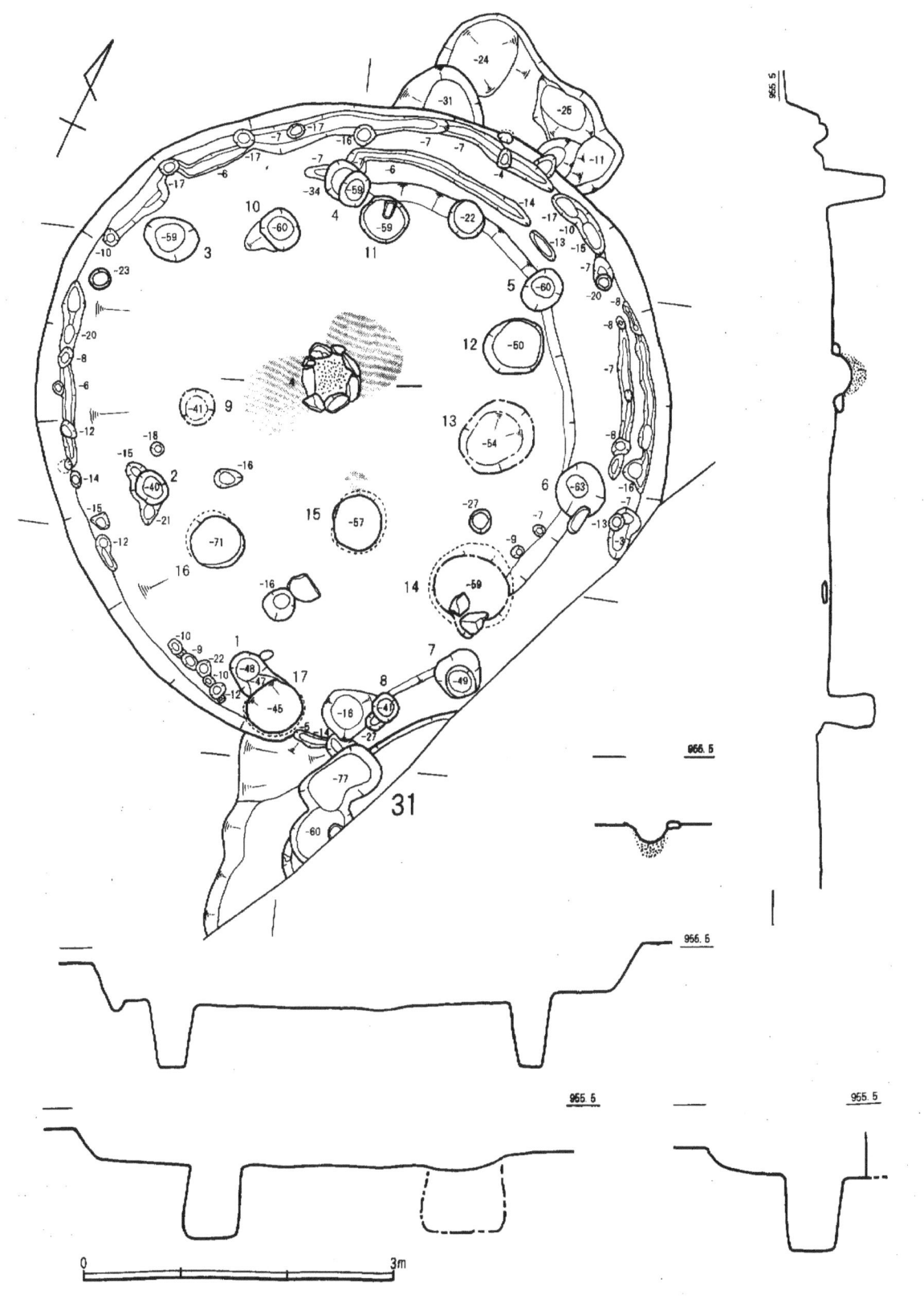

Fig.8 The dwelling site #14 & #31 (1:60), remain number based on "Idojiri"

Catalog

Cylindrical vessel with a statue of God
Tounai ruins
Tounai style I
Dwelling site #32, lower layer
Excavated in 1984
Middle Jomon, Middle
4,700 B.P.
55.7cm(H), 21.5cm(D)
"Tounai Report" P.132
ID-038

This is the most excellent masterpiece of Jomon pottery. Unfortunately, the bottom is missing. On the hollow head are expressed only two eyes. Left eye is round and facing the front. Right eye is vertically long along the lip like a drop, and the outer corner curls at the top of head. On the left rim of the left eye is arranged a small ring. On the back of the head, a spiral ring is arranged and goes through to the left eye. On the nape, a small-hill-like swelling like an oblique oval is arranged symmetrically. The shoulder is plump and roundish. Regarding the both shoulders, the inner wall is made like a hemisphere cave and swells. Both arms curl inwards and hollow to the elbows. Only left arm has a small lump and gets flat and close to the wall from there.

The wide inverted triangular back is almost flat but slightly curving. The back is divided into two and the right edge of the hip close to the body curls and slightly bends. On the legs of the lower half, a wide convex belt rises and curls like a bracken. On the front side of the statue of God, a belt-shaped pattern is carved through the wall obliquely. The upper end is an oblique ring as if it got out of the rim like a thick hoop.

The lower end also has a large ring pattern. By both shoulders, a pair of strange vertically long drawings is arranged symmetrically. On the whole, patterns of the rim extend horizontally and the body is composed of vertical compartment patterns.

Although the bottom area is rough, abrasion is little and slightly shiny. About one fourth of the lower half has turned red due to cooking, and a part close to the rim has some soot. The inner wall is made neat and no scorch is found.

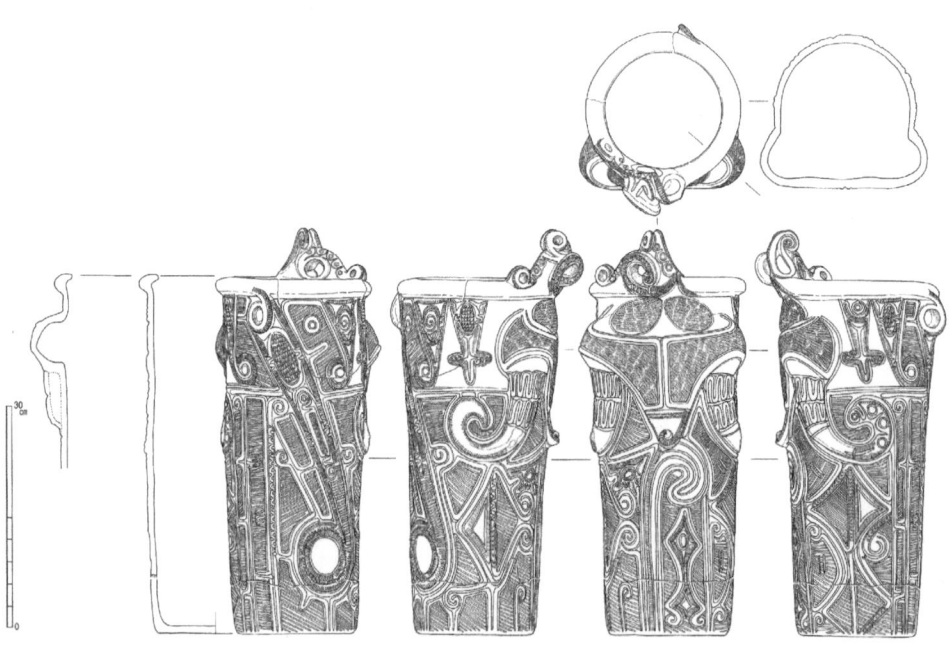

Cylindrical vessel with a statue of God

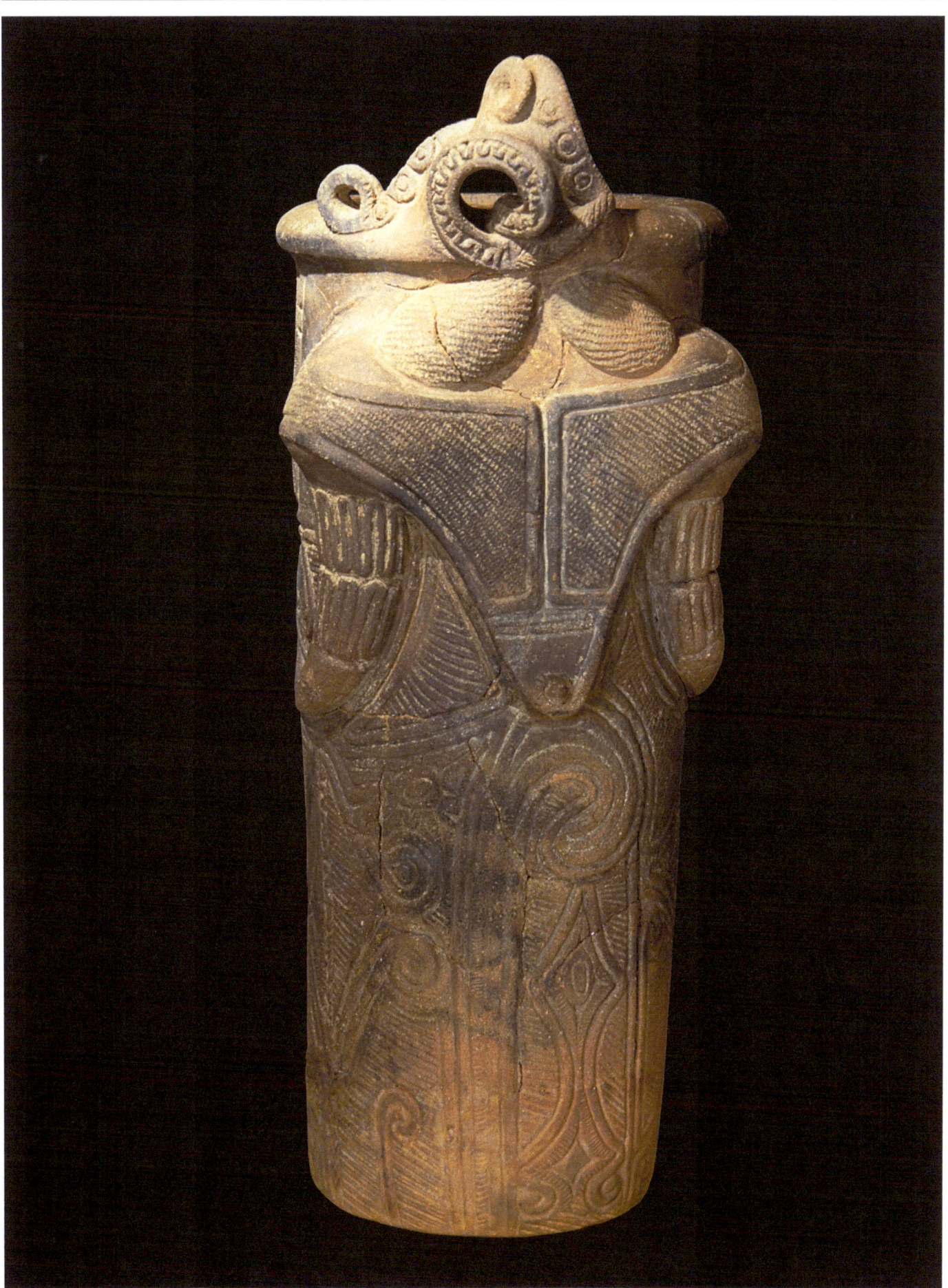

Cylindrical vessel with a statue of God

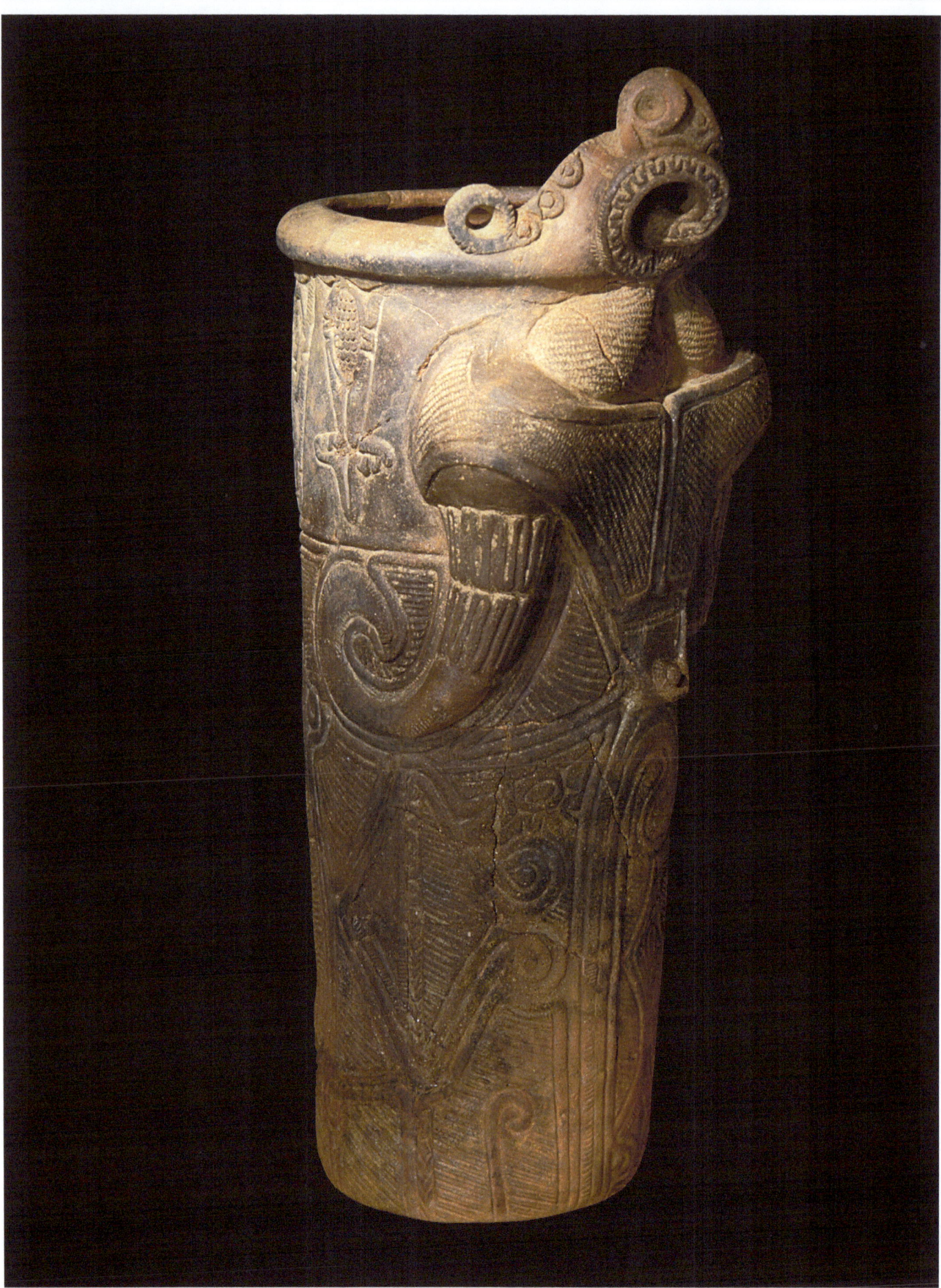

Cylindrical vessel with a statue of God

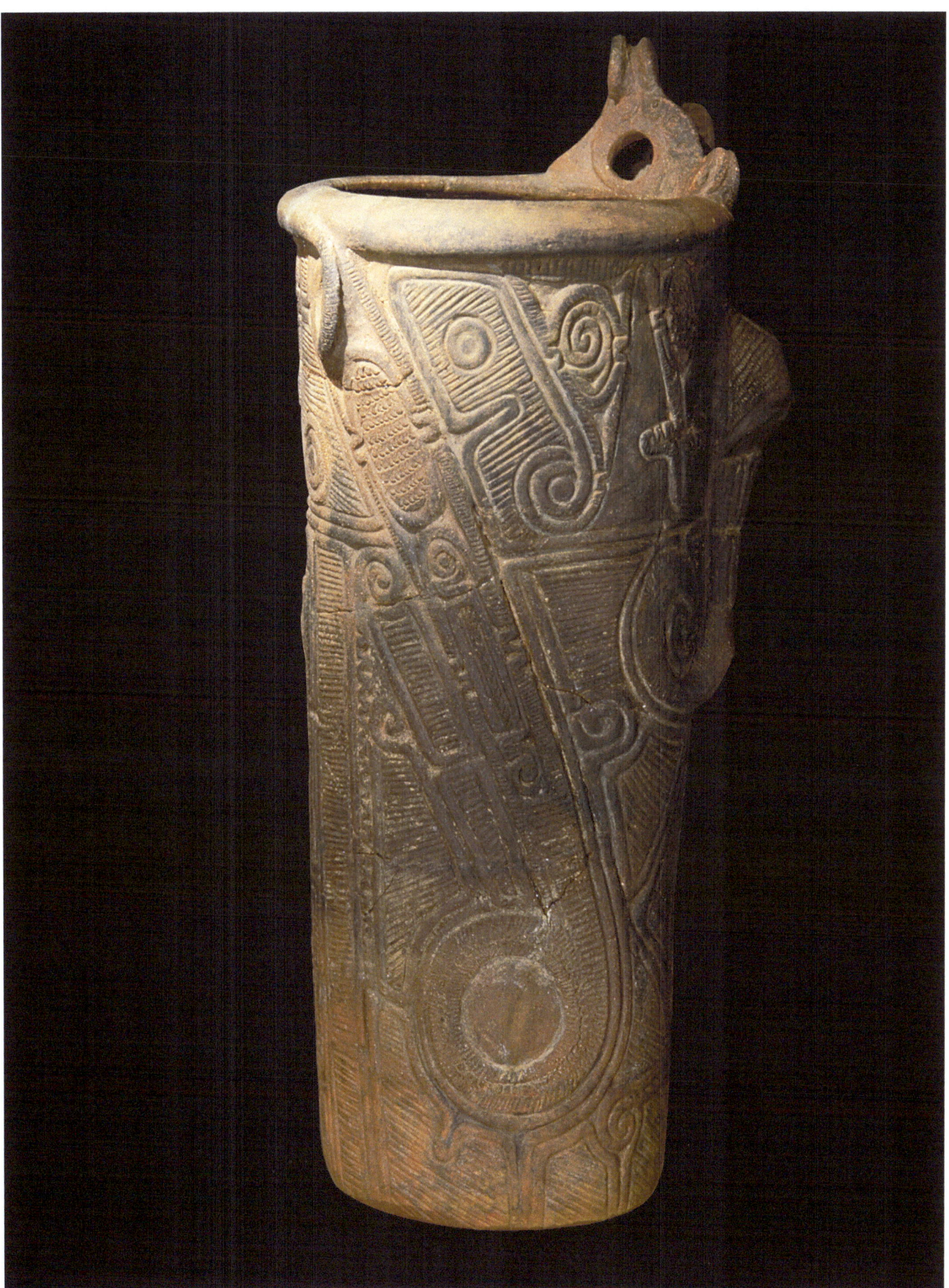

23

Cylindrical vessel with a statue of God

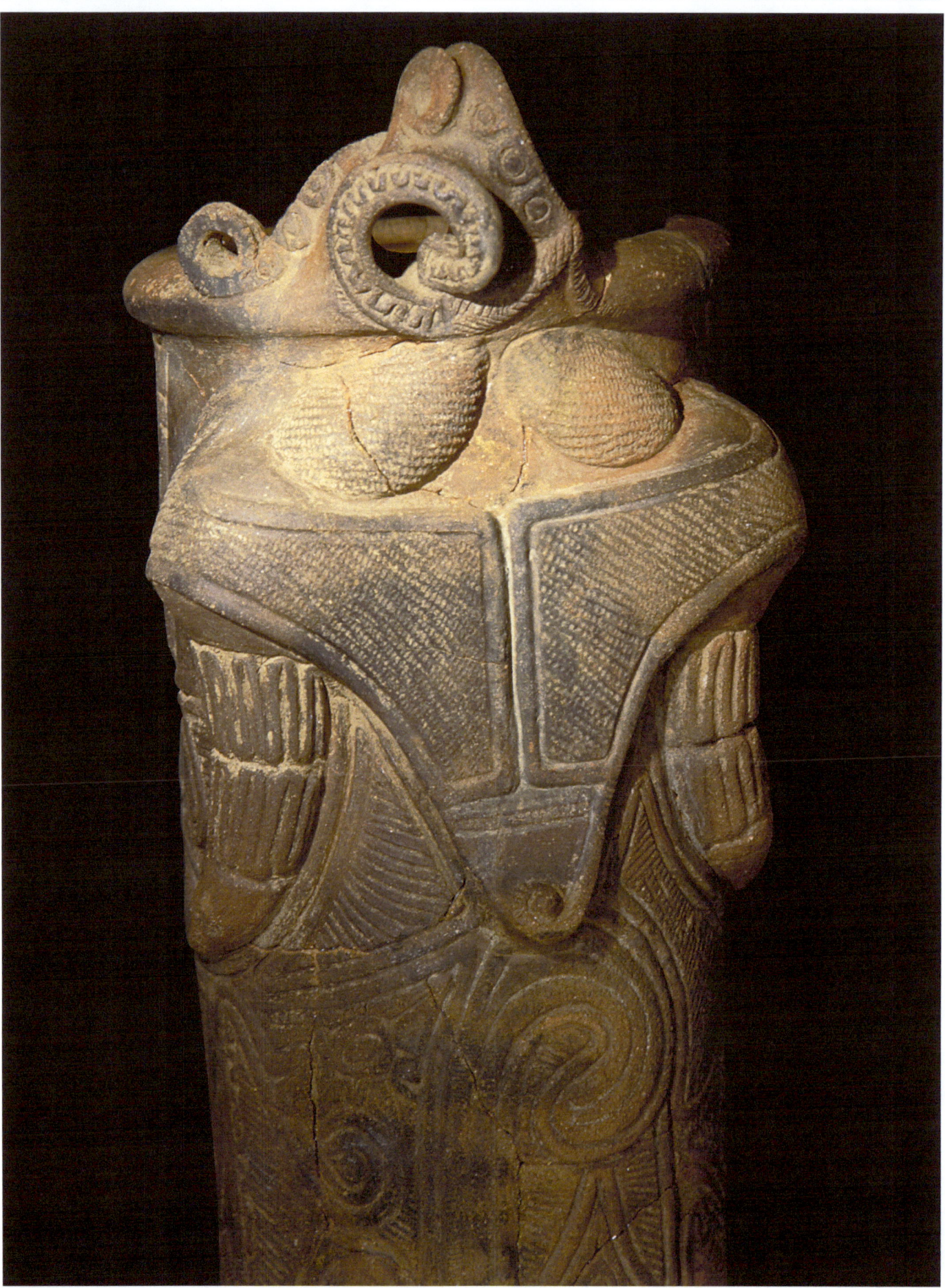

Cylindrical vessel with a statue of God

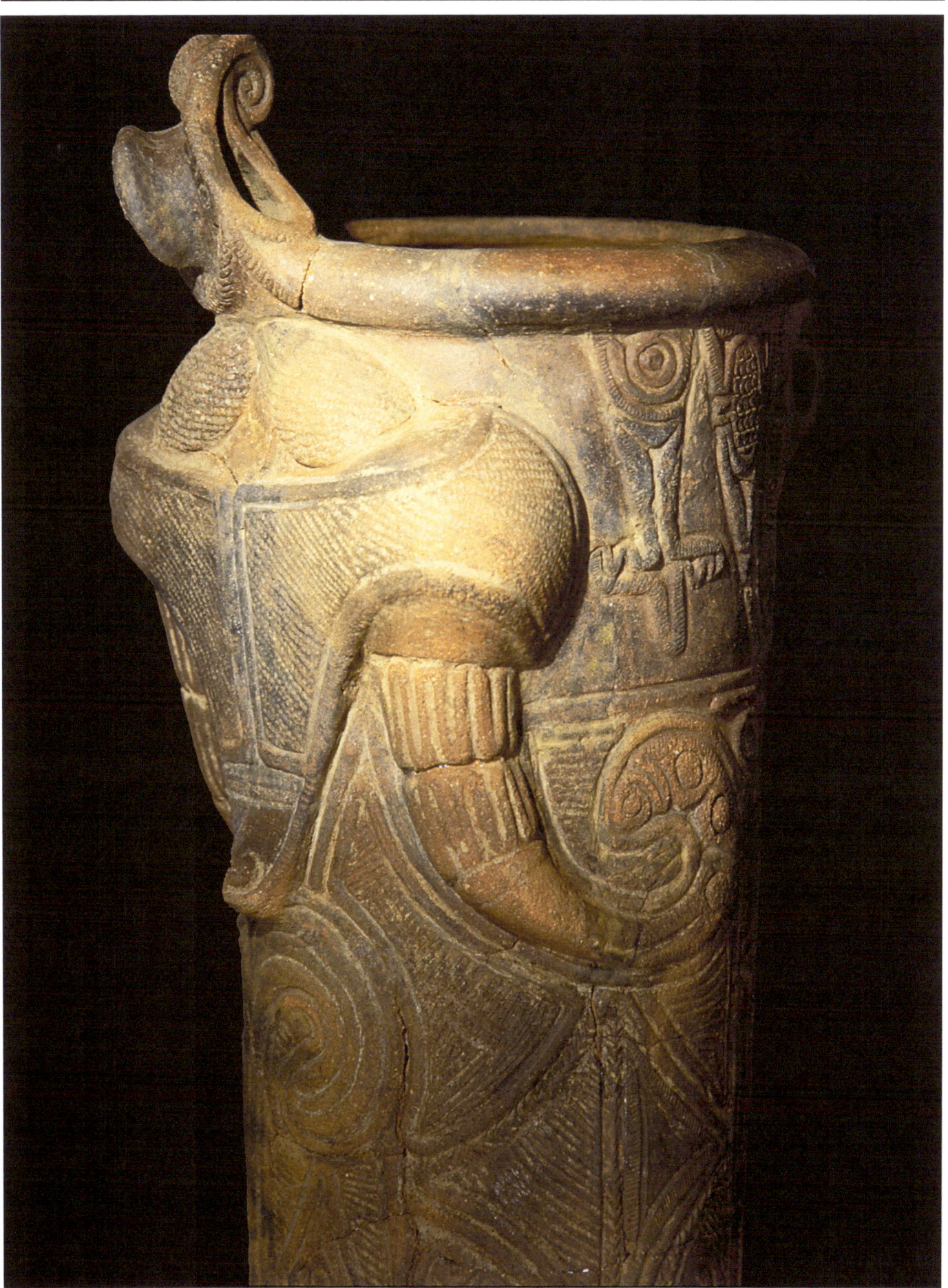

25

Cylindrical vessel with a statue of God

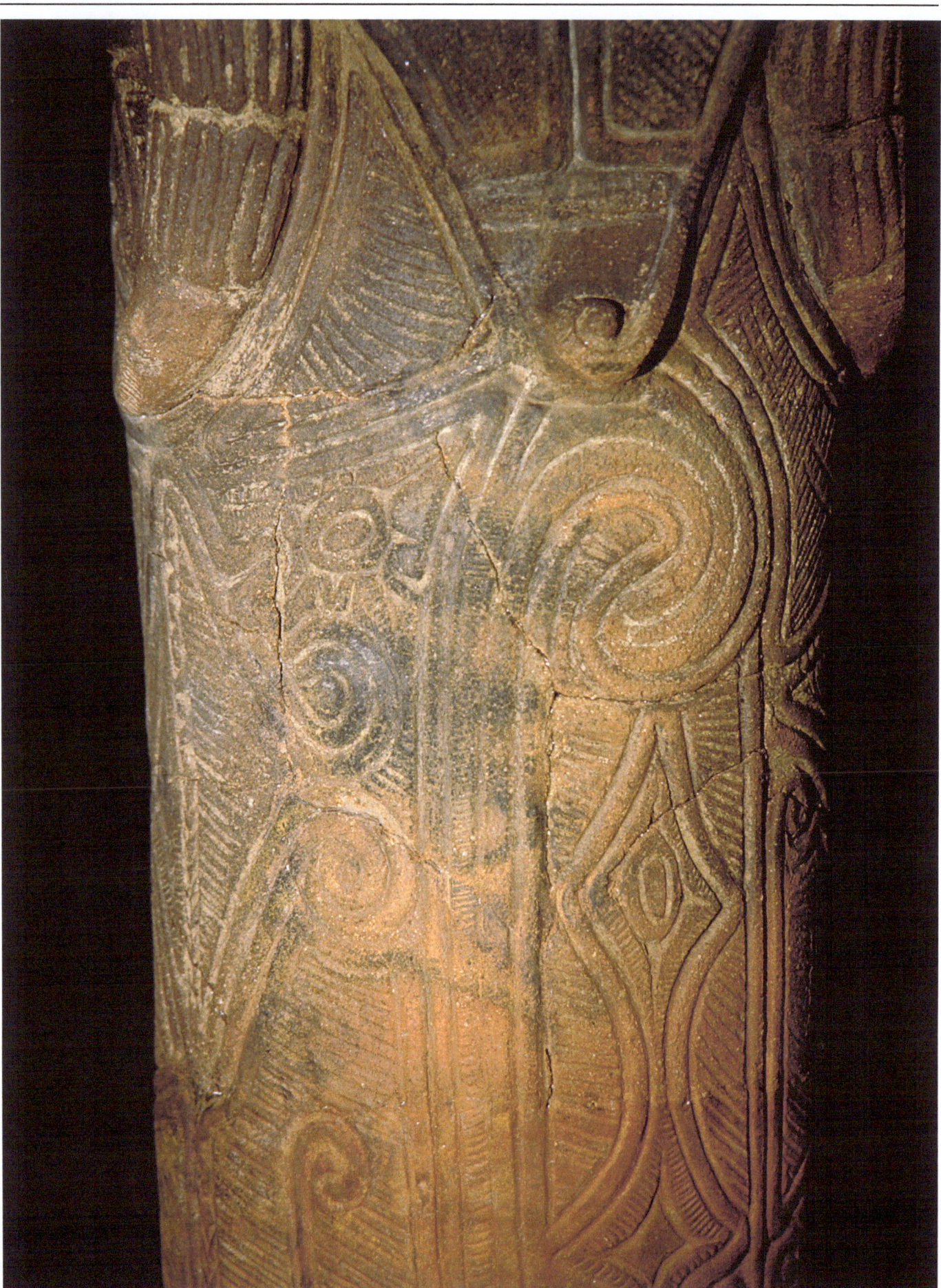

Cylindrical vessel with a statue of God

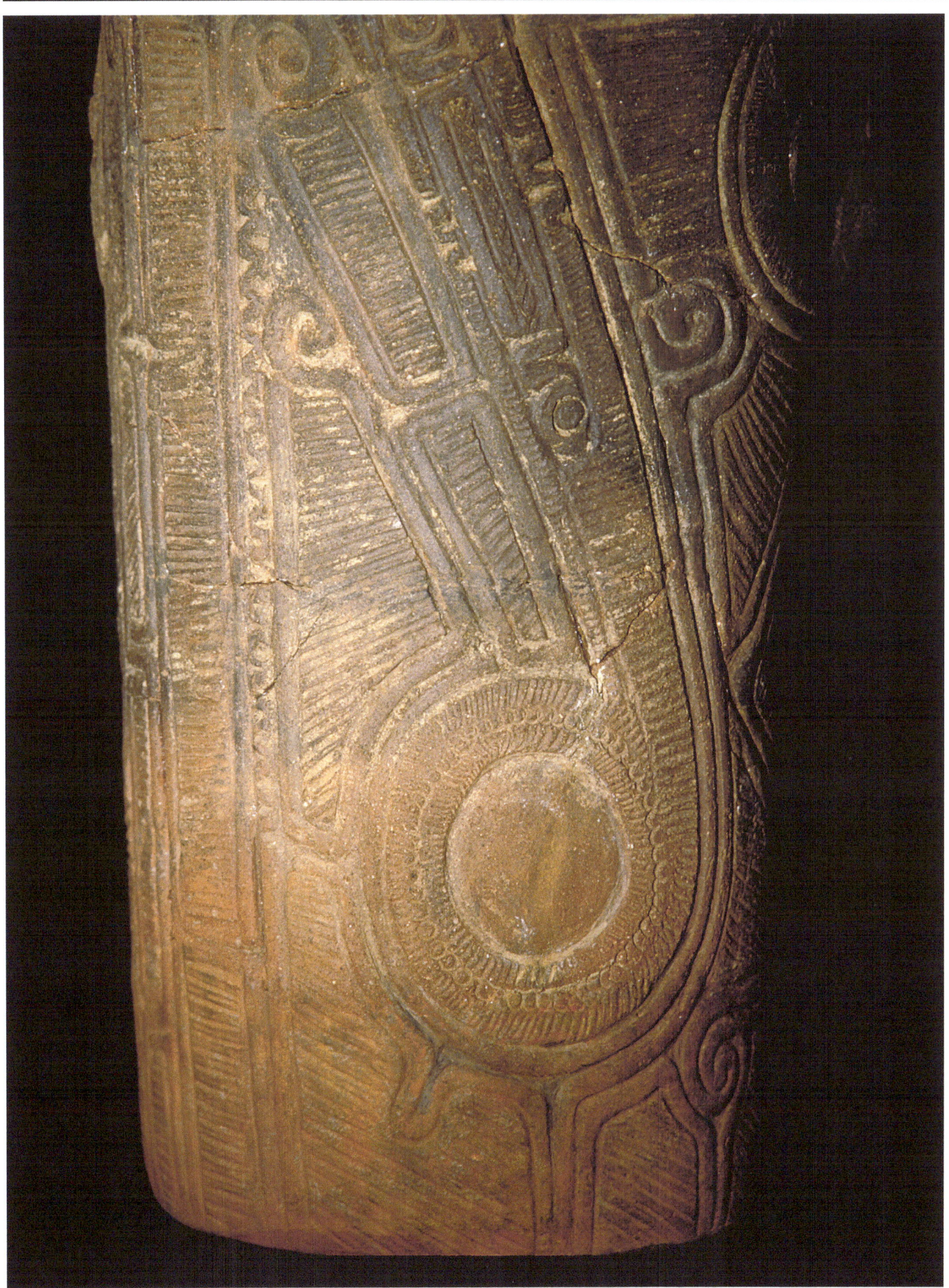

Bowl with a frog pattern
Tounai ruins
Tounai style I
Dwelling site #32, lower layer
Excavated in 1984
Middle Jomon, Middle
4,700 B.P.
18.9cm(H), 16.0cm(D)
"Tounai Report" P.132
ID-045

The frog's proboscis makes a slowly sloping rim of the bowl. Eyes are expressed as rings with notches, and the insides are deeply hollow. The fat body is a pair of half spheres. The part of spine is made as a grip-like shape, and diagonal lines are carved spirally. It resembles the cylindrical earthenware with compartment pattern shown on page 34.

The same kind of eyes can be seen at the right and left side and an eye on the opposite side is arranged obliquely. The upper part has a compartment pattern of horizontal stripes, and the lower part has that of vertical and horizontal stripes.

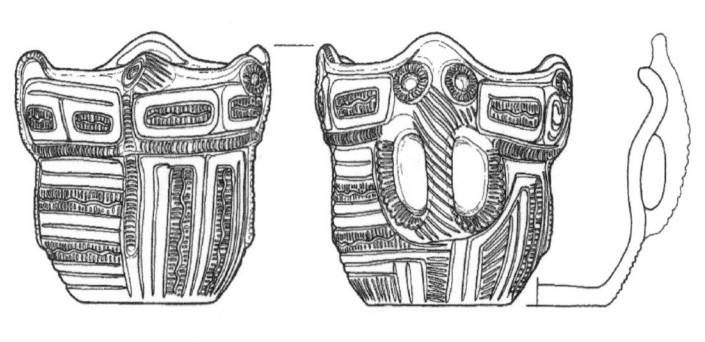

Bowl with a frog pattern

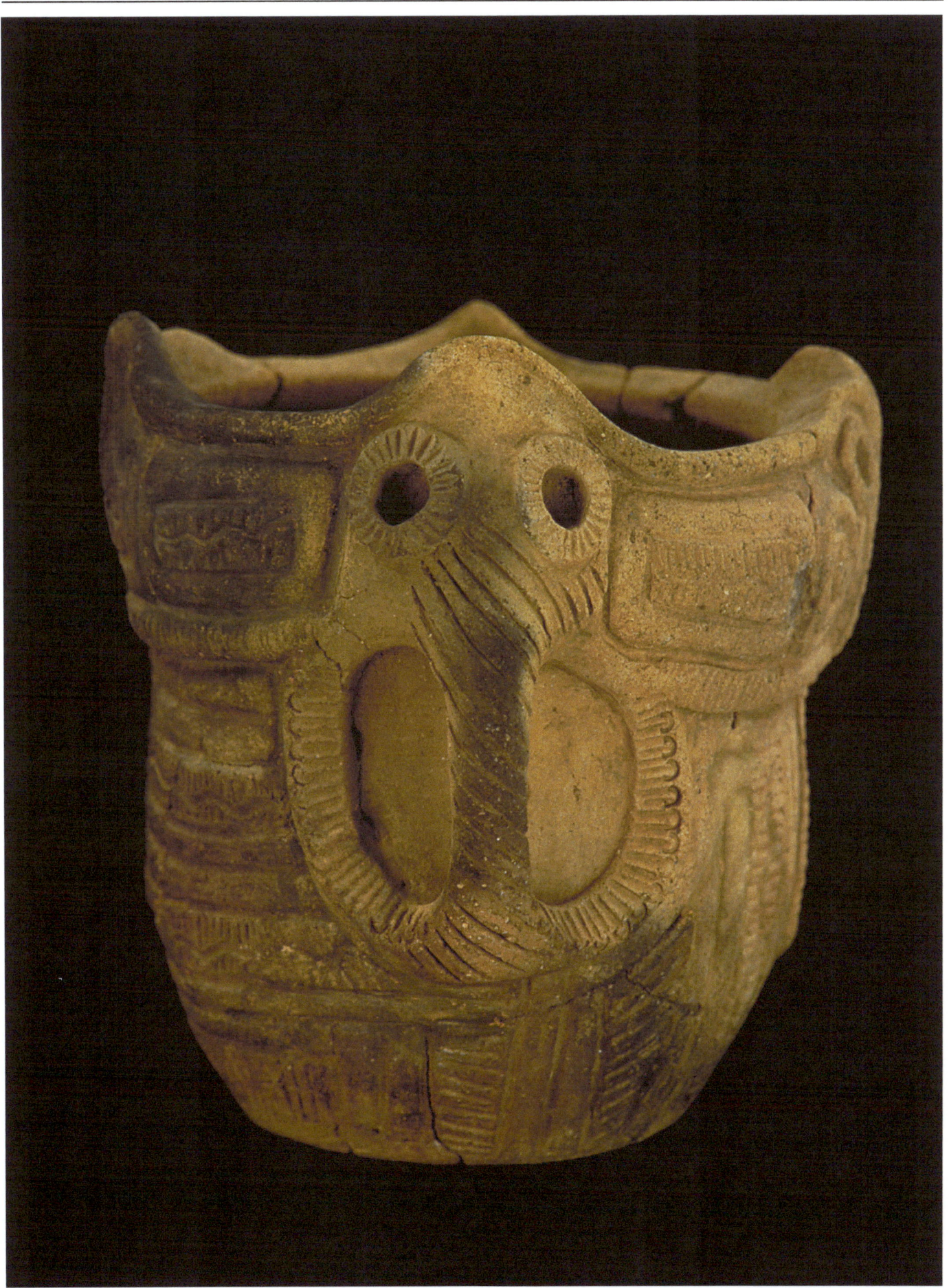

29

Bowl with a frog pattern

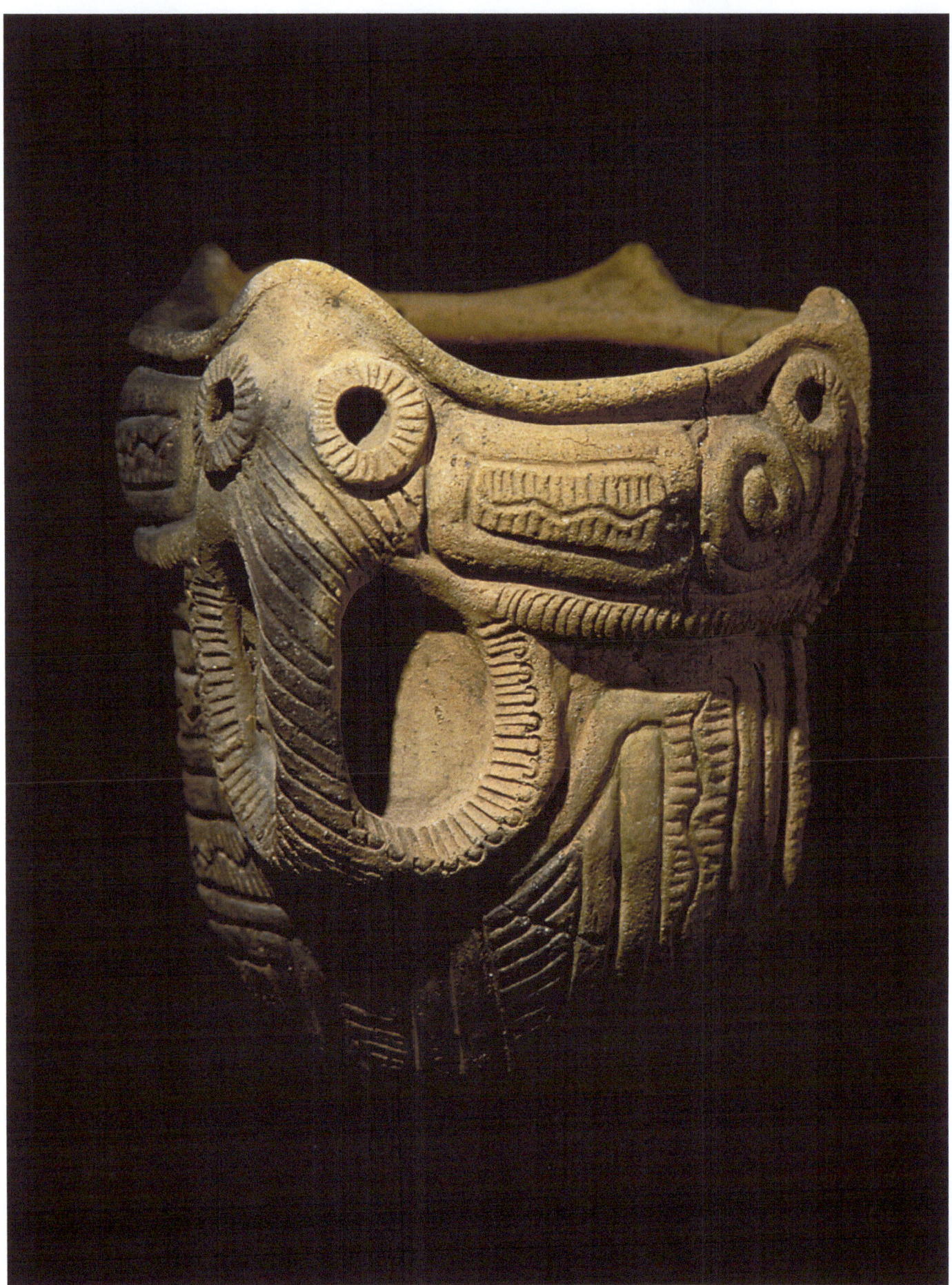

Bowl with a frog pattern

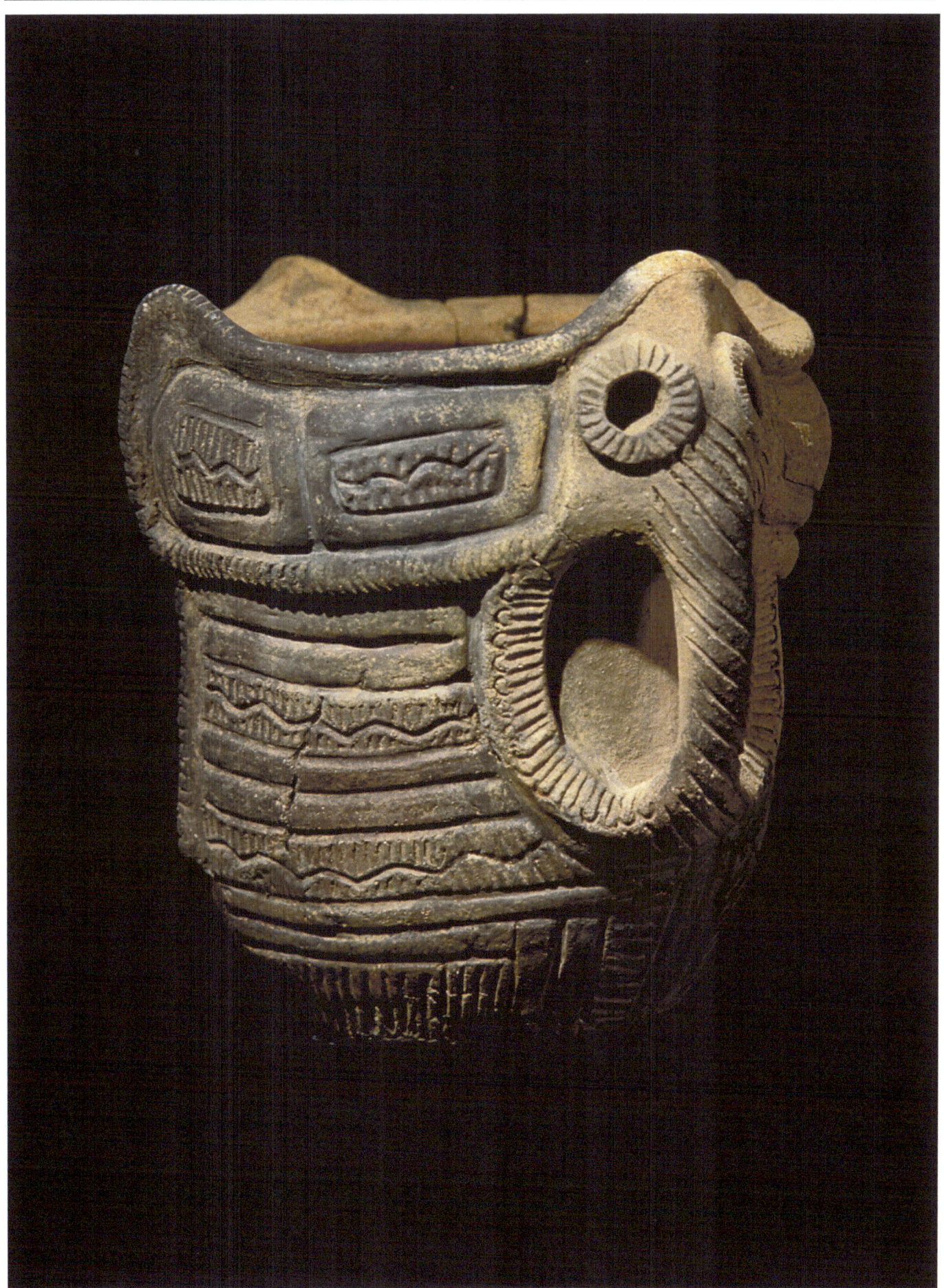

Bowl with a frog pattern

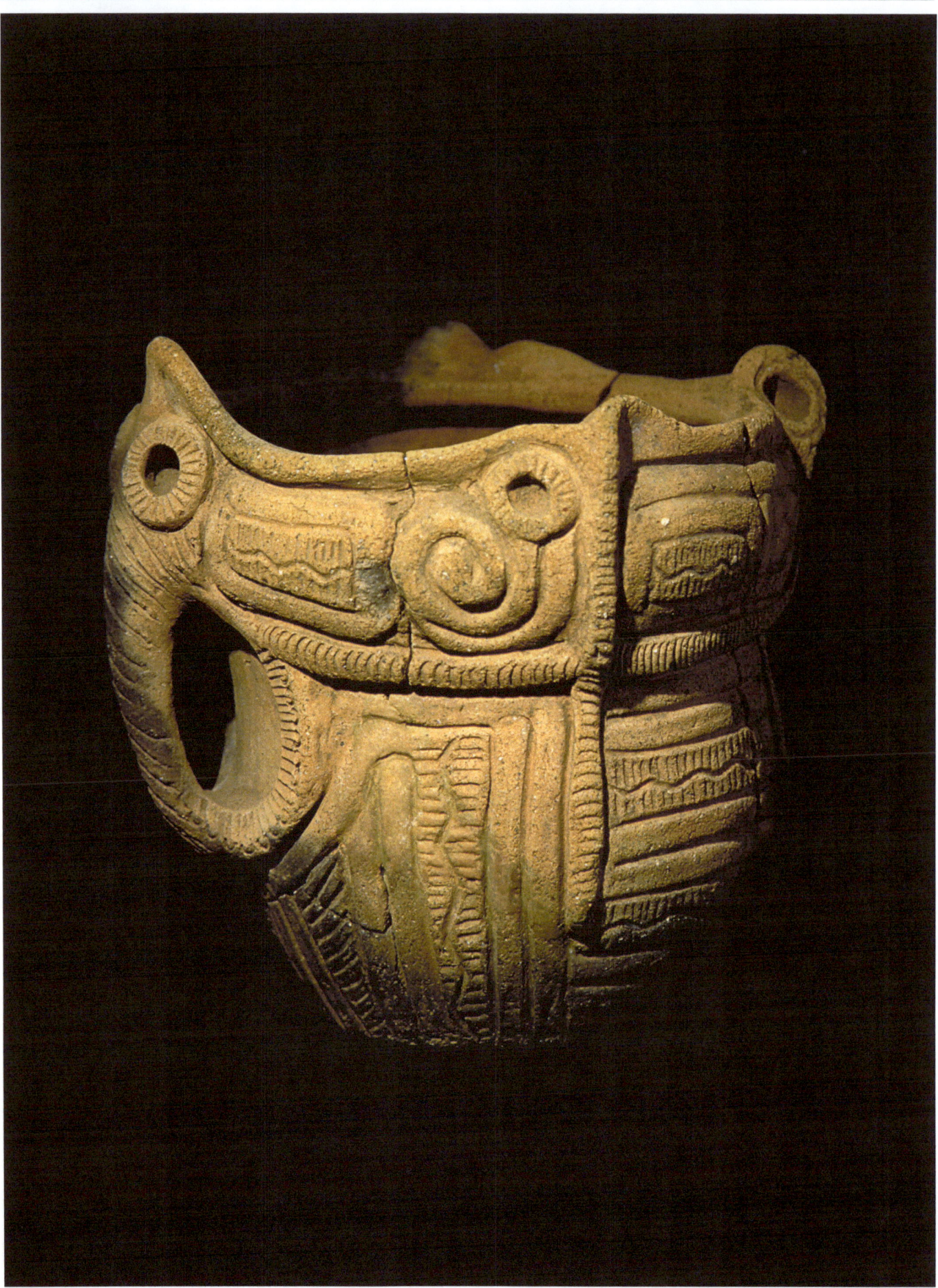

Bowl with a frog pattern

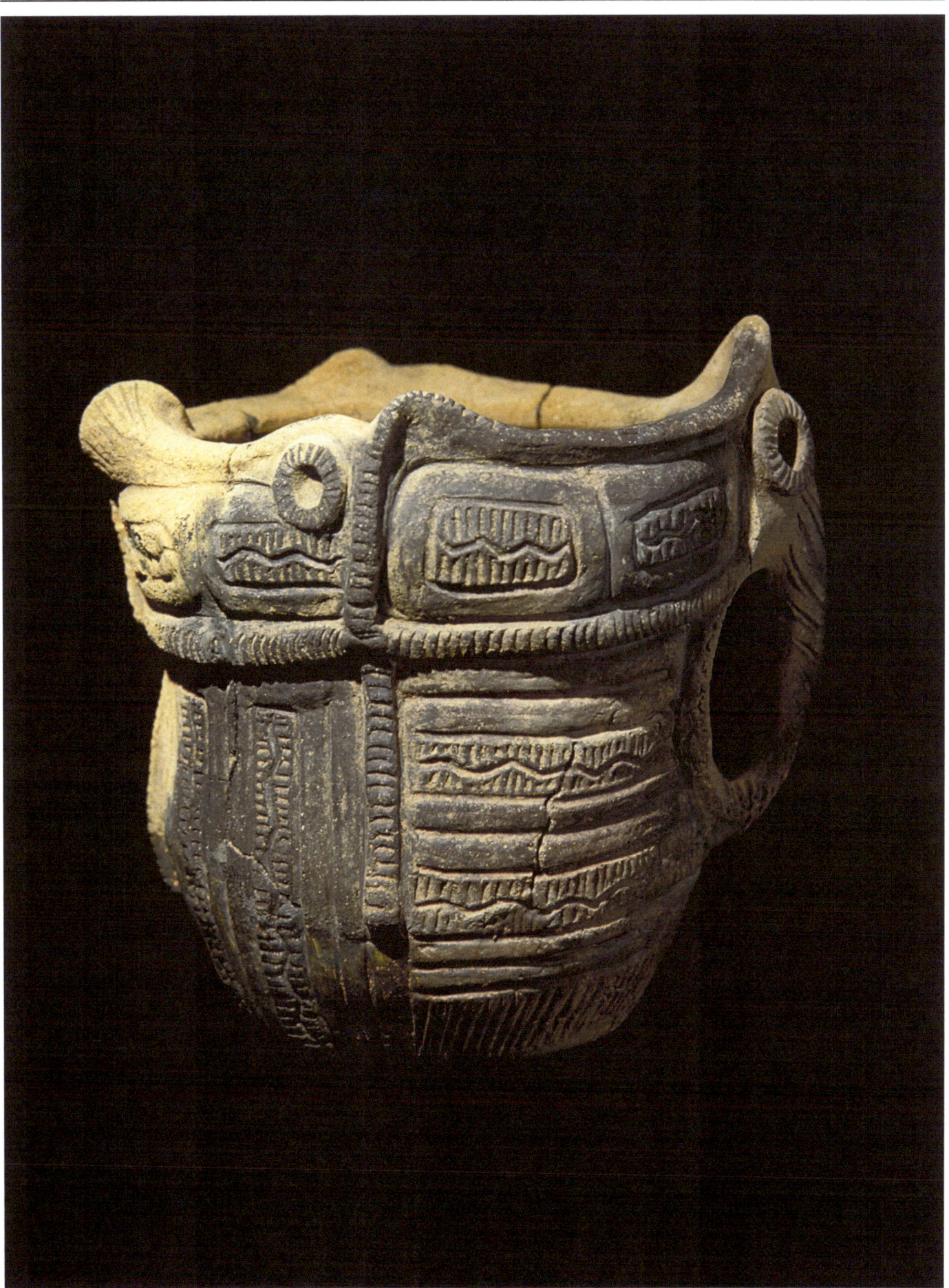

Big bowl with eyes on four sides
Tounai ruins
Tounai style I
Dwelling site #32, lower layer
Excavated in 1984
Middle Jomon, Middle
4,700 B.P.
24.0cm(H), 48.7cm(D)
"Tounai Report" P.137
ID-065

This is a large-sized shallow bowl with the inside diameter of 48.7cm and the height of 24cm.

On the four points of the rim can be seen a couple of eyes whose inner corner is wide and outer corner is narrow. Between the eyes, meandering convex belts and crescent patterns are arranged alternately. Push-pull patterns fringing them are wide, fine, and designed carefully.

The inside is smooth, made neat, and wholly blackish. Coating layers regarded as black lacquer are remaining in places. As they are found on the edge of the rim, they are thought to have been applied generally at first.

Repairing holes are pierced on both sides of a crack under the shoulder. Outer periphery of the bottom touching the ground is rough with the width of 1.5cm. This pottery must be the most representative shallow bowl of the first period of Tounai.

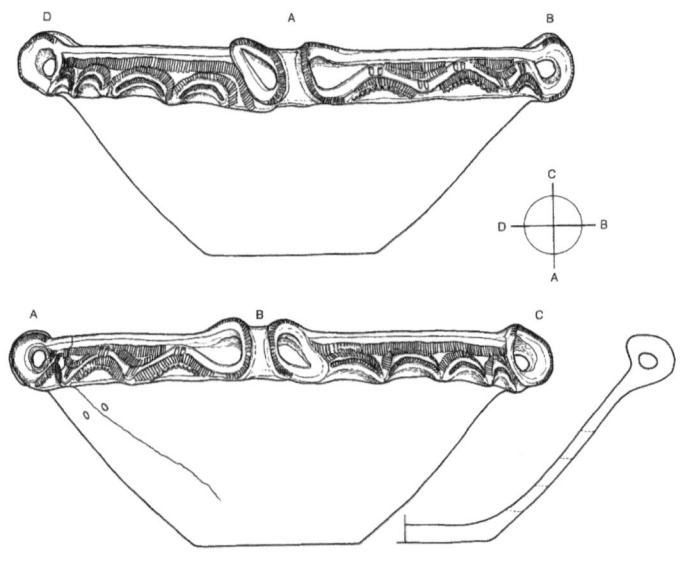

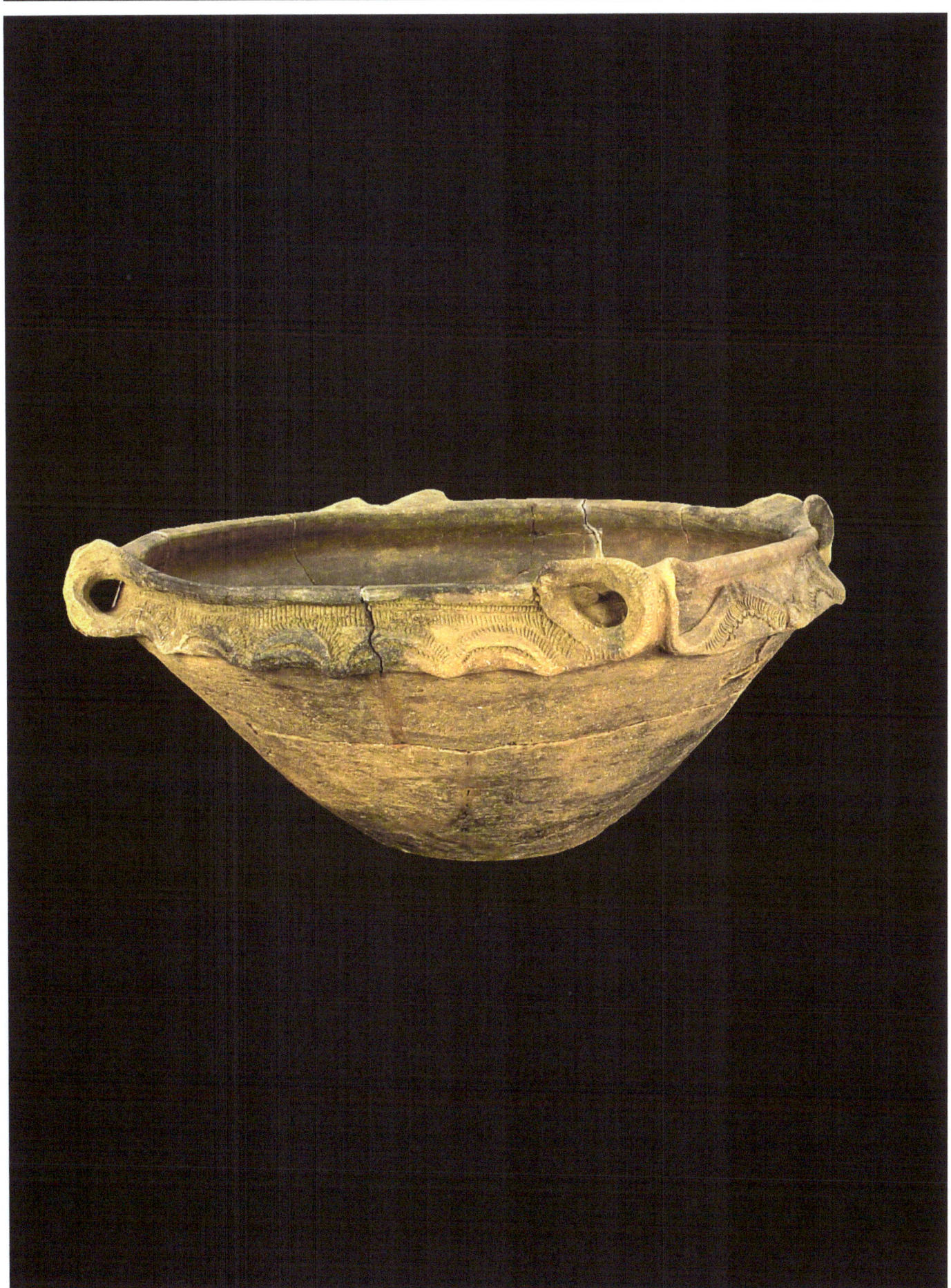

Big bowl with eyes on four sides

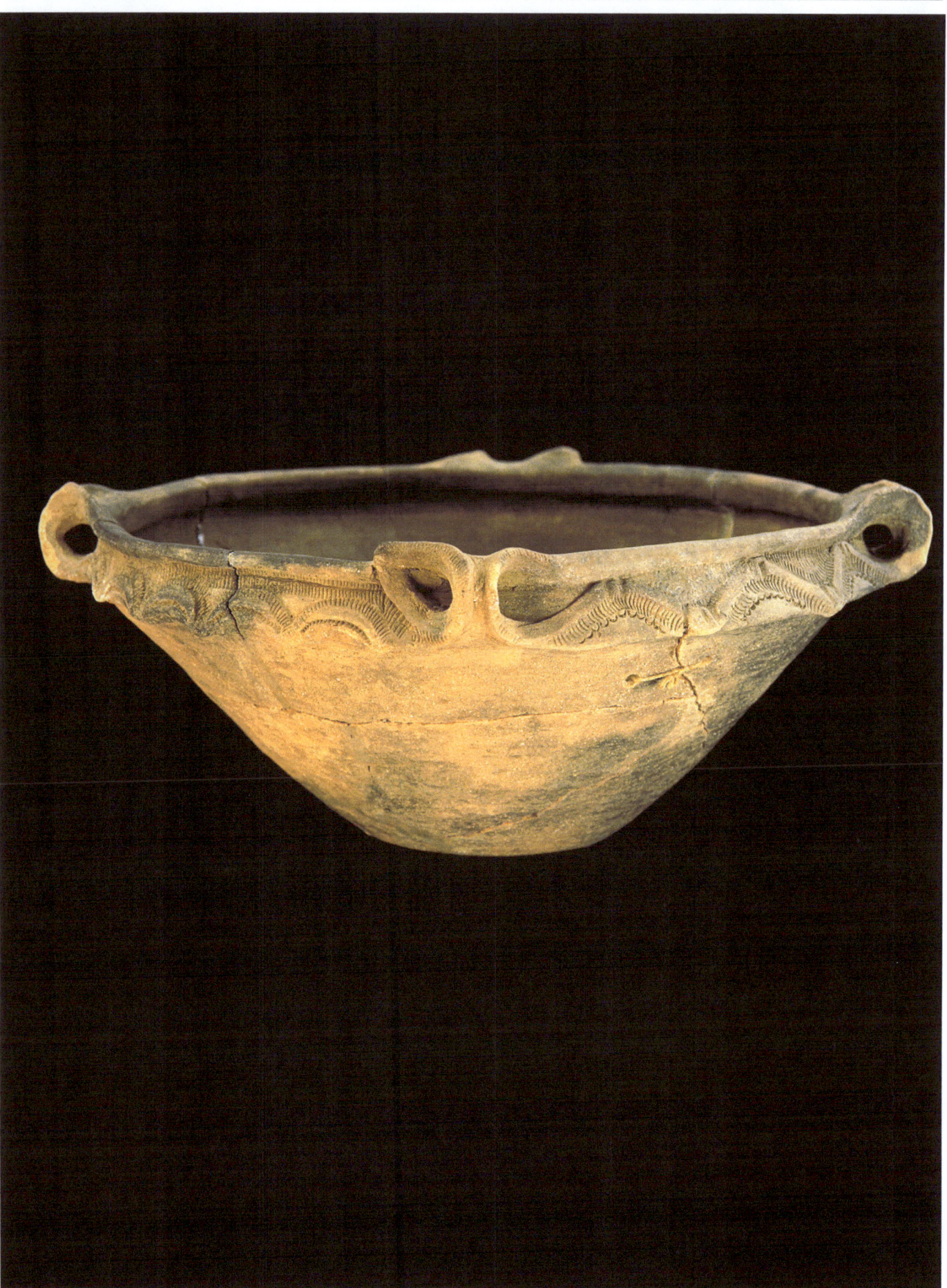

Big bowl with eyes on four sides

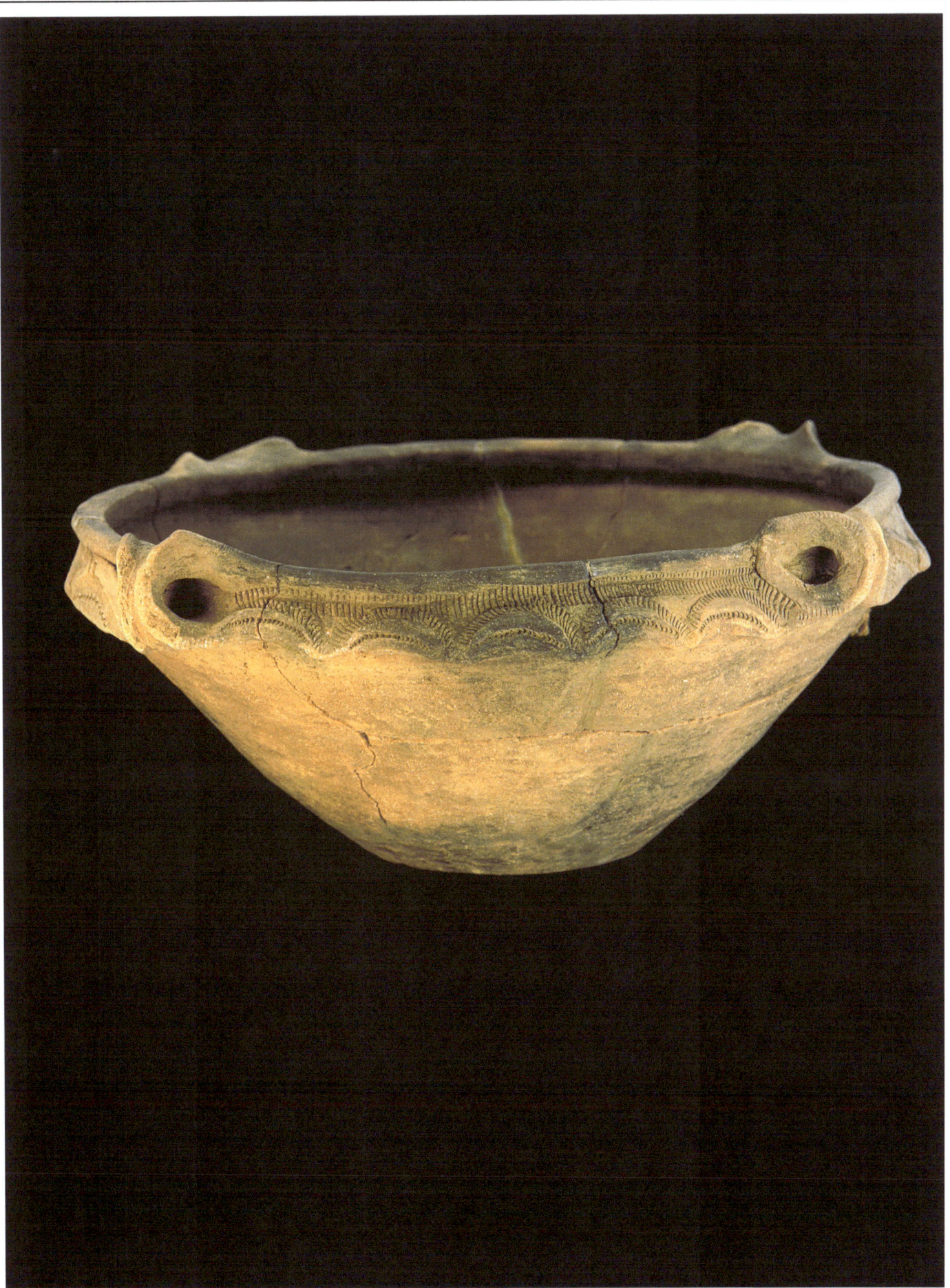

Cylindrical vessel with compartment patterns
Tounai ruins
Tounai style I
Dwelling site #32, lower layer
Excavated in 1984
Middle Jomon, Middle
4,700 B.P.
30.0cm(H), 15.6cm(D)
"Tounai Report" P.131
ID-076

The cylindrical body has an incurved rim. Four columnar protrusions rising from four sides stick out their heads over the rim and the tops are sunken. On the four sides of the body, convex lines hang and vertical compartments patterns mainly with rhombuses are engraved.

Two thirds of lower side of the outer wall has turned orange, and one third of the upper side has belt-shaped soot. In addition, the edge of 1cm in width of the bottom is slightly rough. On the other hand, two thirds of lower side of the inner wall is scorched, and one fourth close to the bottom has belt-shaped scorches.

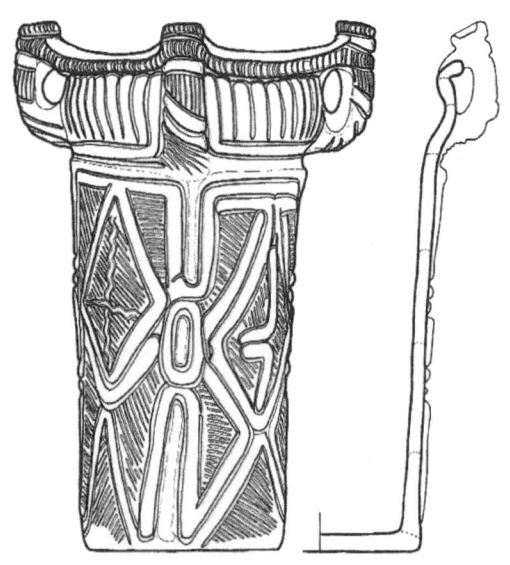

Cylindrical vessel with compartment patterns

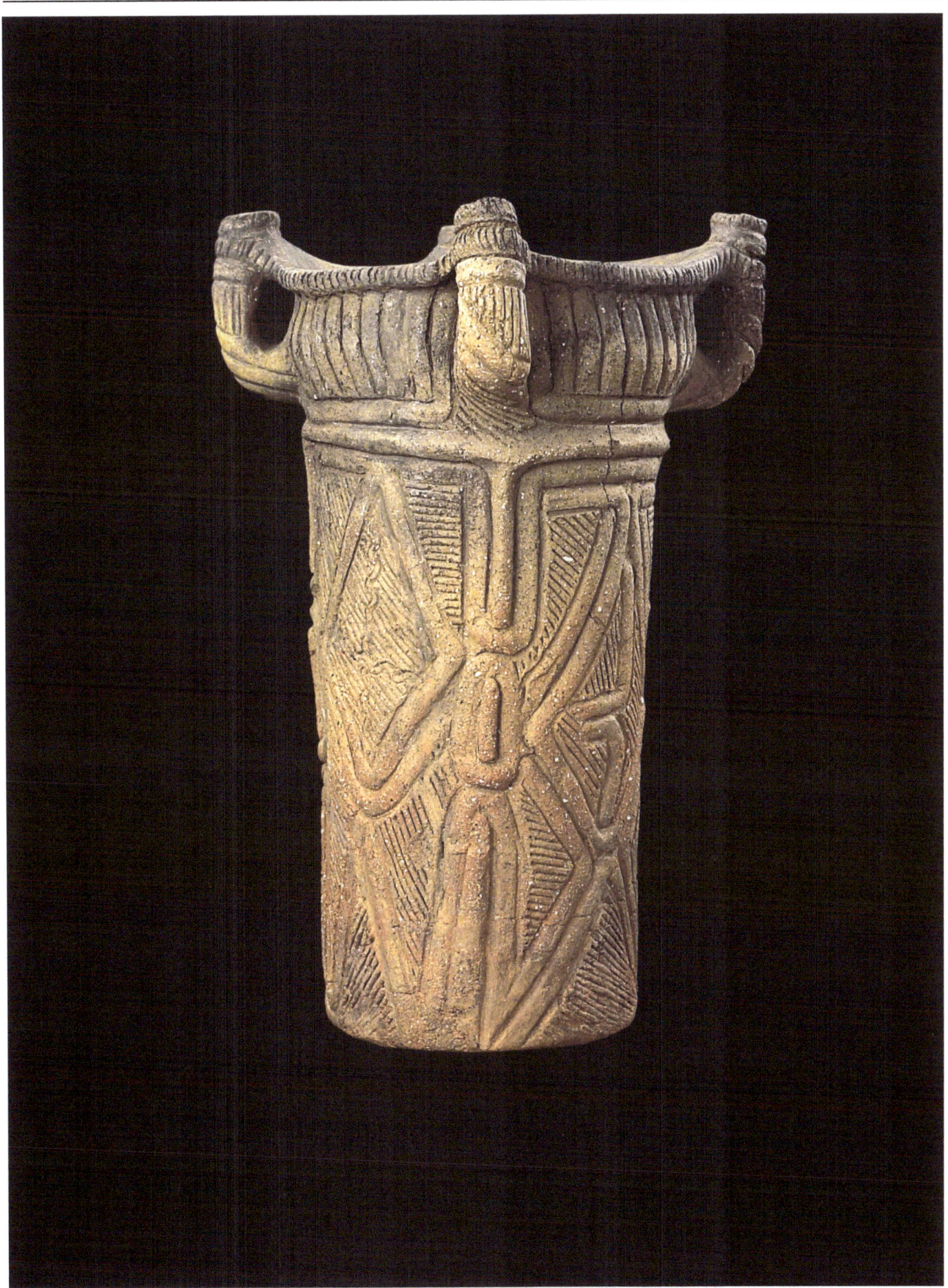

Cylindrical vessel with compartment patterns

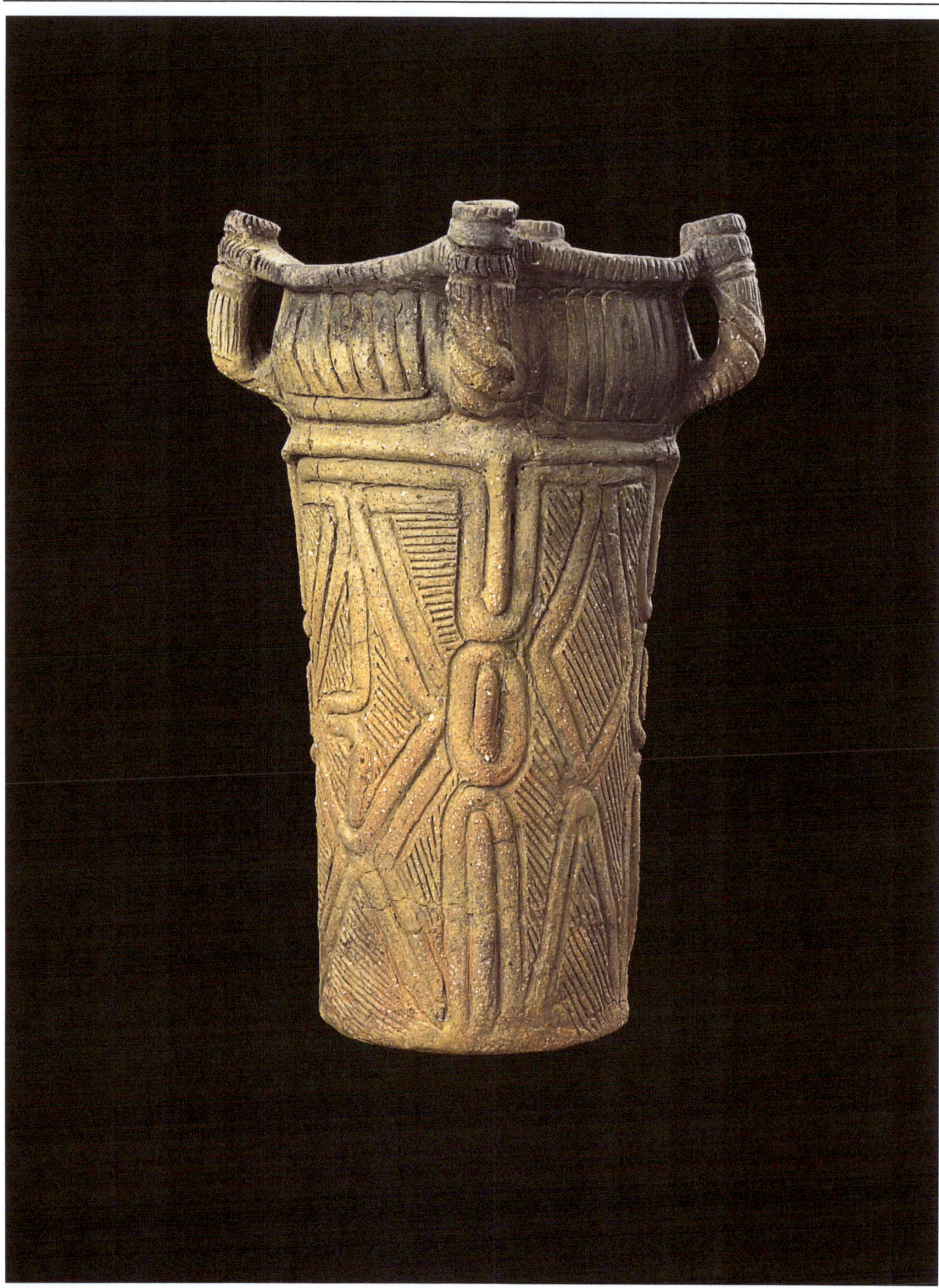

Cylindrical vessel with compartment patterns

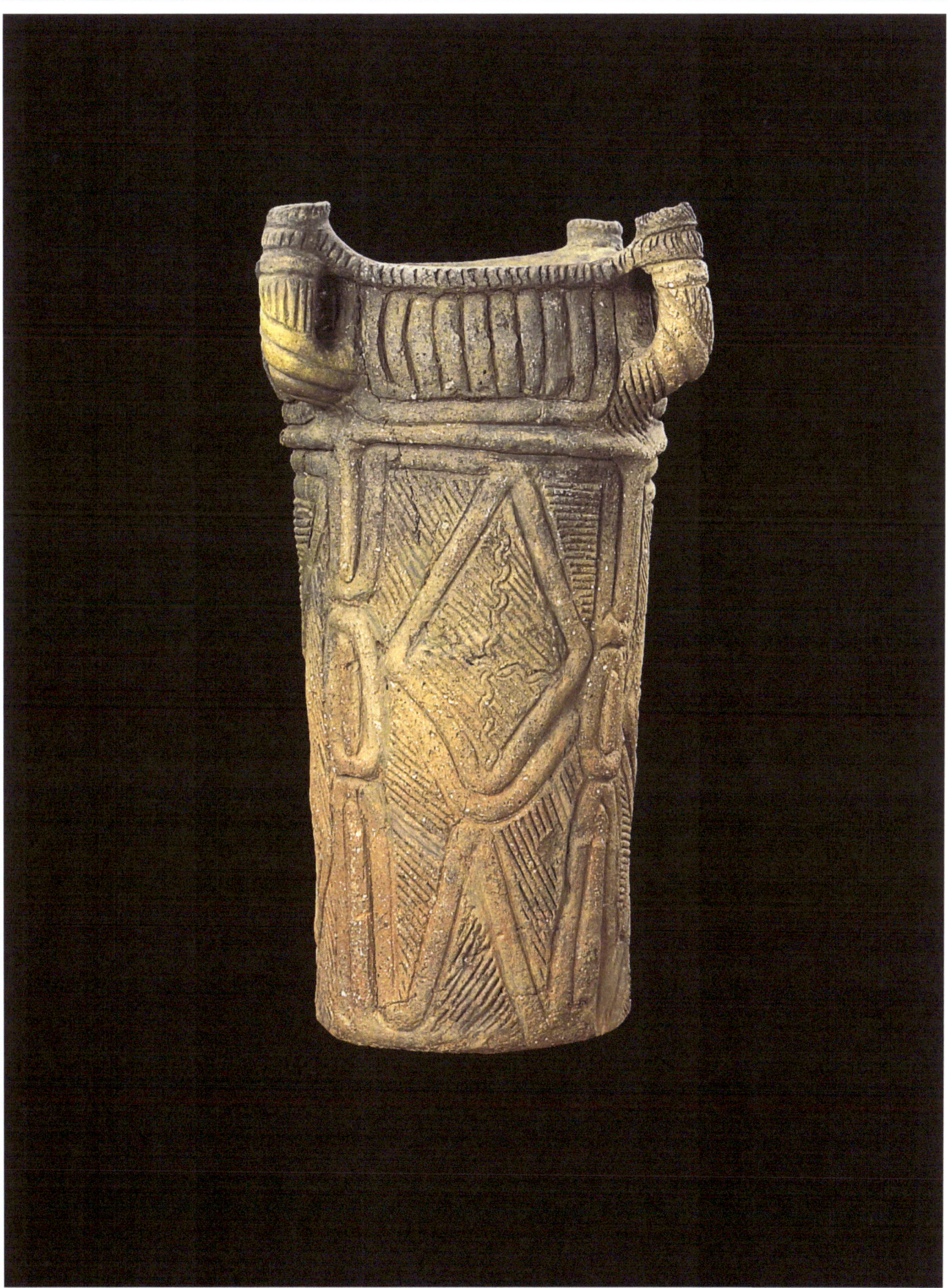

Cylindrical vessel with cross patterns
Tounai ruins
Tounai style I
Dwelling site #32, lower layer
Excavated in 1984
Middle Jomon, Middle
4,700 B.P.
32.3cm(H), 18.2cm(D)
"Tounai Report" P.131
ID-077

Fine Jomon patterns are marked without a break except the bottom. Three pupa-like convex shapes with notches are formed vertically on all sides. Four scraped cross patterns are arranged between them.

The upper half of outer wall is slightly sooty and the lower half is turned red. One third is quite red and has rough skin. In accordance with it, the inner wall is turned black and scorched along the border of the bottom.

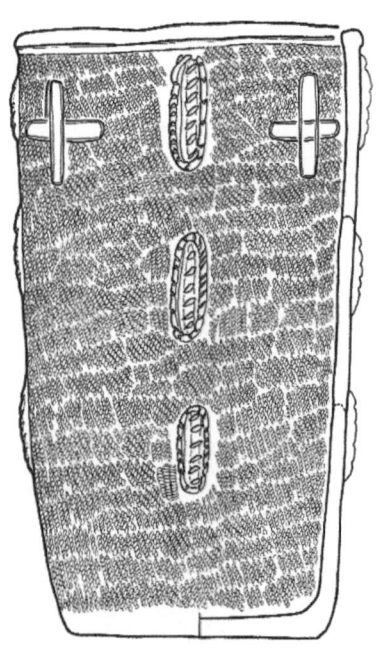

Cylindrical vessel with cross patterns

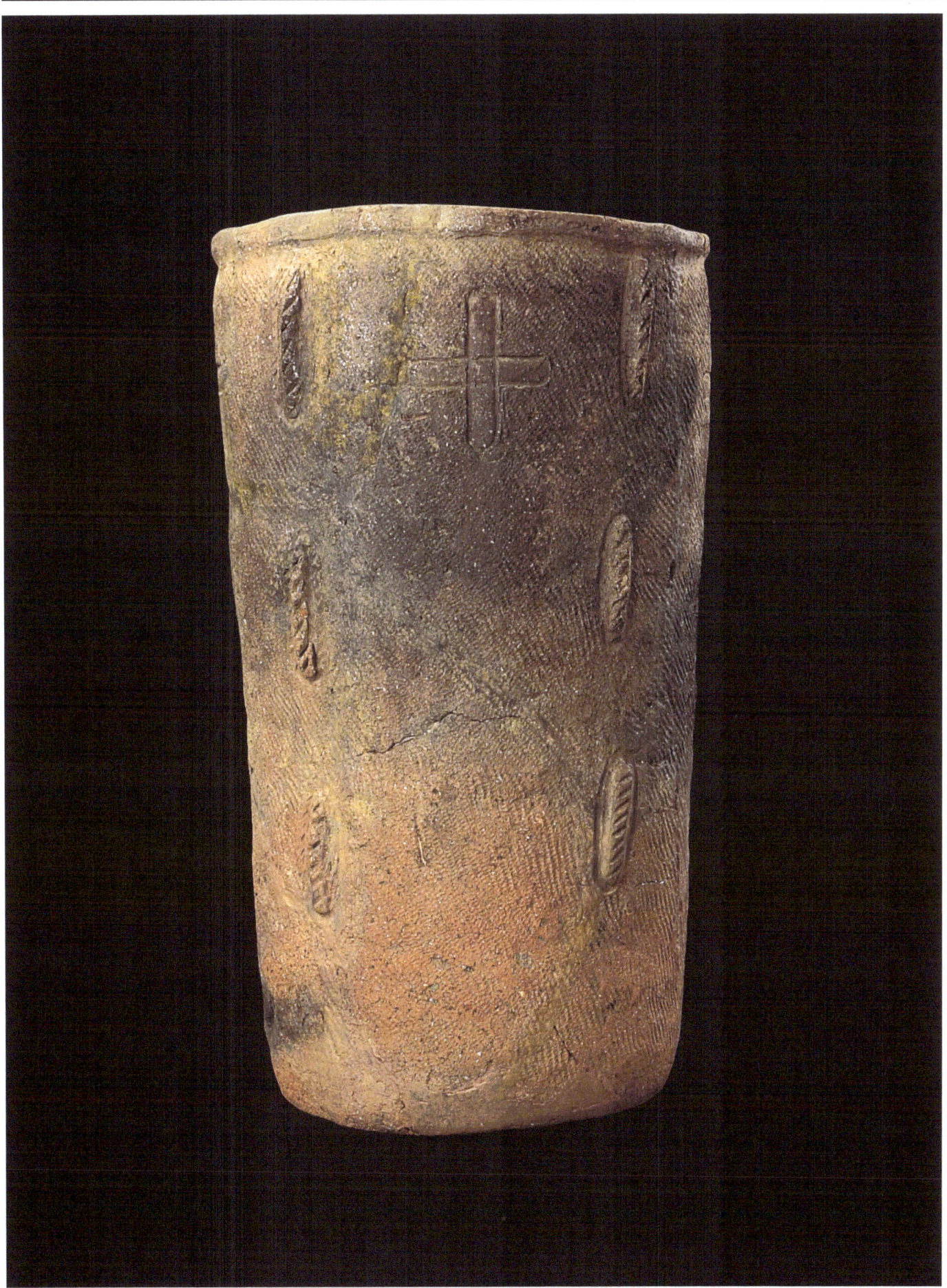

Cylindrical vessel with cross patterns

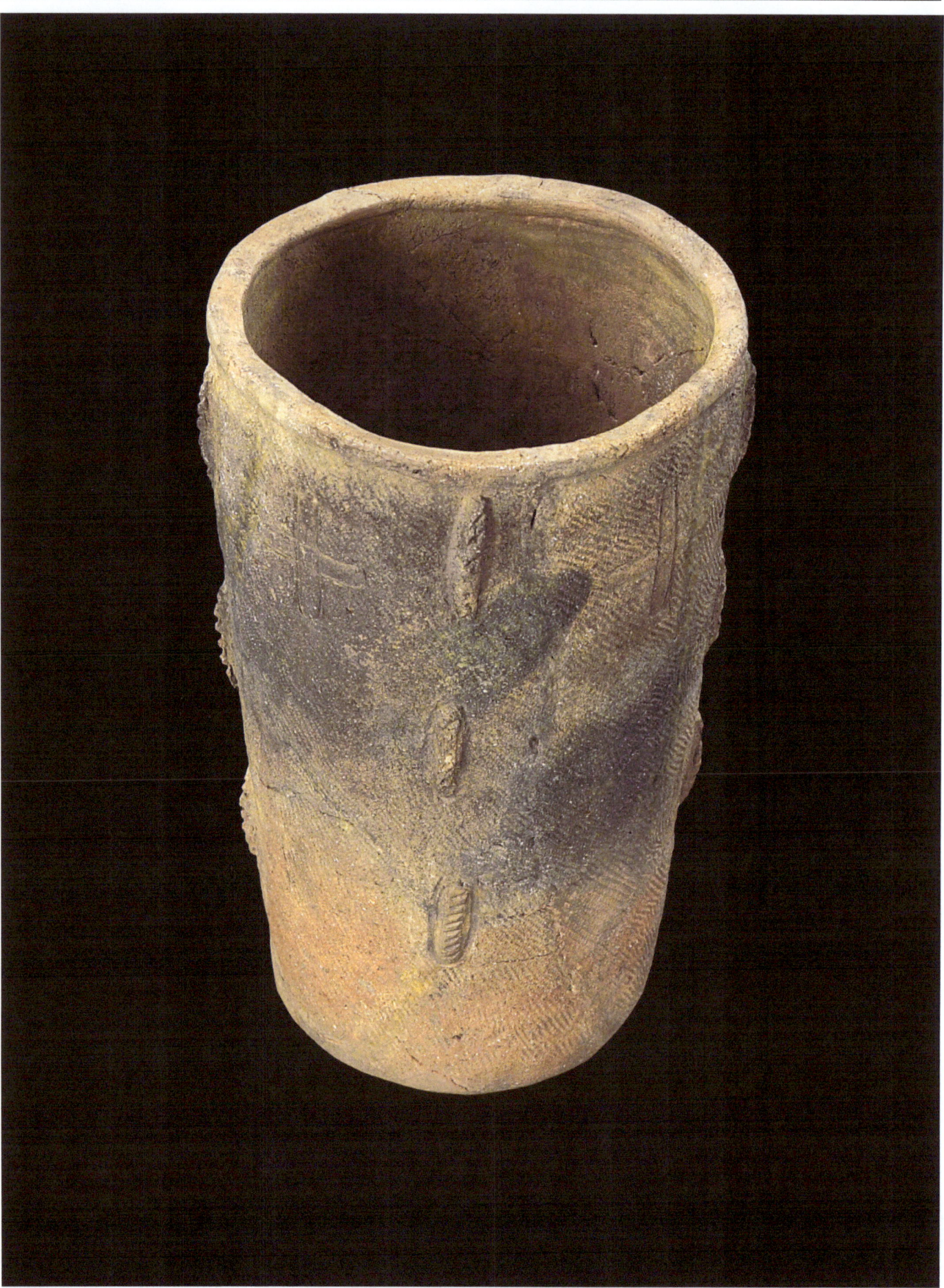

Cylindrical vessel with cross patterns

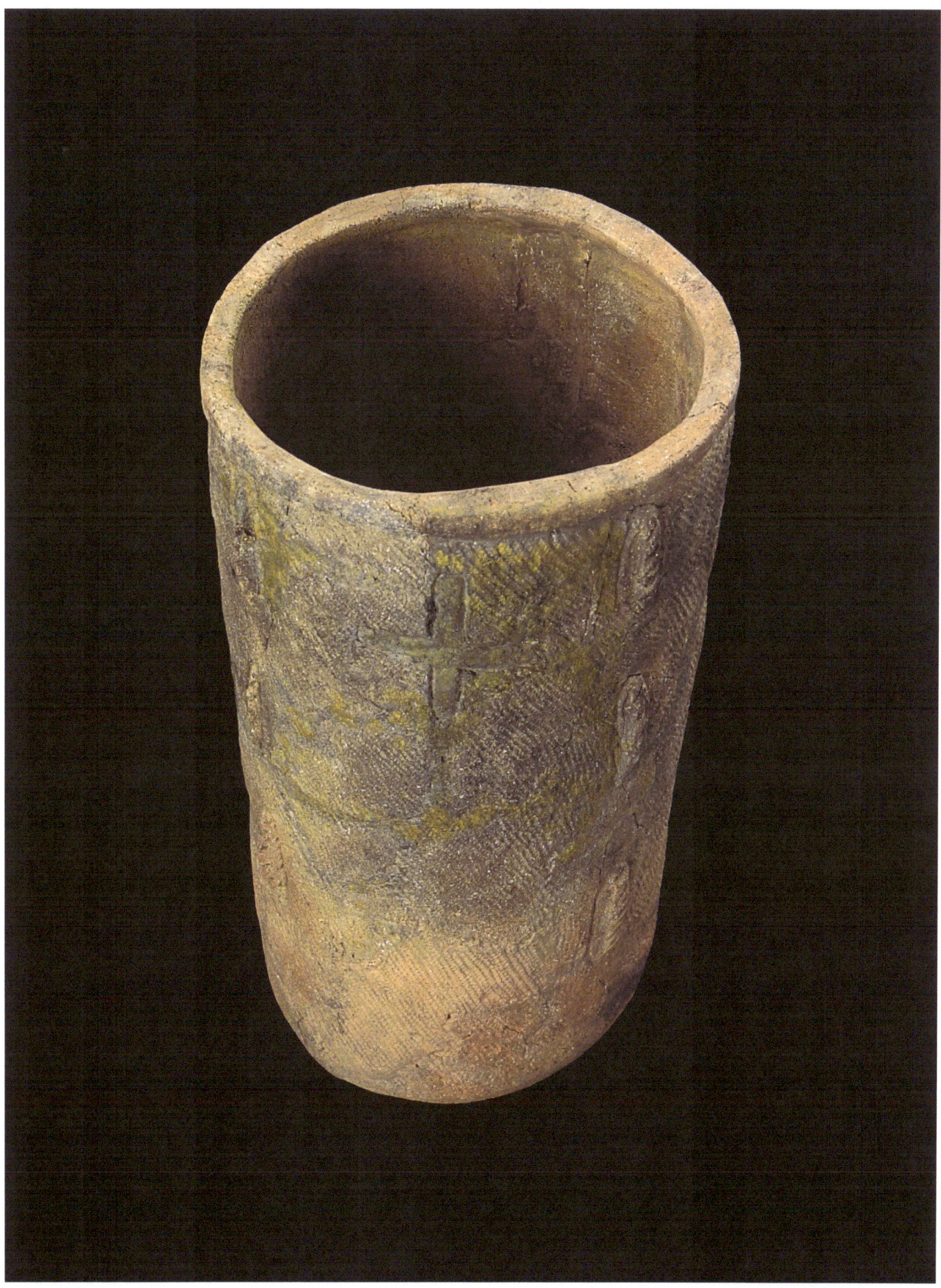

Deep bowl with a statue of one-eyed God
Tounai ruins
Tounai style II
Dwelling site #32, lower layer
Excavated in 1984
Middle Jomon, Middle
4,700 B.P.
34.4cm(H), 19.8cm(D)
"Tounai Report" P.133
ID-078

This is a deep bowl with an umbrella-shaped convex band and has a pointed protrusion. One side has a small round shape. At one side of the protrusion can be seen a concave ring-shaped eye. A similar ring-shaped eye can be seen at the base of the rim section as well. A pair of J-shaped bulges and I-shaped bulges is hanging from umbrella-shaped convex band. The bottom curves gently like the " く (ku)"-shape. It is a beautiful molding and slightly lustrous.

The upper half of the outer wall has light soot, and one third from the bottom of the inner wall has belt-shaped scorches like paste.

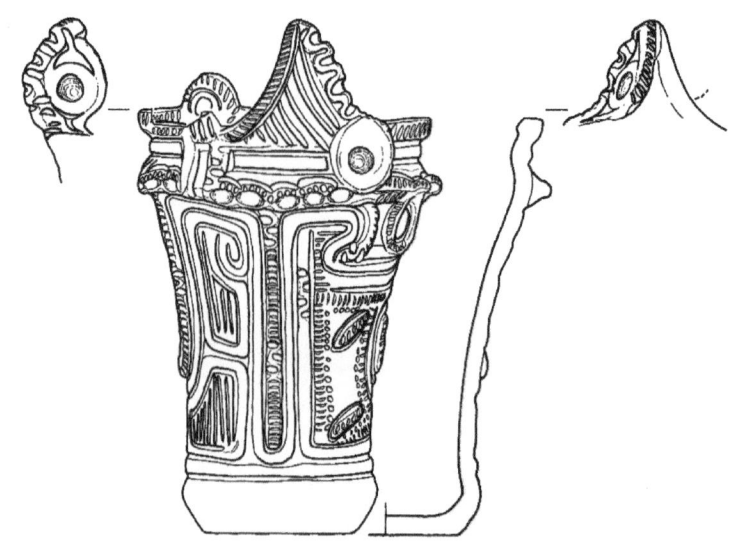

Deep bowl with a statue of one-eyed God

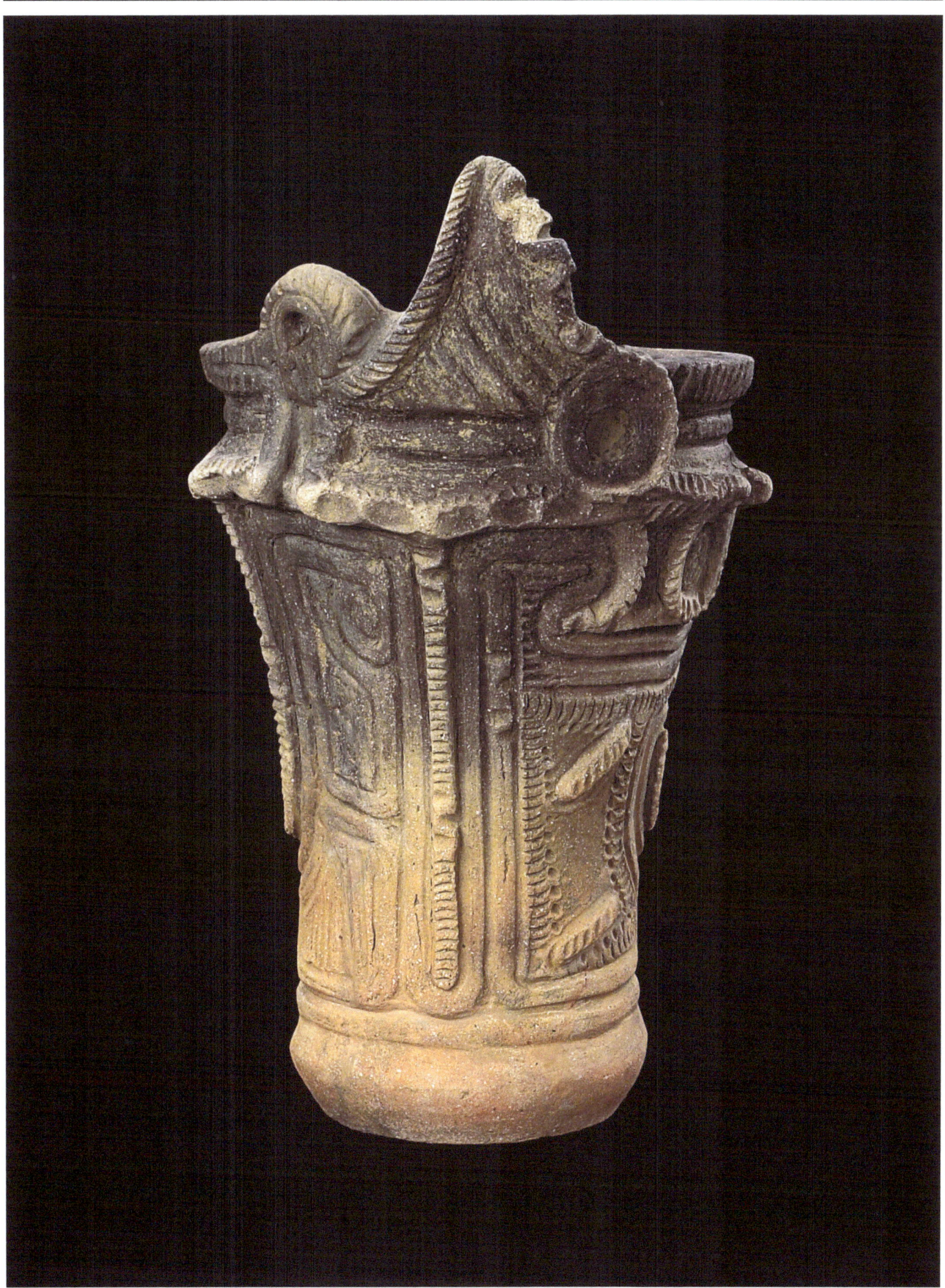

47

Deep bowl with a statue of one-eyed God

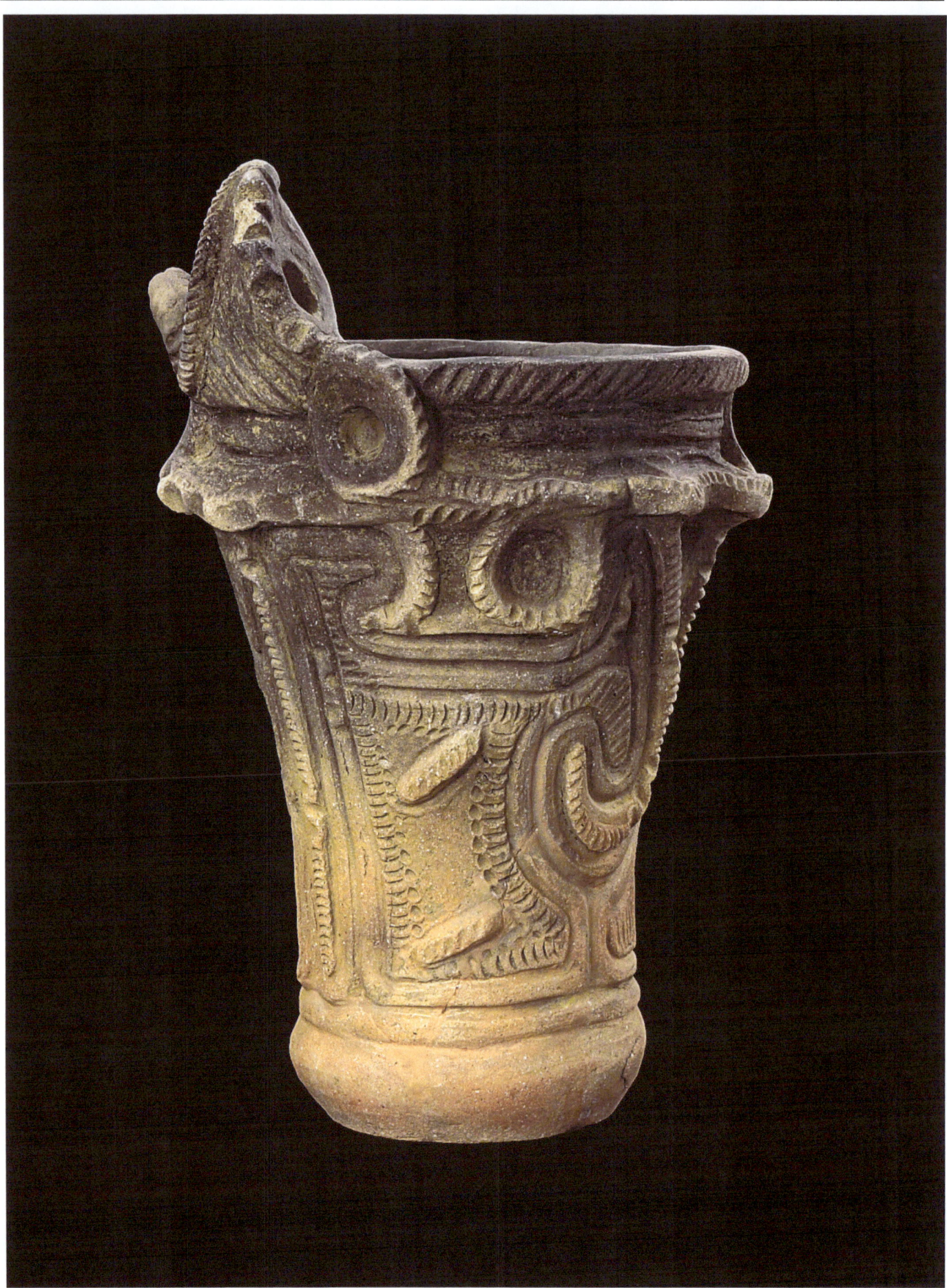

Deep bowl with a statue of one-eyed God

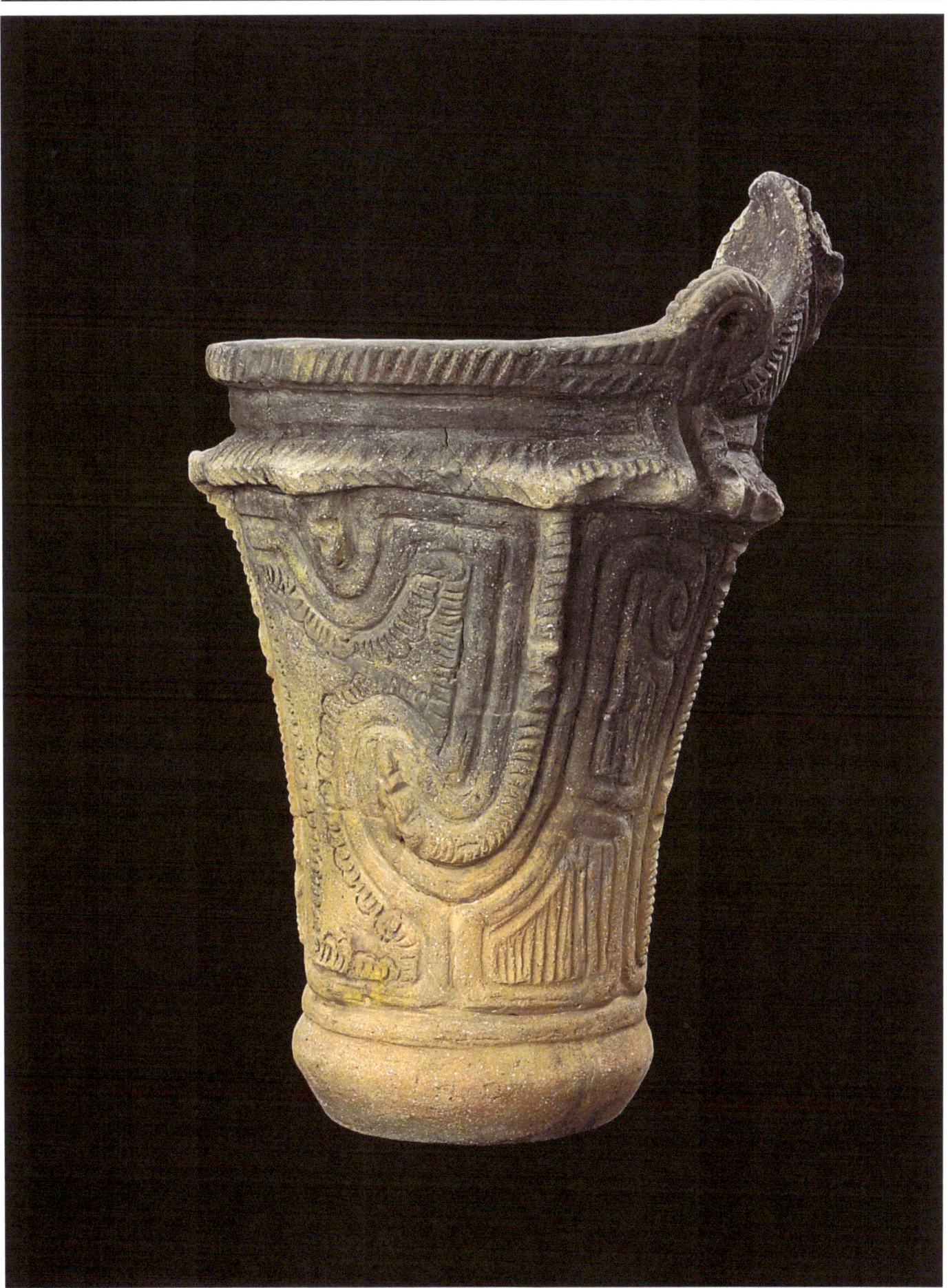

Deep bowl with a statue of one-eyed God

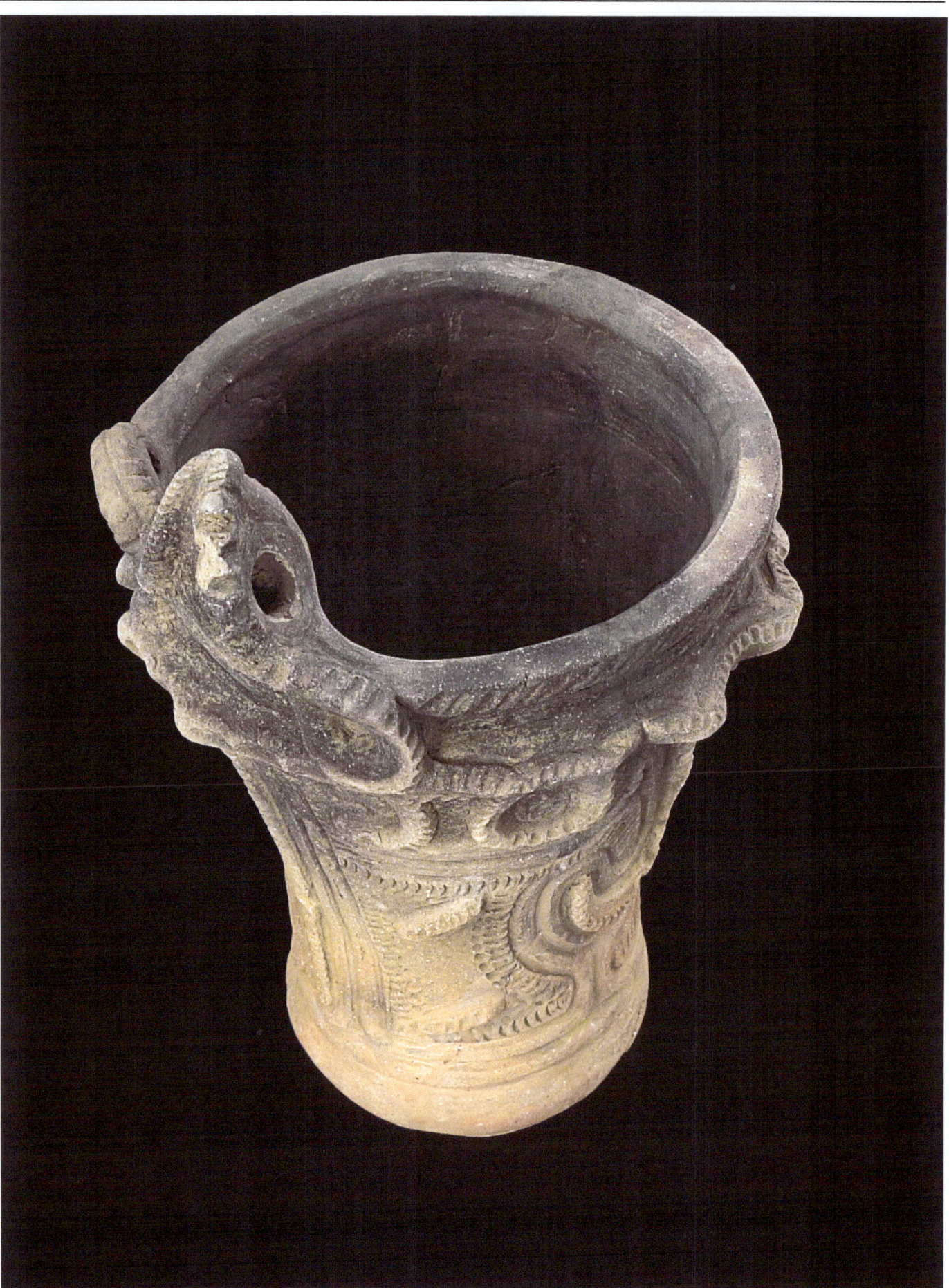

Deep bowl with a statue of one-eyed God

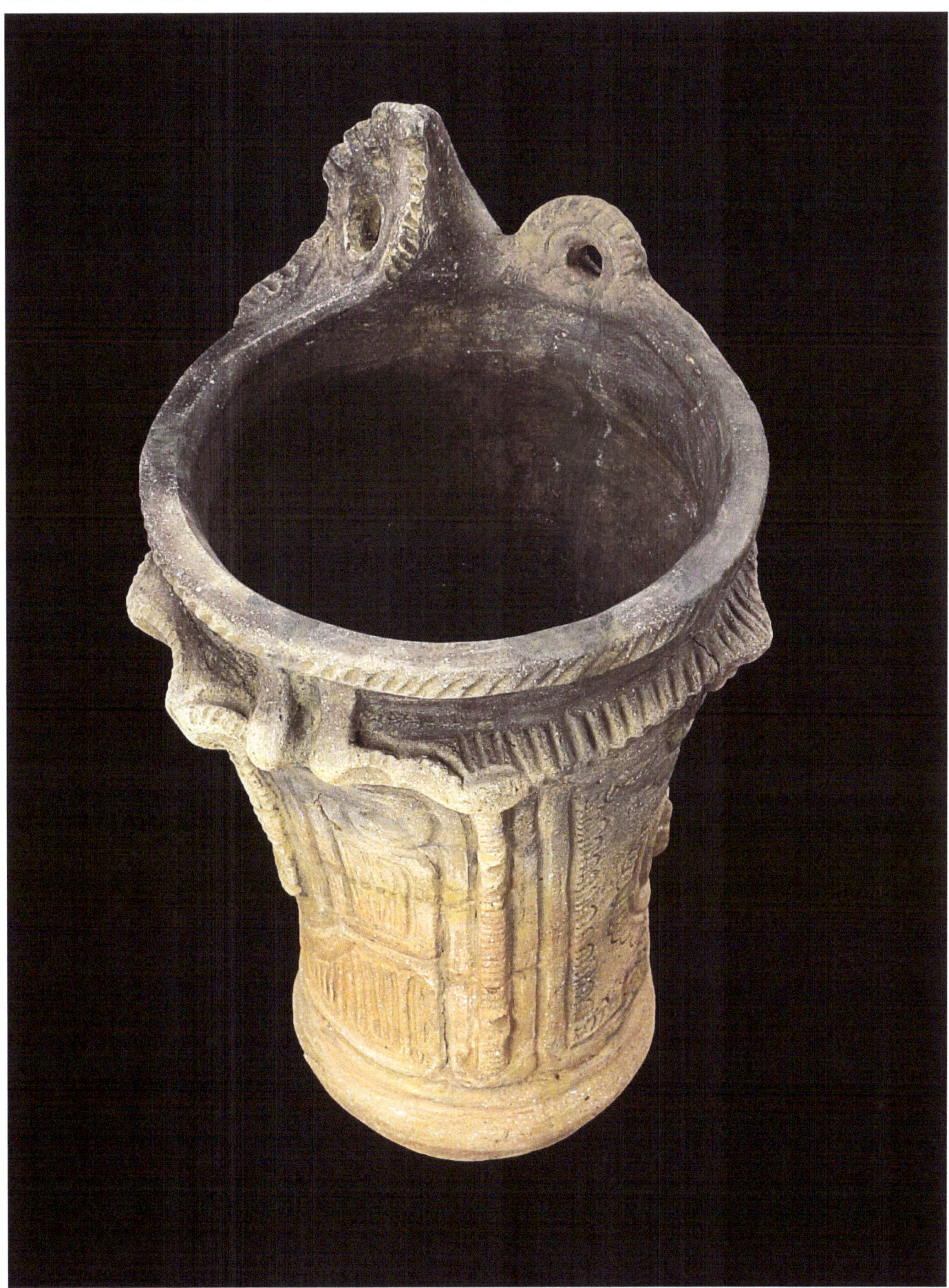

Cylindrical deep bowl with oval compartment patterns
Tounai ruins
Tounai style II
Dwelling site #32, lower layer
Excavated in 1984
Middle Jomon, Middle
4,700 B.P.
33.2cm(H), 23.3cm(D)
"Tounai Report" P.135
ID-079

Four sides of the rim are formed in the peak shape. However, a facing pair seems to have been lost with some reason, the cracks are rubbed flat carefully. The pattern on the rim is a mixture of triangles and crescents, and convex lines hang down from the tops of the peaks. The lower ends of the lines curl like brackens. The bottom slightly incurves at the lowest part and widen gradually up to the shoulder, and it forms an upstanding rim in a slight curve. The body consists of three steps of horizontal blocks and each one has five oval compartment patterns.

This pottery has left the typical appearance of scorching marks. Near the outside of the bottom has not been completely exhausted. The outer wall of the lower body has turned orange and the entire periphery is rough. Above it, thick soot is adhered on the whole including the top of the rim. In the other hand, the bottom of the inner wall is extremely clean and not exhausted at all. One third of the inner wall slightly above the bottom has scab-like soot. Incidentally, this position perfectly corresponds to the lower end which has soot on the outer wall. In the upper can be seen a dark adsorption discoloration like a stain of juice. Also, the incurved part of the rim has slight soot of 3cm in width.

In addition, the outer periphery of the bottom, the corner of the rising portion is rubbed with a width of 1.5cm.

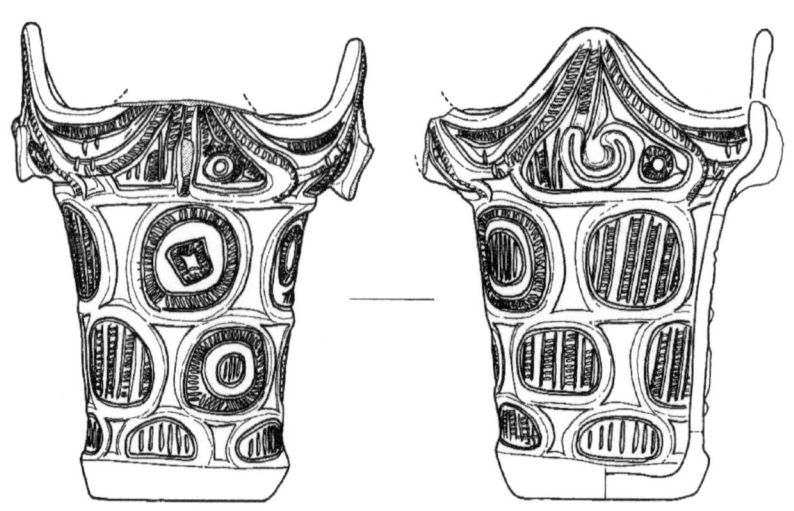

Cylindrical deep bowl with oval compartment patterns

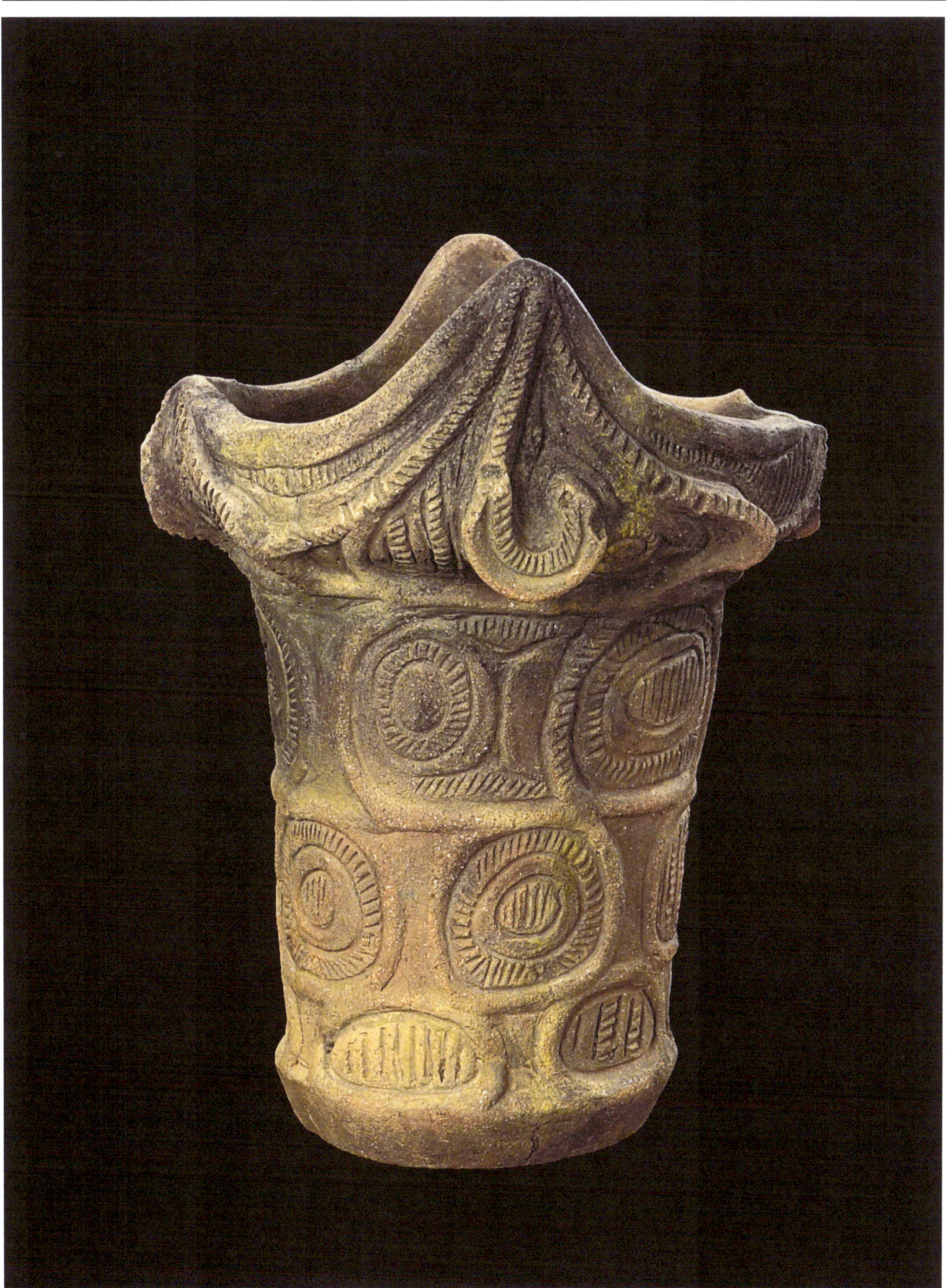

Cylindrical deep bowl with oval compartment patterns

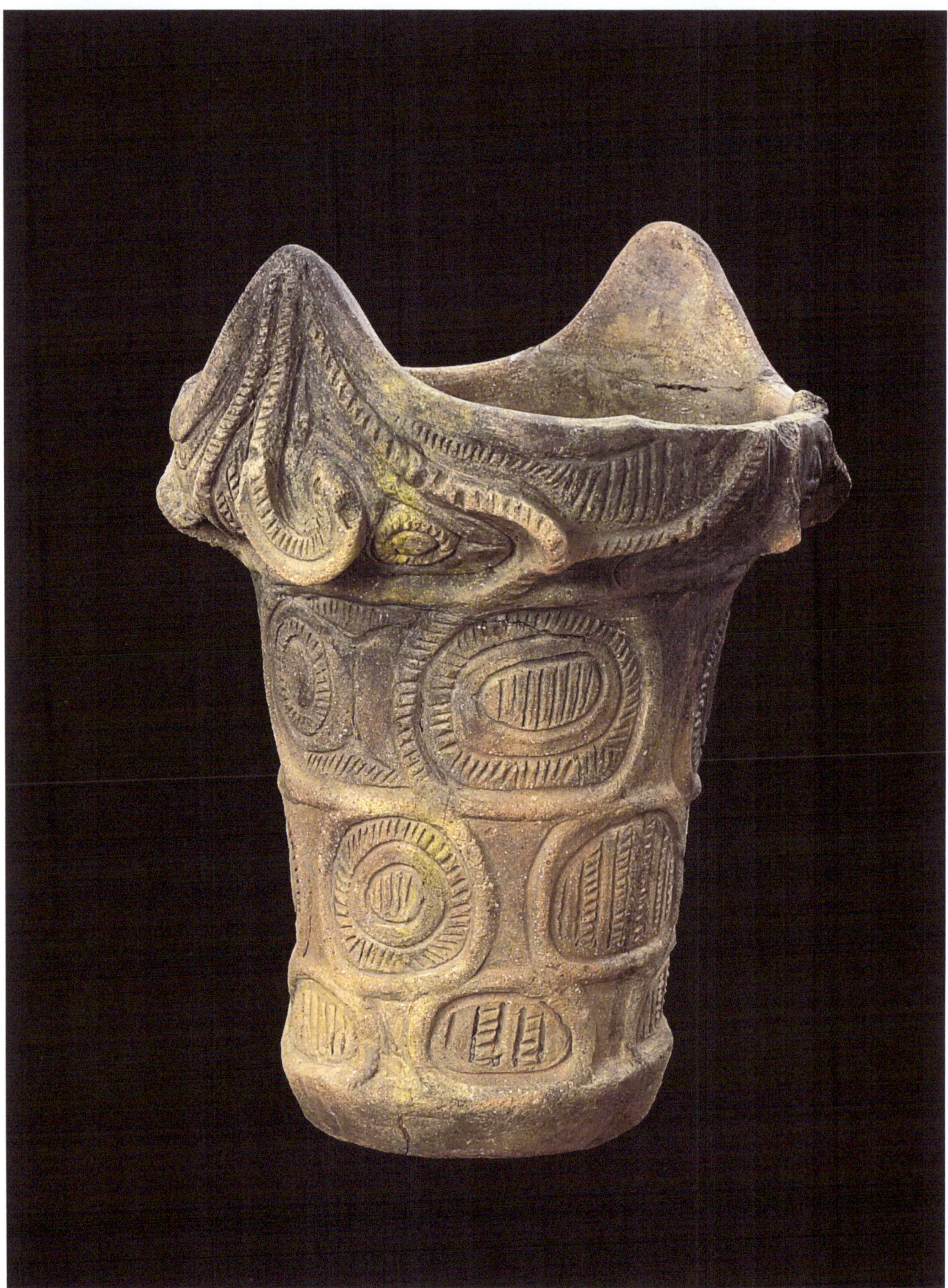

Cylindrical deep bowl with oval compartment patterns

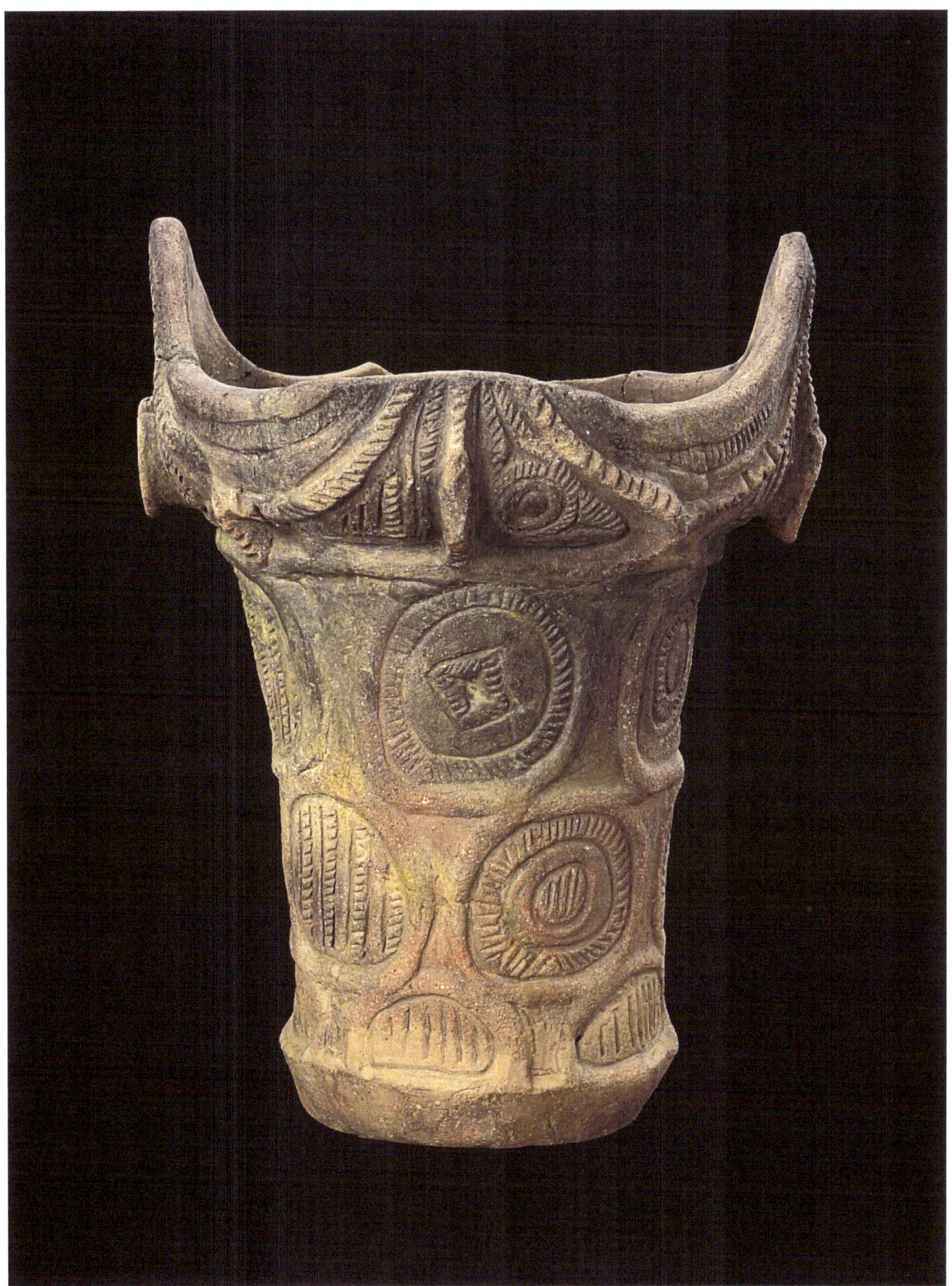

Cylindrical deep bowl with oval compartment patterns

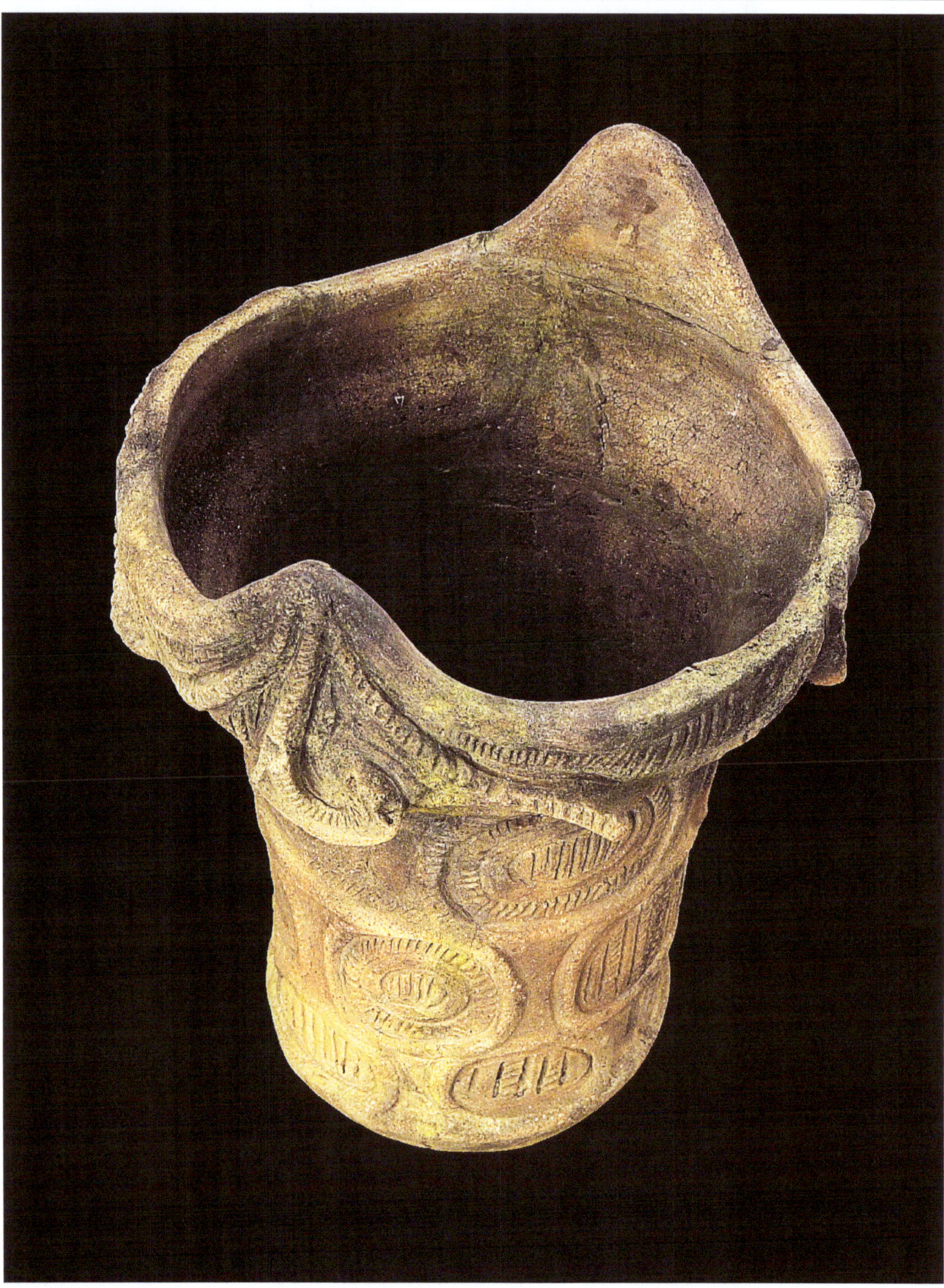

Cylindrical deep bowl with oval compartment patterns

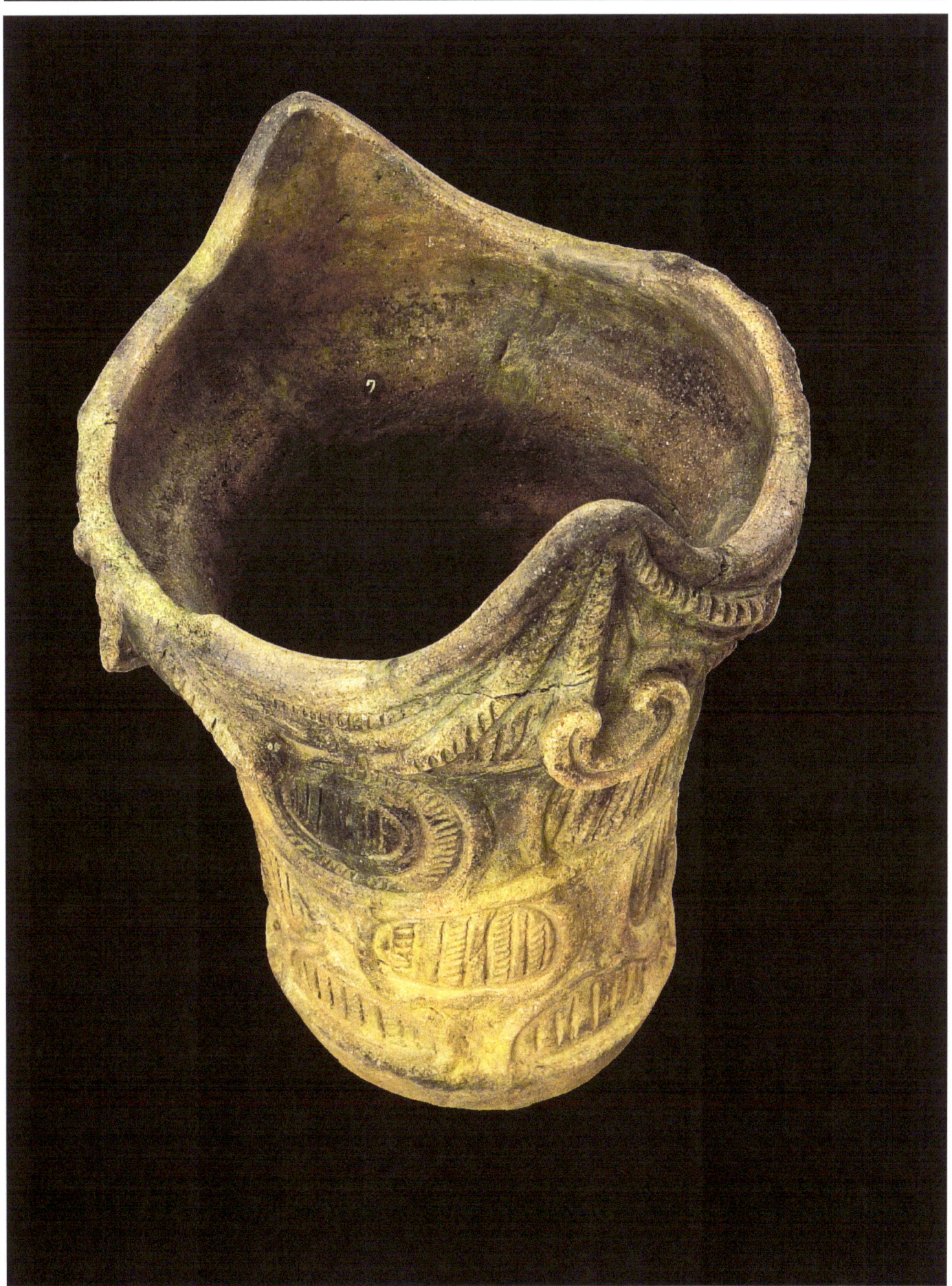

Deep bowl with non-decorative rim
Tounai ruins
Tounai style I
Dwelling site #32, storage hole
Excavated in 1984
Middle Jomon, Middle
4,700 B.P.
39.2cm(H), 22.5cm(D)
"Tounai Report" P.134
ID-081

This is a deep bowl with non-decorative incurved rim that was found in a storage hole. On every side of the neck, narrow oval patterns are arranged. The right side of the oval is made higher and notches are formed on the edges. Below them are formed similar patterns by using thinner ridges. A facing pair of the pattern has a shape of right half rhombus. One is a curled-pattern of right side that is coming up from below, and the end has a circular pattern.

Another one has much loss, but seems to be Y-shape. Around them, it has a rough texture with the ring and padding marks. On the upper right of the half rhombus with no pattern inside, double circles and an arrow-shaped pattern are formed with fine triangular lines. A similar arrow-shaped pattern is formed at the left side as well, but the circular part is missing.

The lower half of the outer wall has turned orange, and the upper half has clear soot on the whole. The inner wall has belt-shaped scorches of 8cm in width from the part 2cm above the bottom.

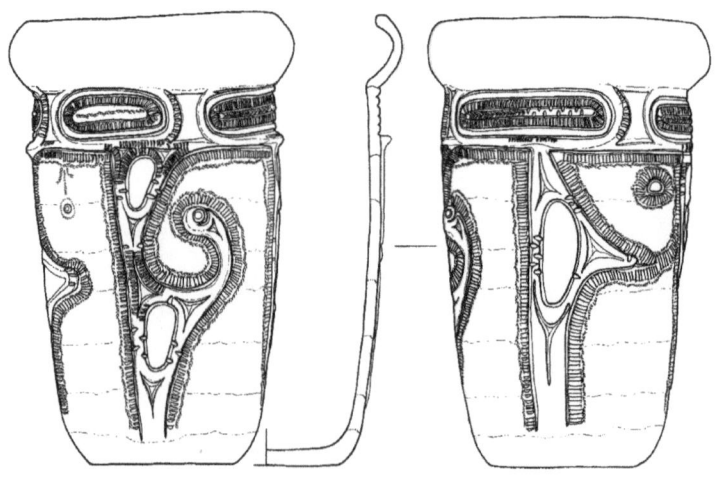

Deep bowl with non-decorative rim

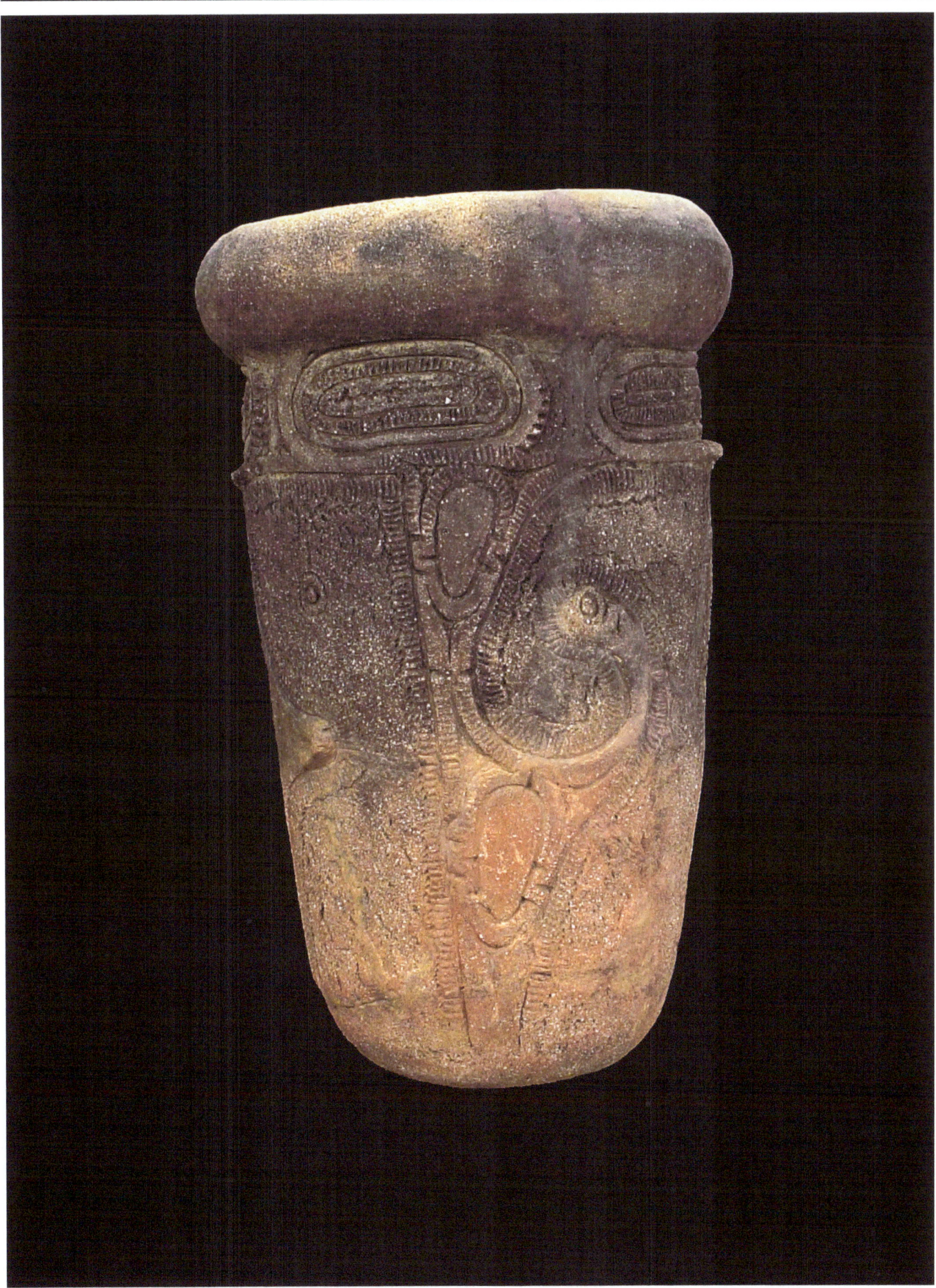

Deep bowl with non-decorative rim

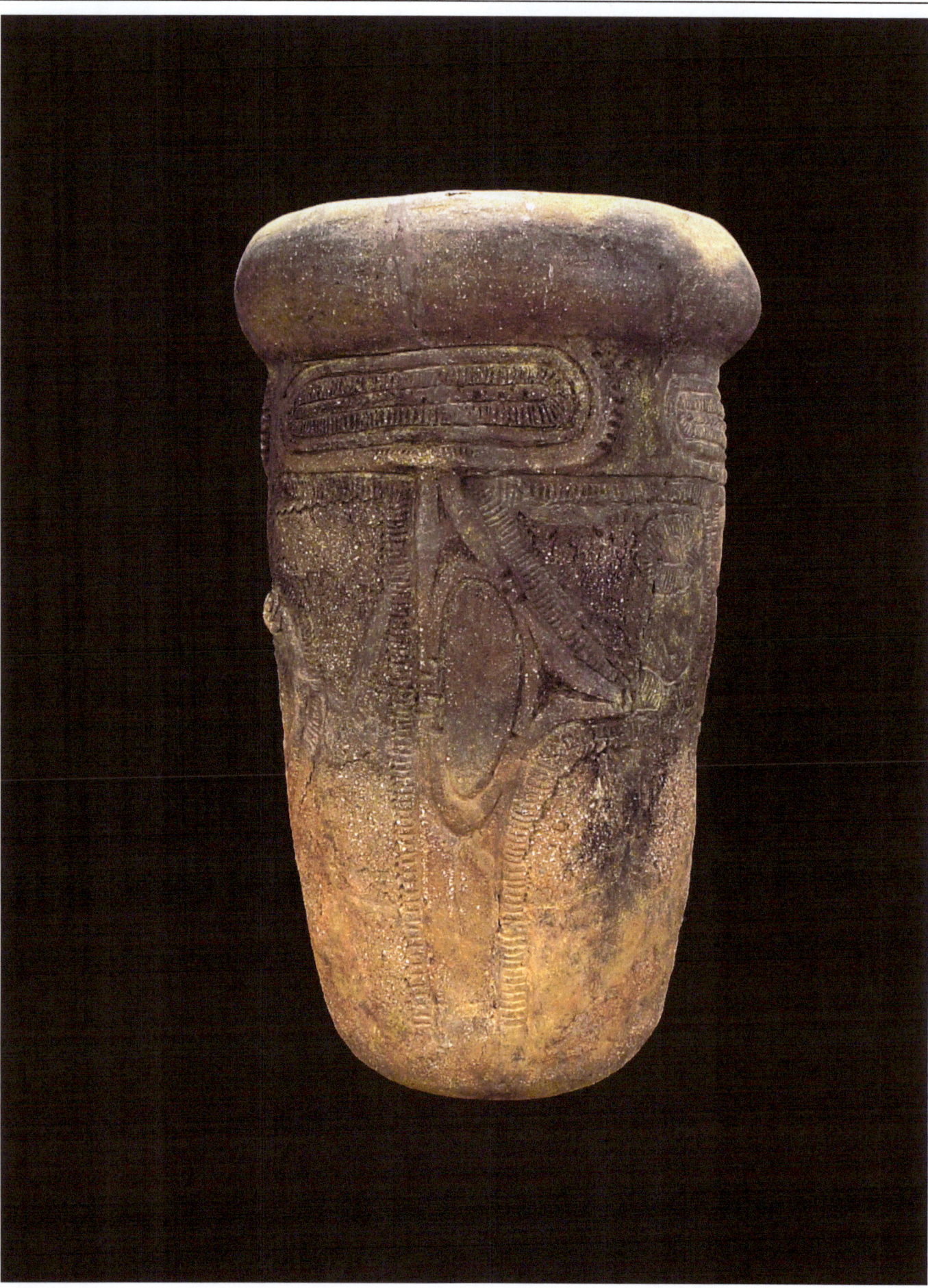

Deep bowl with non-decorative rim

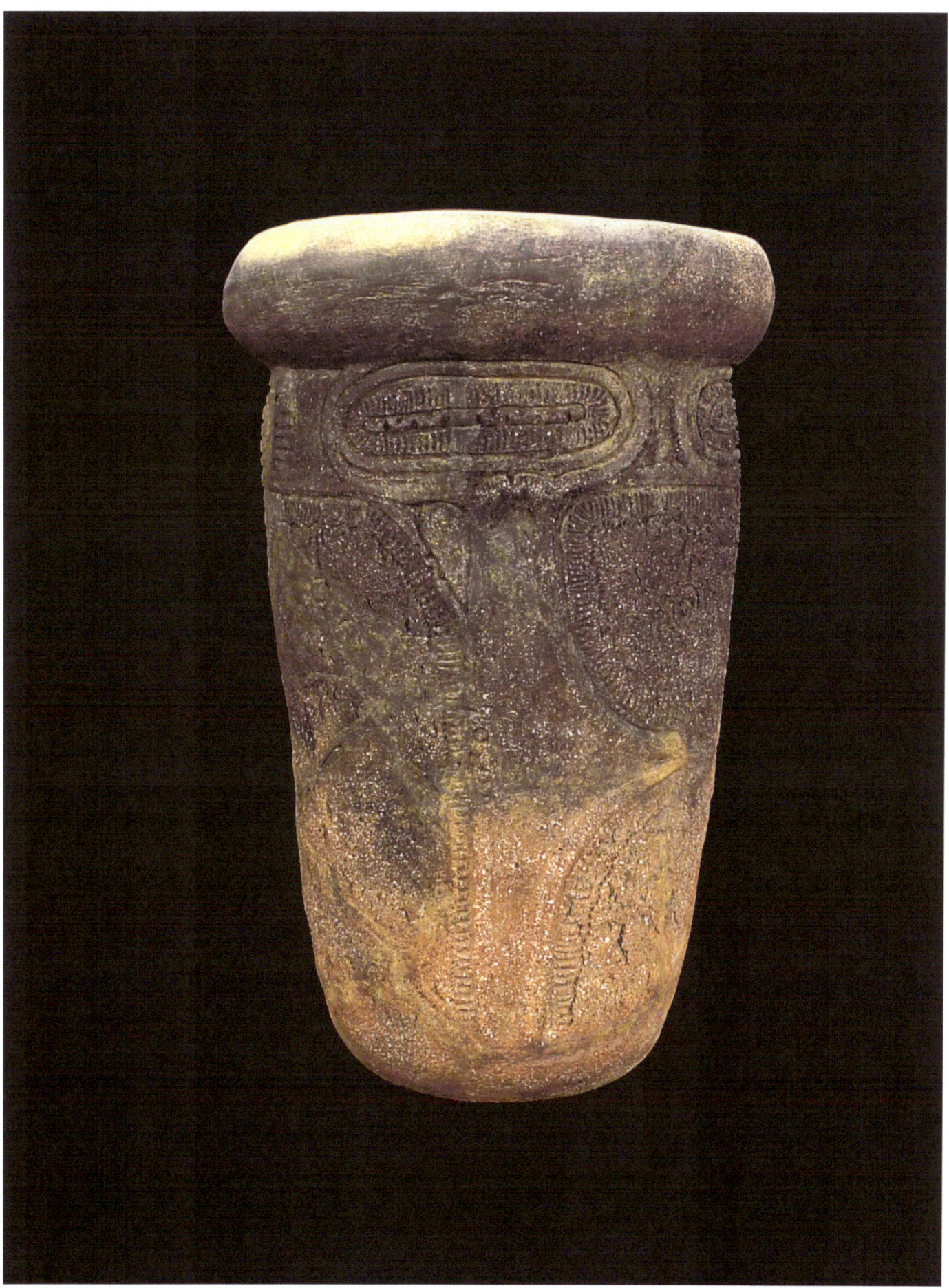

Deep bowl with dual eyes and snake pattern
Tounai ruins
Idojiri style I
Dwelling site #32, upper layer
Excavated in 1984
Middle Jomon, Middle
4,500 B.P.
48.6cm(H), 28.0cm(D)
"Tounai Report" P.137
ID-082

This is a deep bowl of rope-patterns with swollen shoulder and constricted bottom. The non-decorative short edge is incurved horizontally and dual eyes are formed on it. Dual rings of the neck, the tip of dual eyes and the bottom are chipped. At the slightly left side with the dual eyes in front is formed a pattern that is assumed as a snake crawling up on the body from the bottom with its mouth open toward the left.

The lower half has remarkable rough skin, and the upper half has soot in places. It seems to have been used often, and the surface is worn.

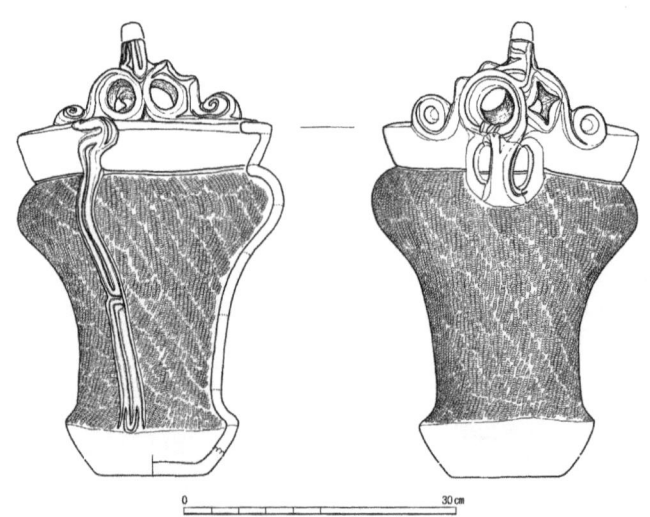

Deep bowl with dual eyes and snake pattern

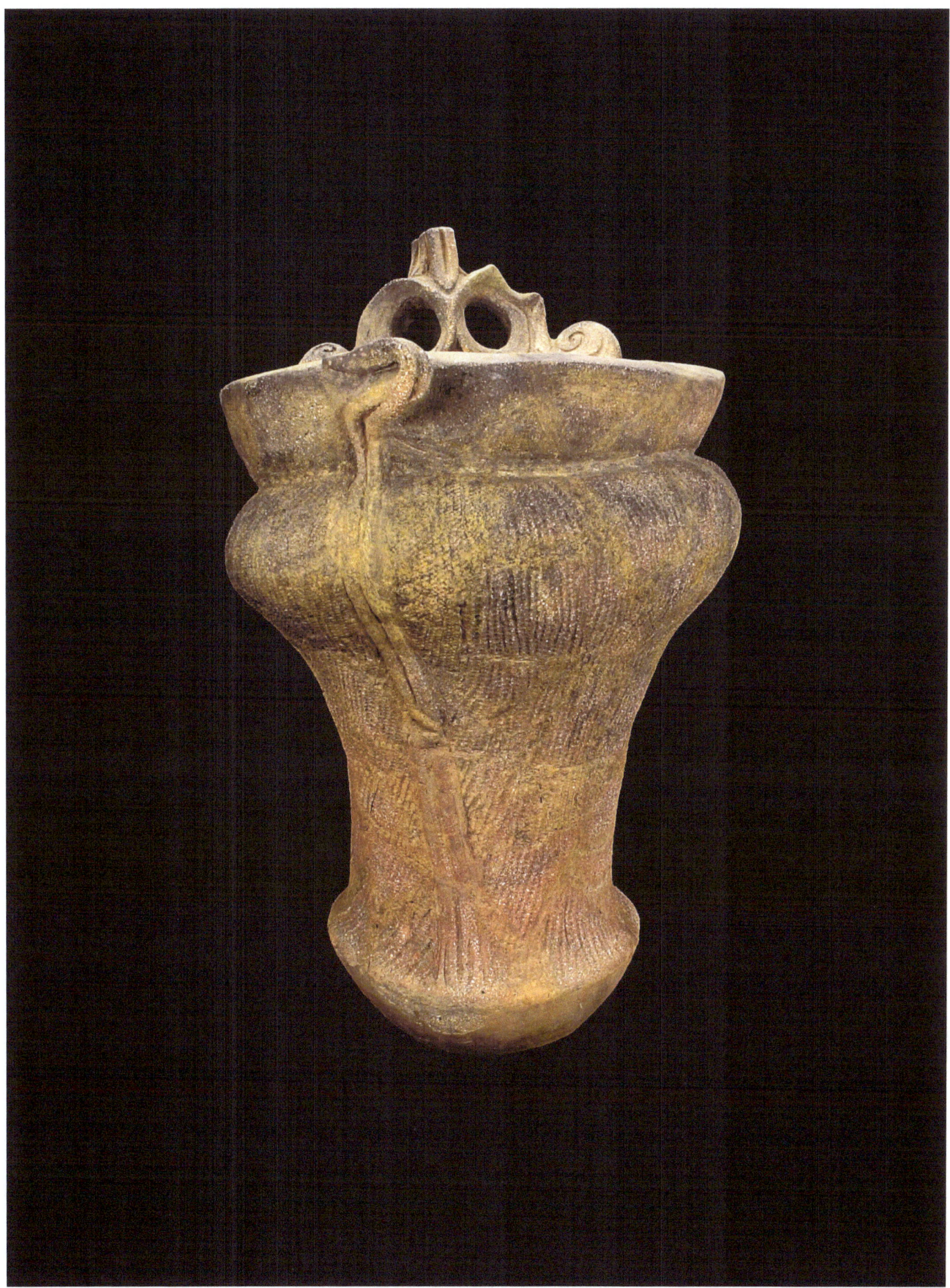

Deep bowl with dual eyes and snake pattern

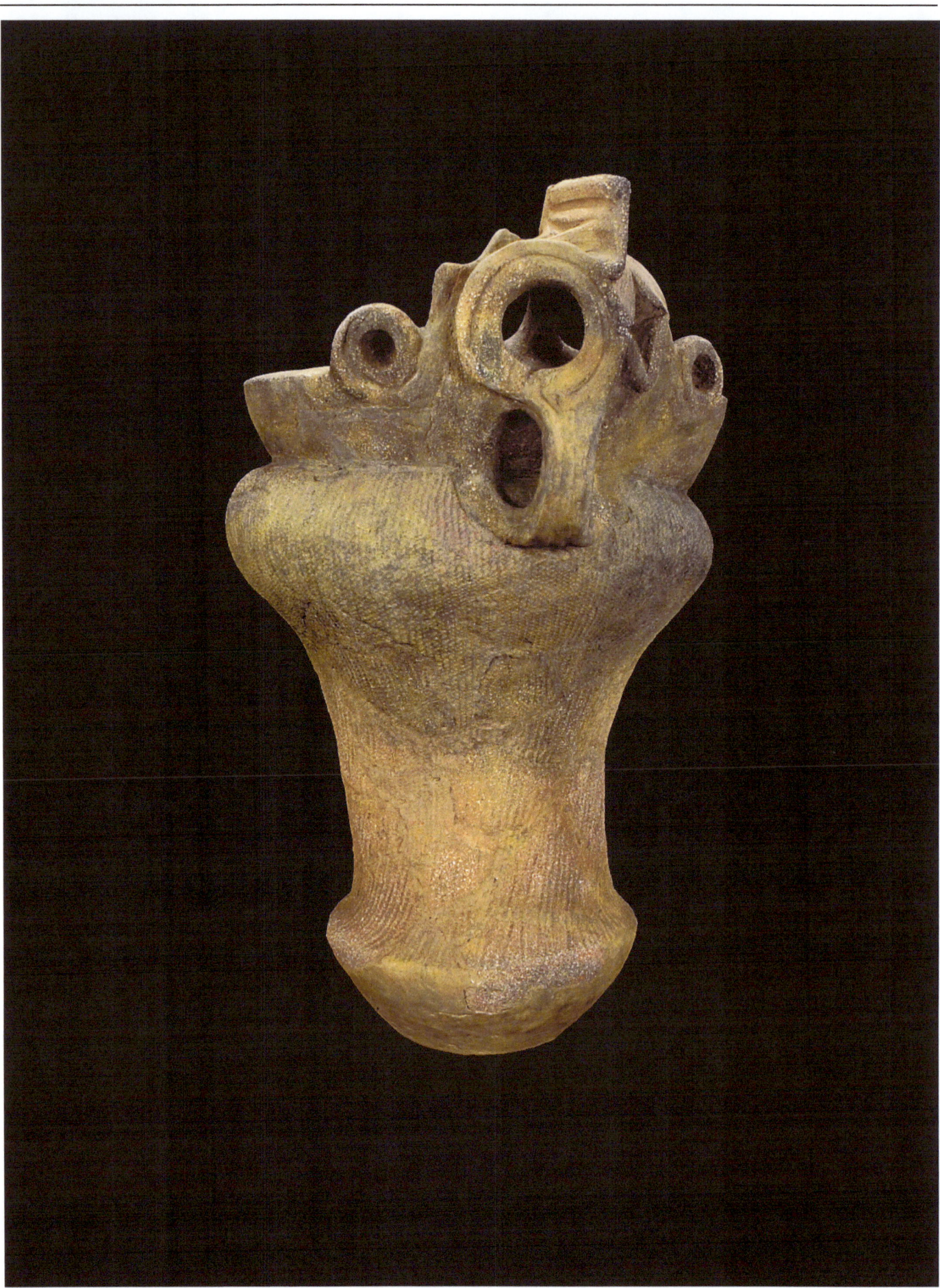

Deep bowl with dual eyes and snake pattern

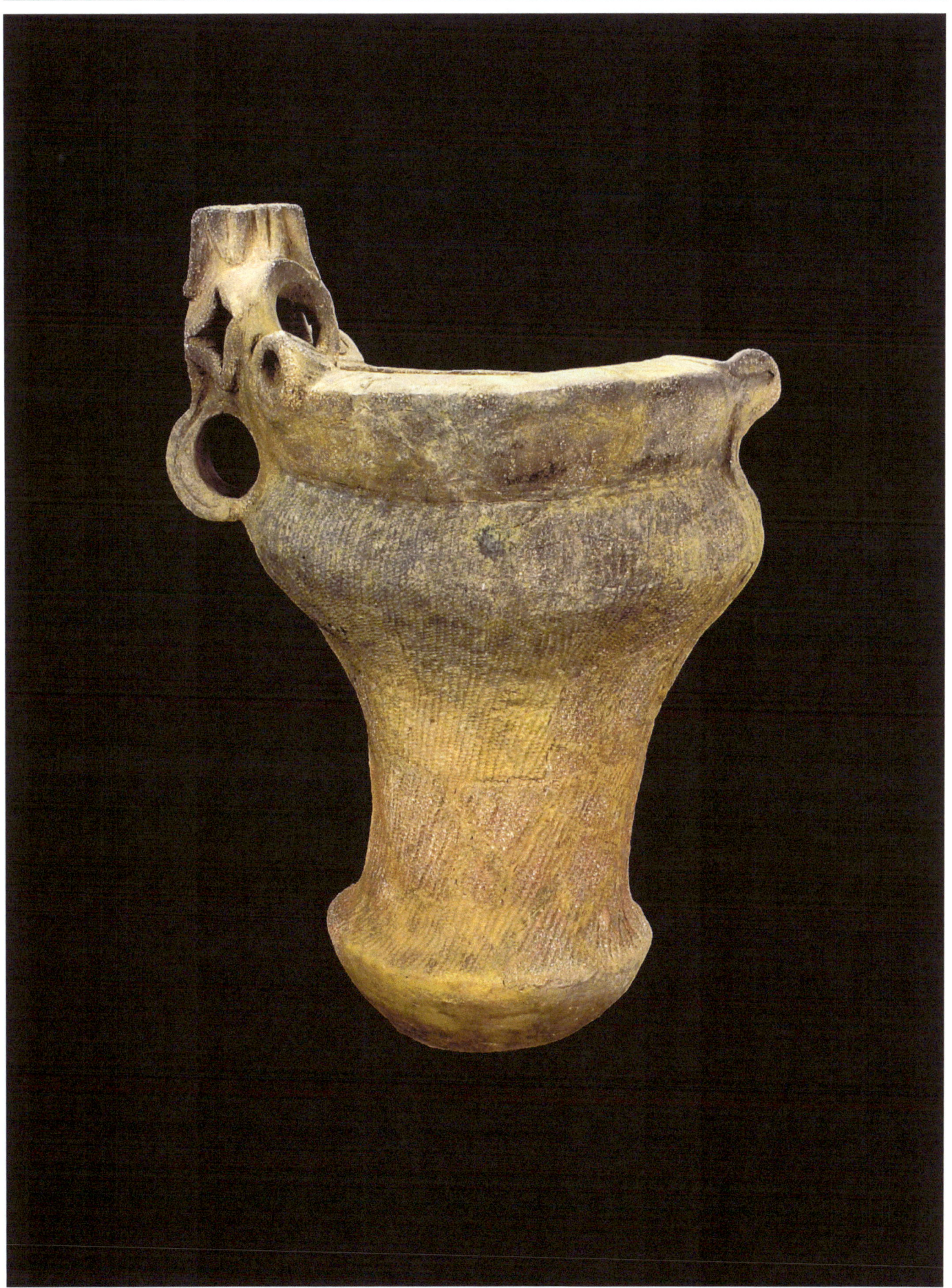

Deep bowl with dual eyes and snake pattern

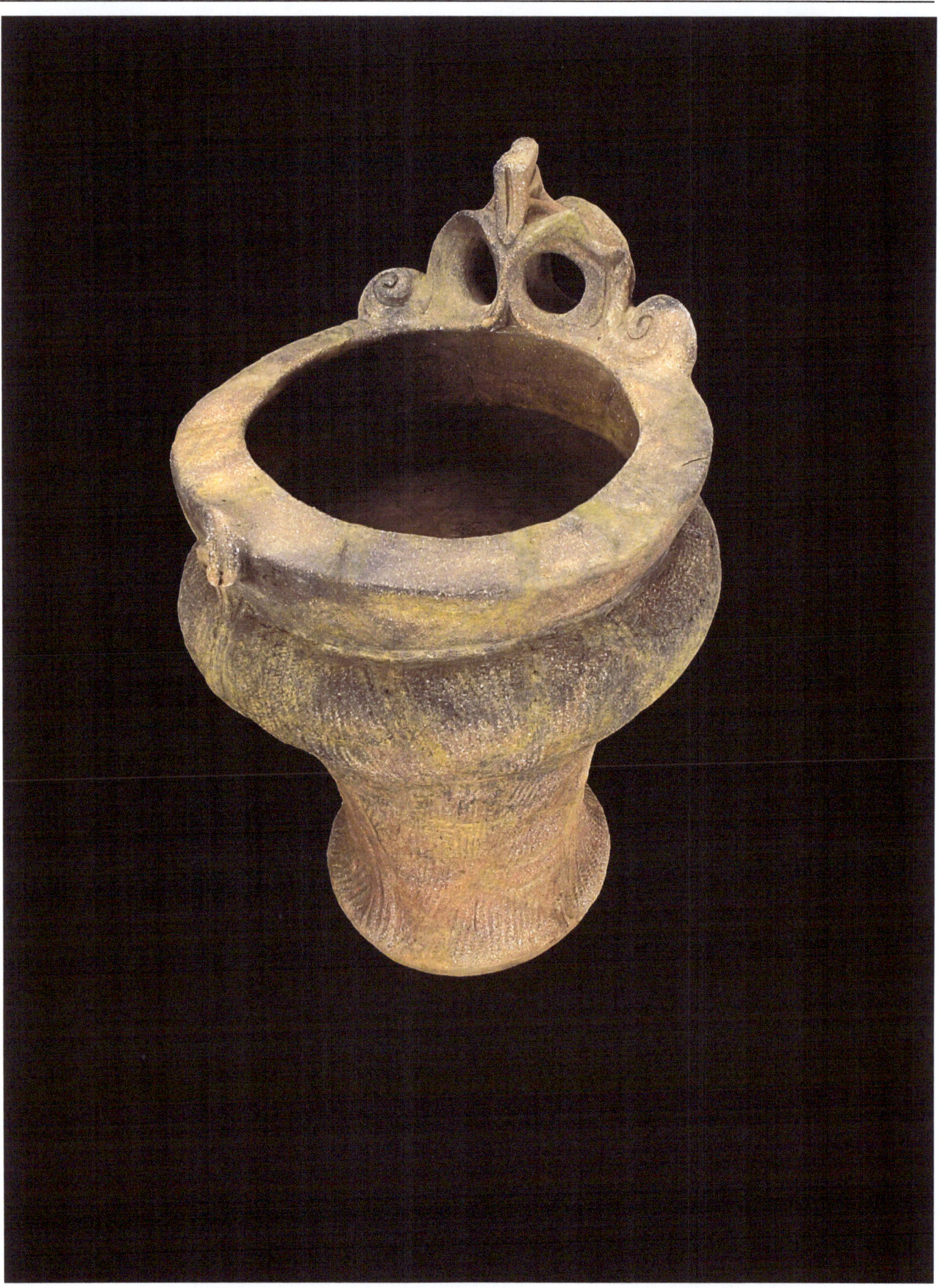

Deep bowl with dual eyes and snake pattern

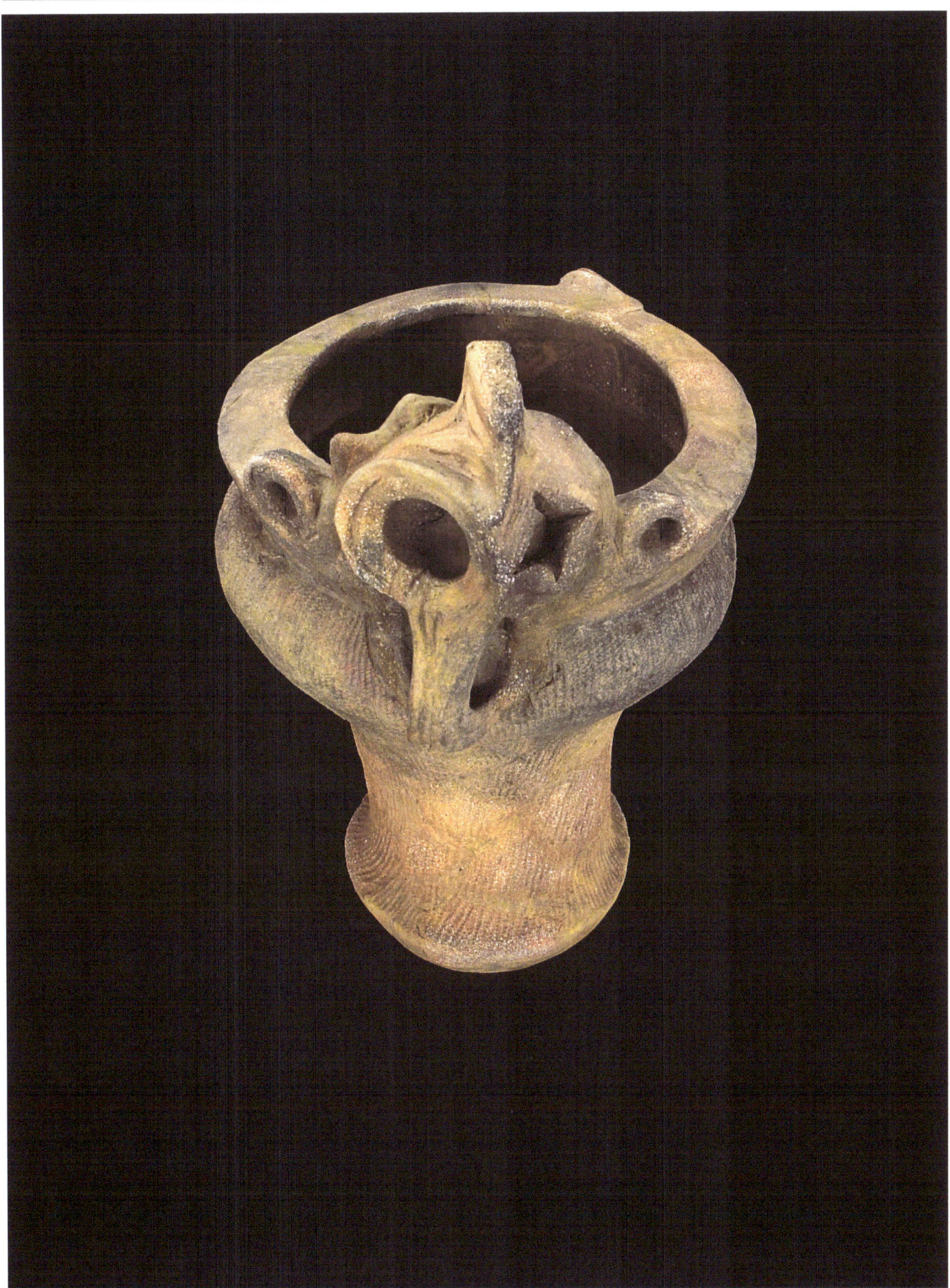

Deep bowl with deformed Mizuchi patterns
(legendary mythical dragon or snake-like beast)
Tounai ruins
Tounai style I
Dwelling site #32, lower layer
Excavated in 1984
Middle Jomon, Middle
4,700 B.P.
48.4cm(H), 30.0cm(D)
"Tounai Report" P.134
ID-083

This is a deep bowl with a hoop-shaped rim. On the rim can be seen a cone projection with a reverse drop shaped hole so as to match the lips from both sides and it is accompanied with a pair of small circles and a small triangle projection. The body consists of three steps of patterns. The upper step is finished in the style of openwork engraving the surface into triangles and diamonds after drawing fine parallel lines.

The second step has four oblongs. On the third step of lower half of the body can be seen a pair of patterns which is like abstraction of Mizuchi. At the bottom can be seen marks of ring and padding.

One third of the lower part of the body has turned red and the upper part of it is blackish. The inner wall has turned black close to the half except the bottom.

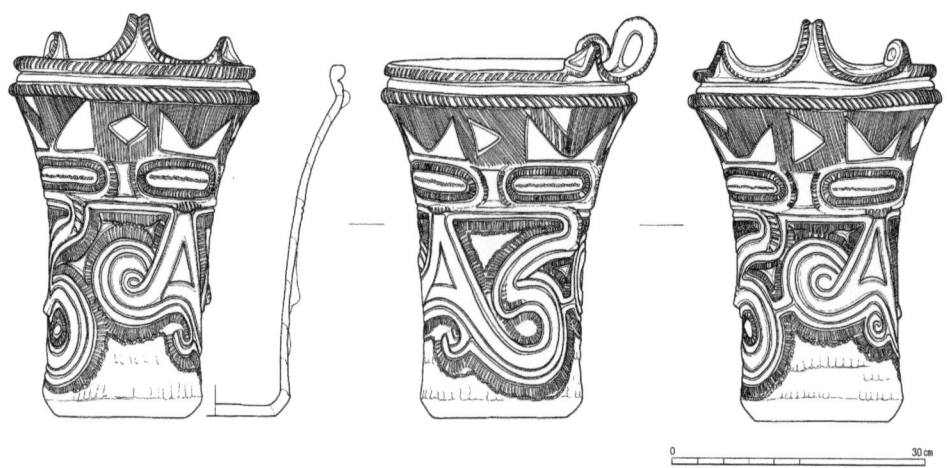

Deep bowl with deformed Mizuchi pattern

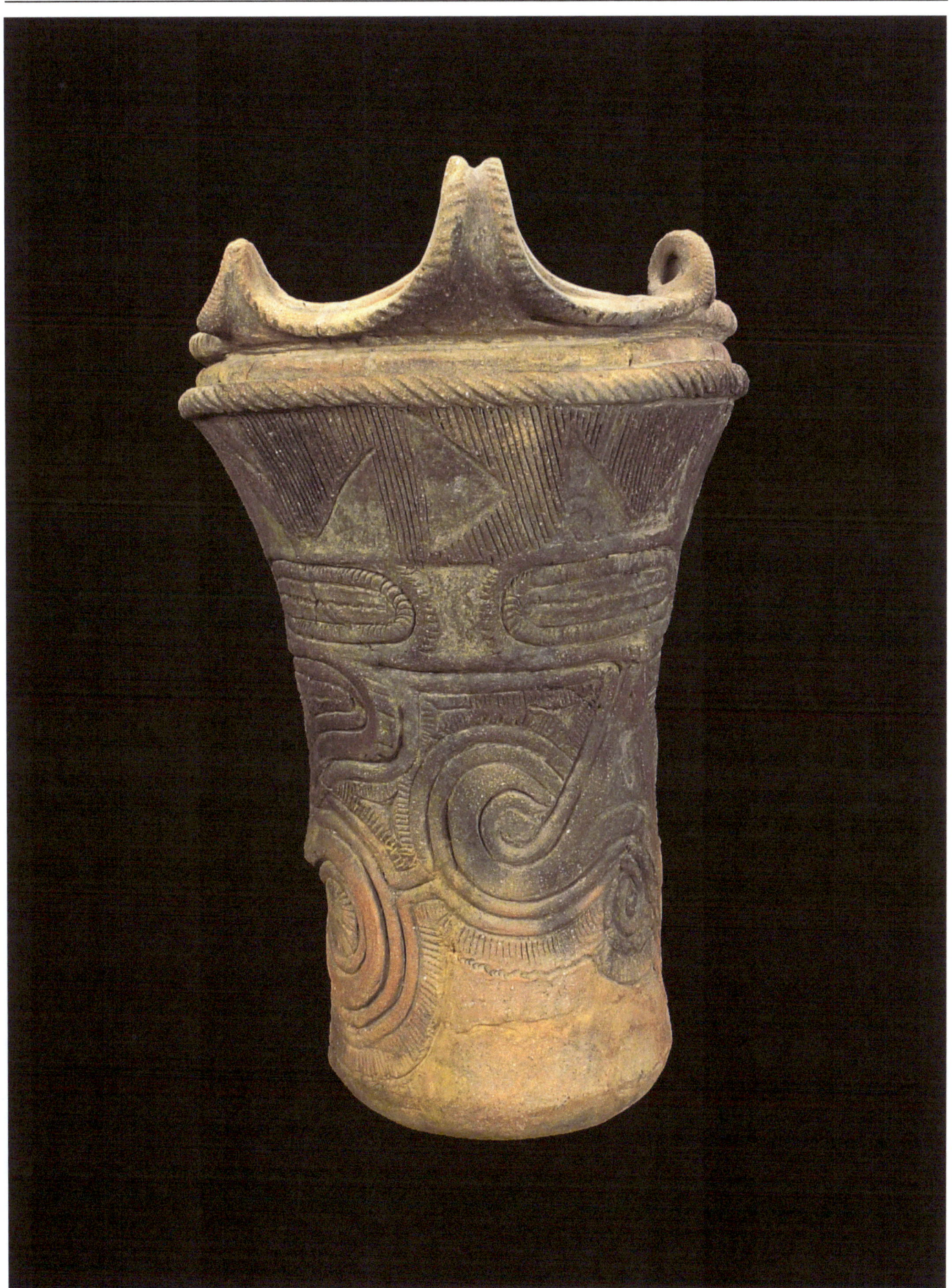

Deep bowl with deformed Mizuchi pattern

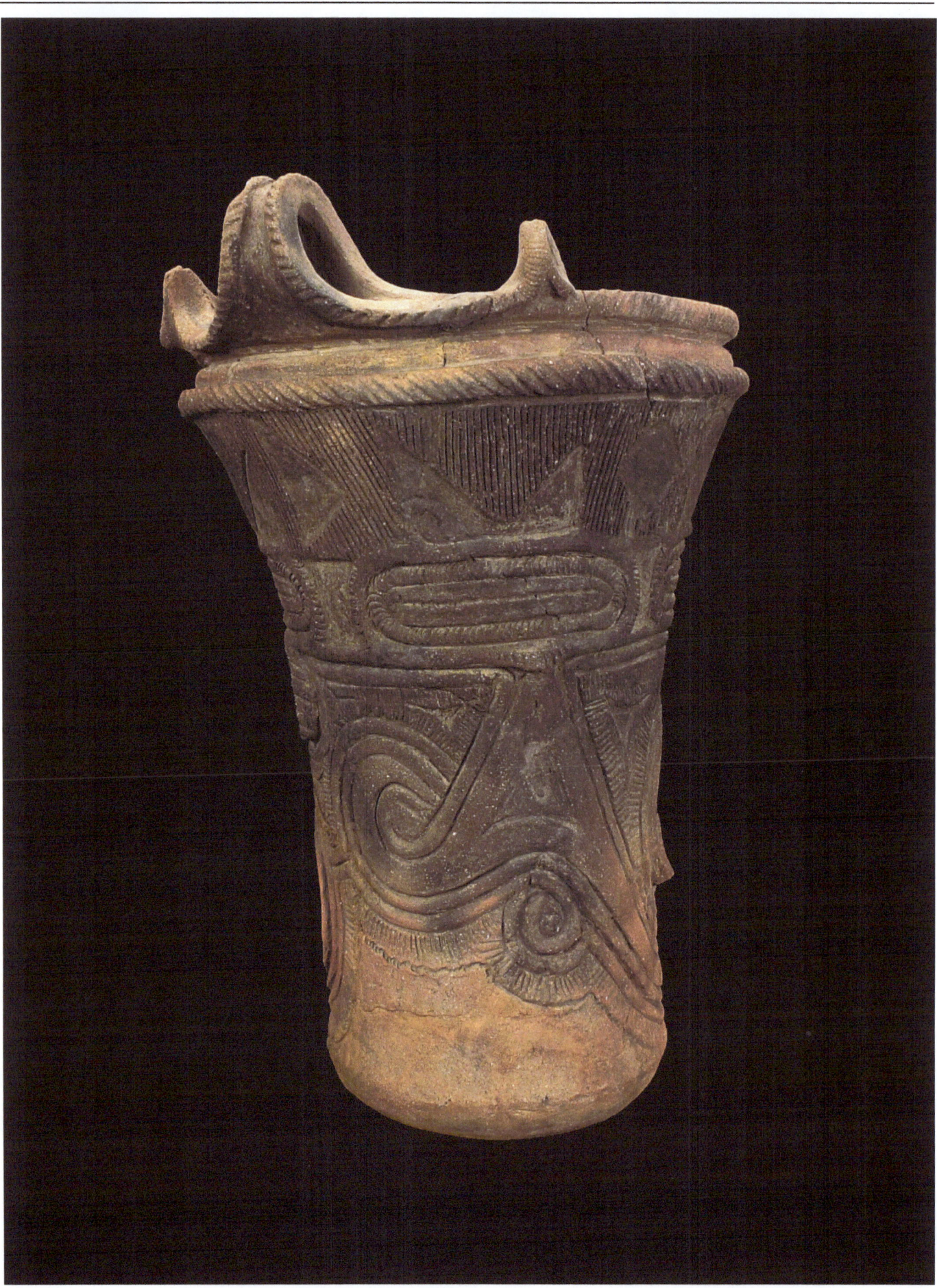

70

Deep bowl with deformed Mizuchi pattern

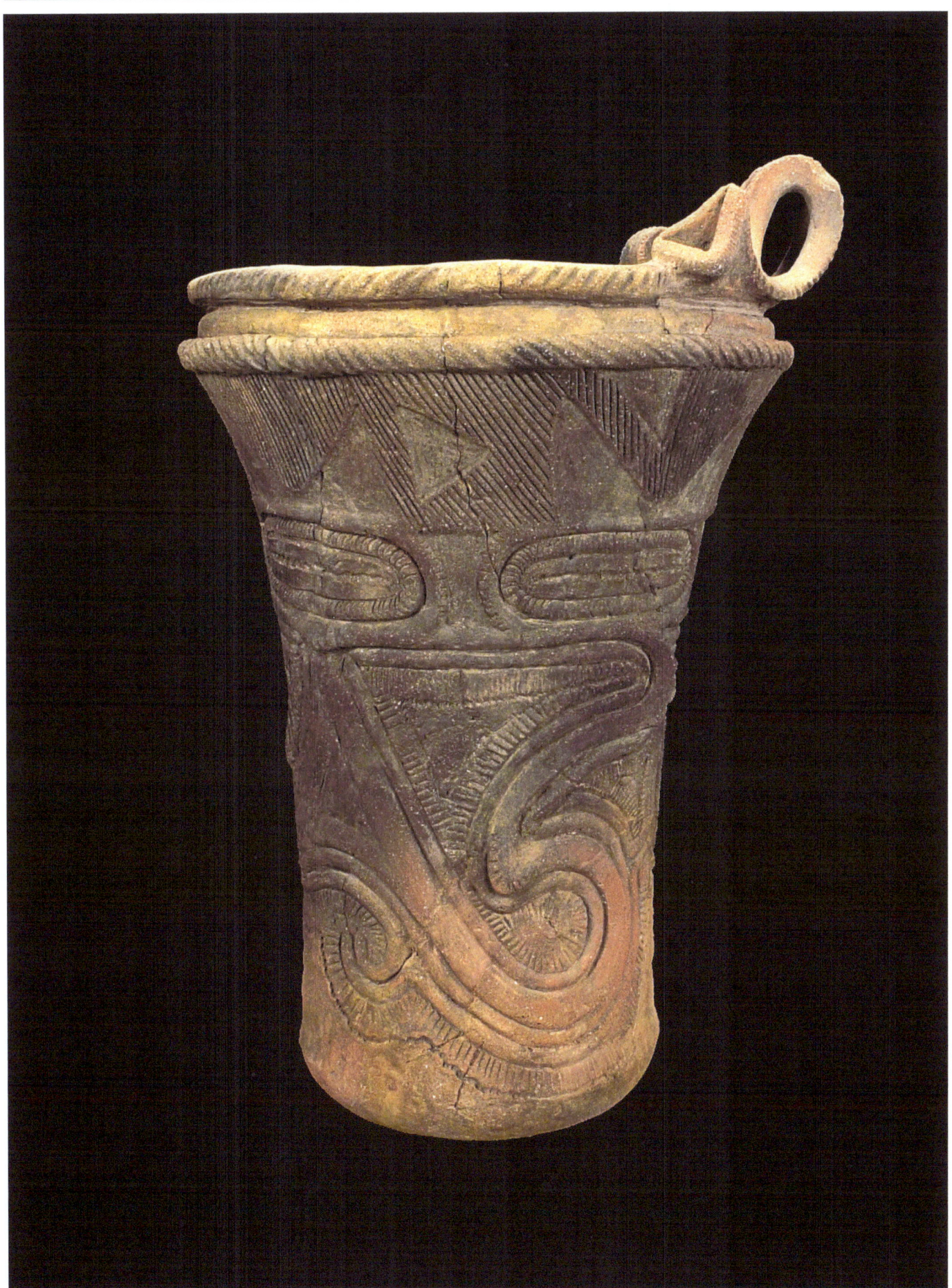

Deep bowl with deformed Mizuchi pattern

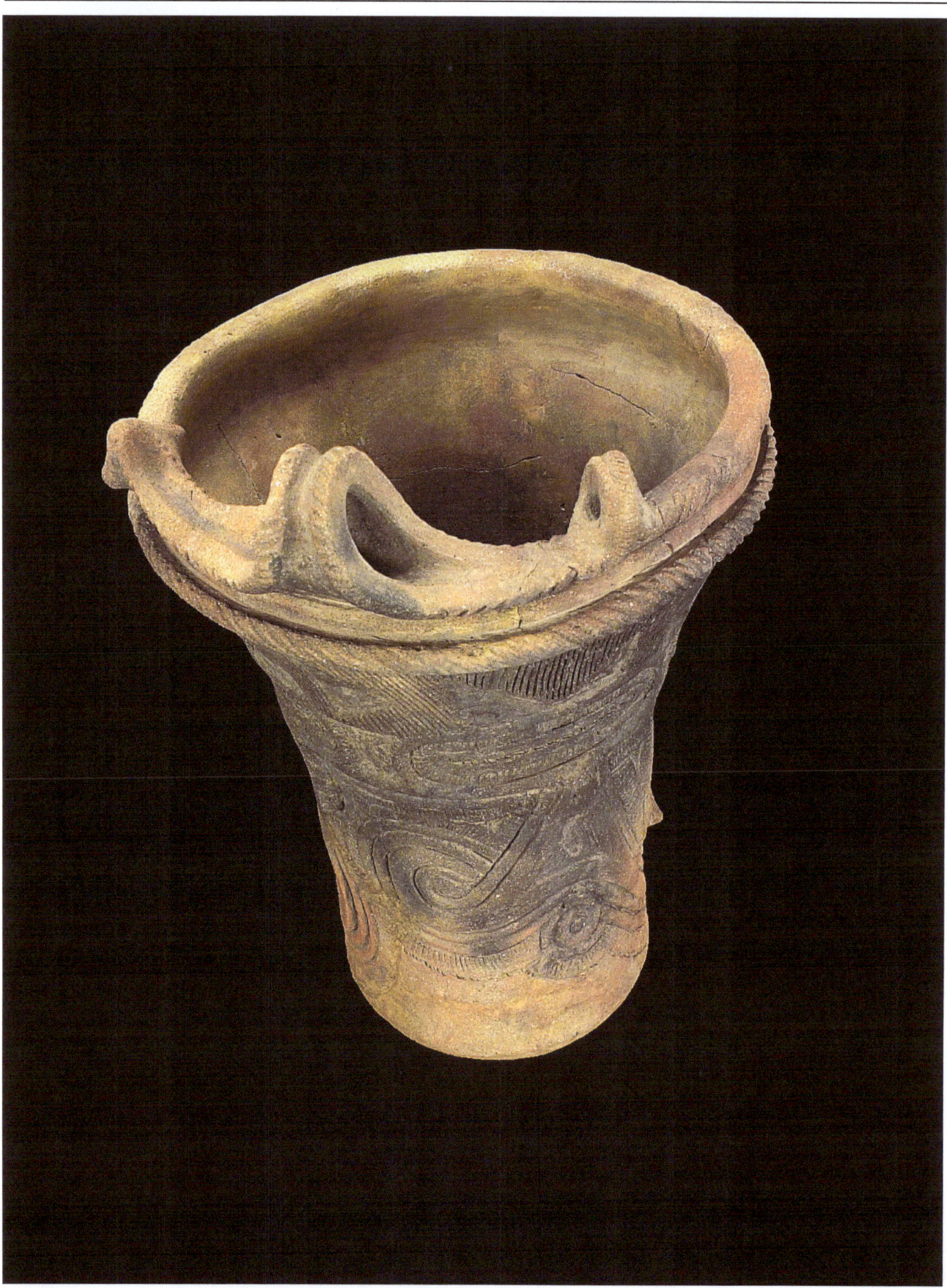

Deep bowl with deformed Mizuchi pattern

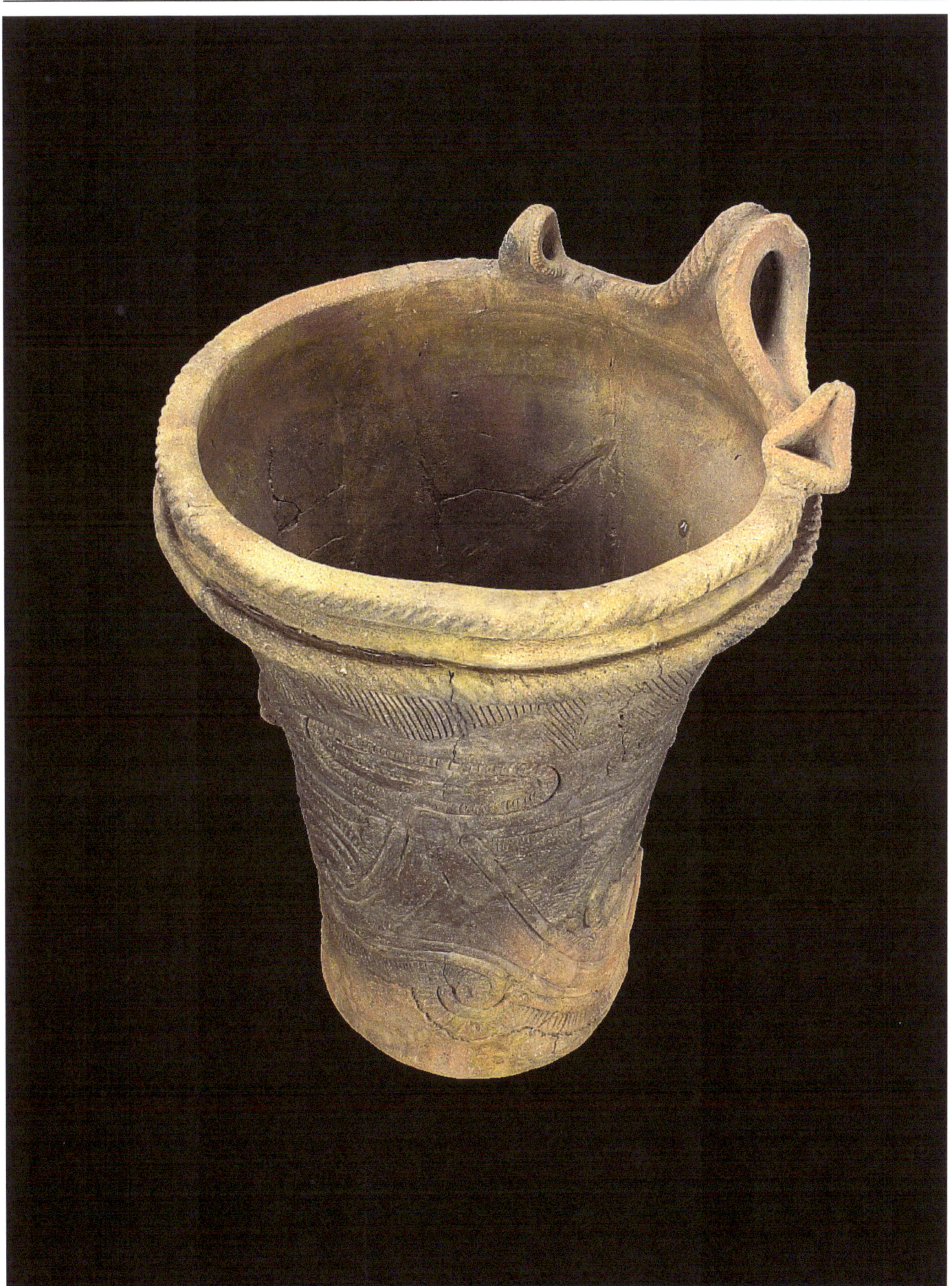

Steamer type deep bowl with snake pattern
Tounai ruins
Idojiri style I
Dwelling site #9
Excavated in 1962
Middle Jomon, Middle
4,500 years B.P.
32.4cm(H), 24.5cm(D)
"Idojiri Report" P97, No.314 ; "Tounai Report" P.315, No.221
ID-029

Half of this steamer type deep bowl exists now. Square plates with dual rings are arranged at the four side of the rim and a circular hole penetrates the square plates. In contact with the dual rings are formed distorted circle patterns and in the middle are arranged in a snake-shaped form with a triangle head.

Among those four sides, the perfect one is only one side and only a part of head remains on the right. On the left remains a part of spiral pattern that represents 3 fingers at the tip. Another is completely missing. At the waist part are arranged six so-called comb-shaped forms.

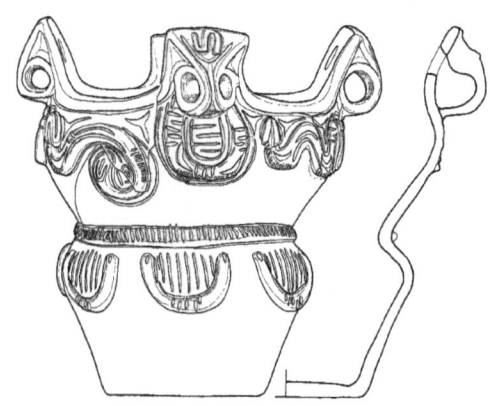

Steamer type deep bowl with snake pattern

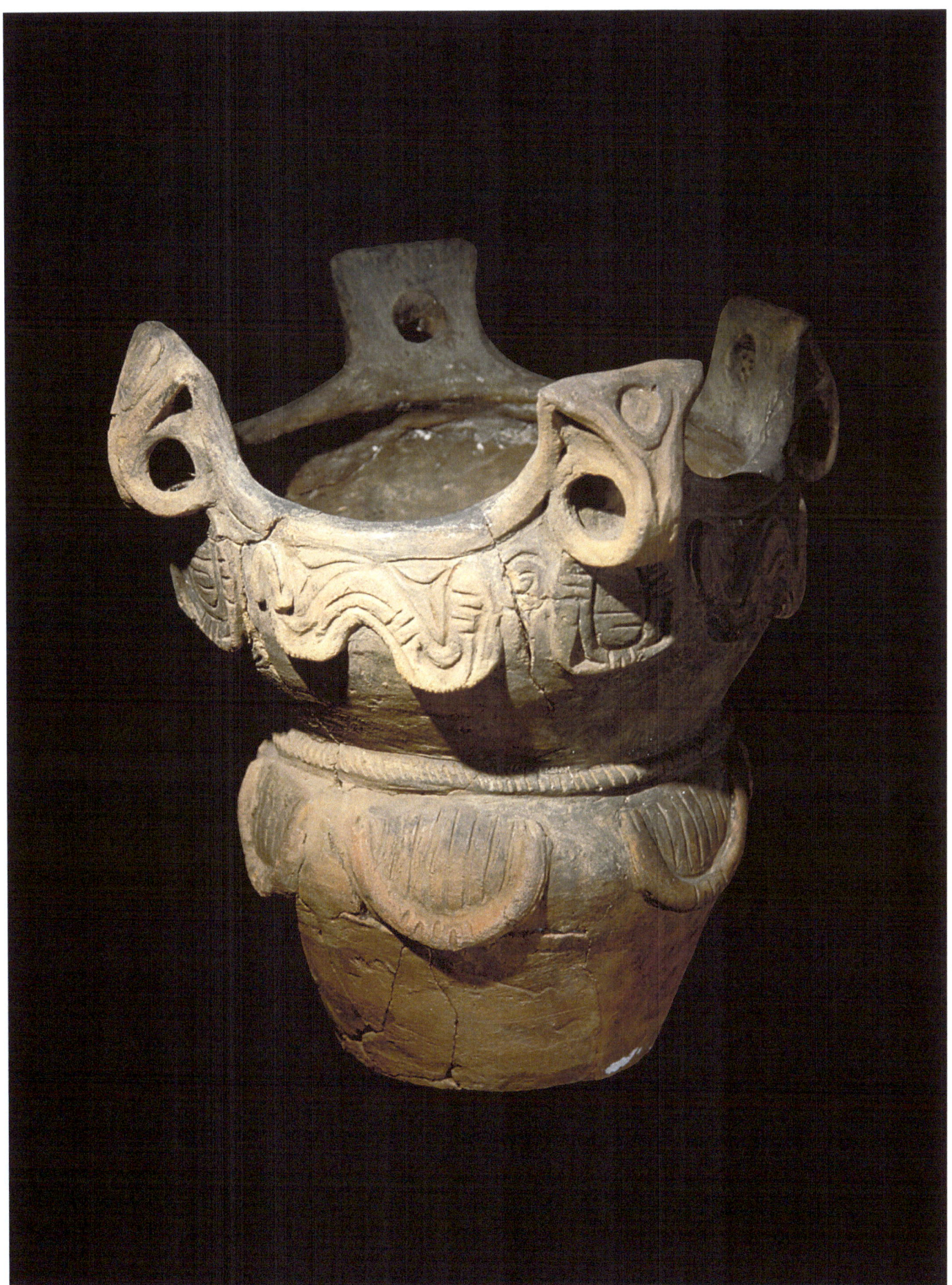

Steamer type deep bowl with snake pattern

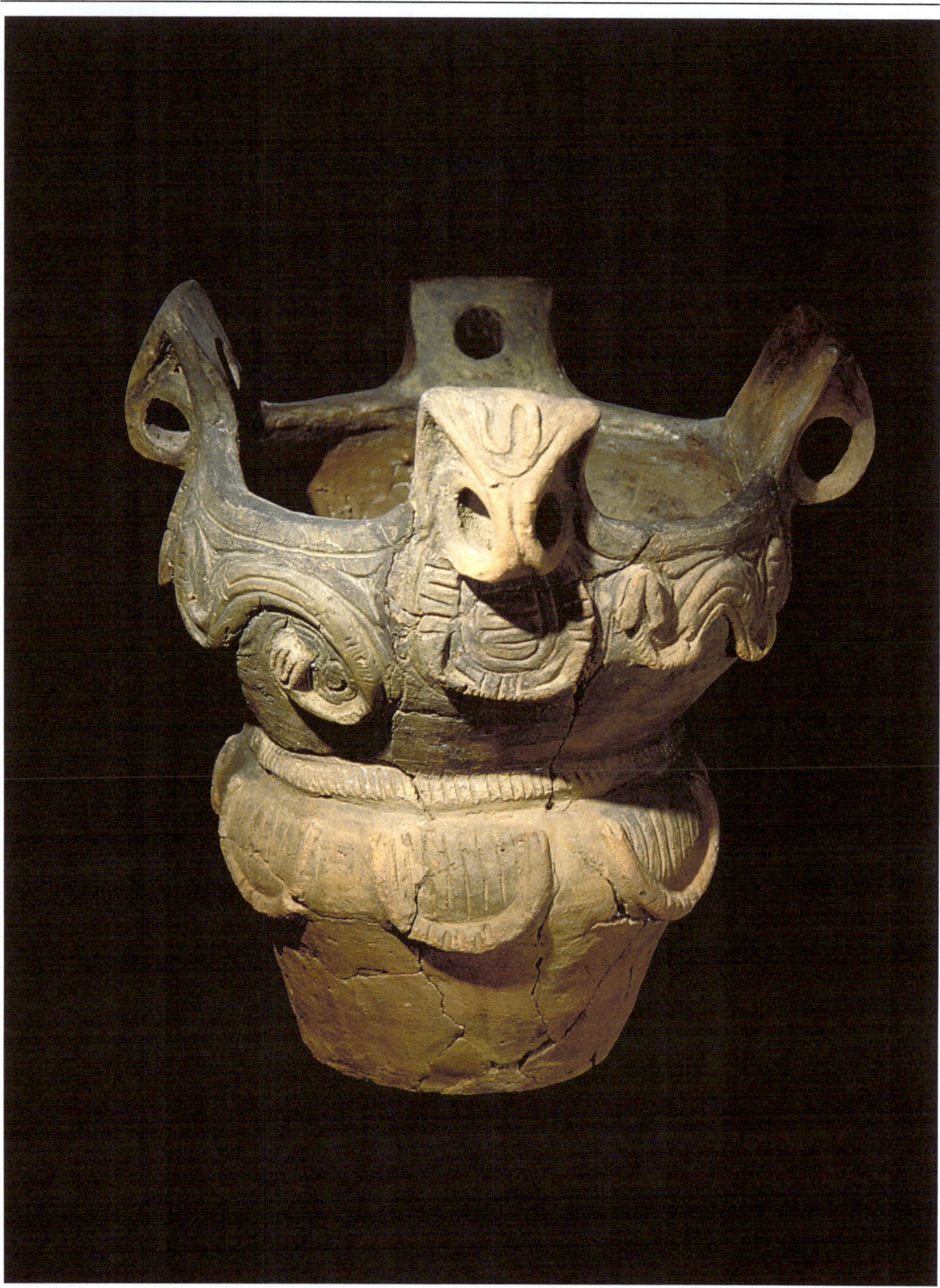

Steamer type deep bowl with snake pattern

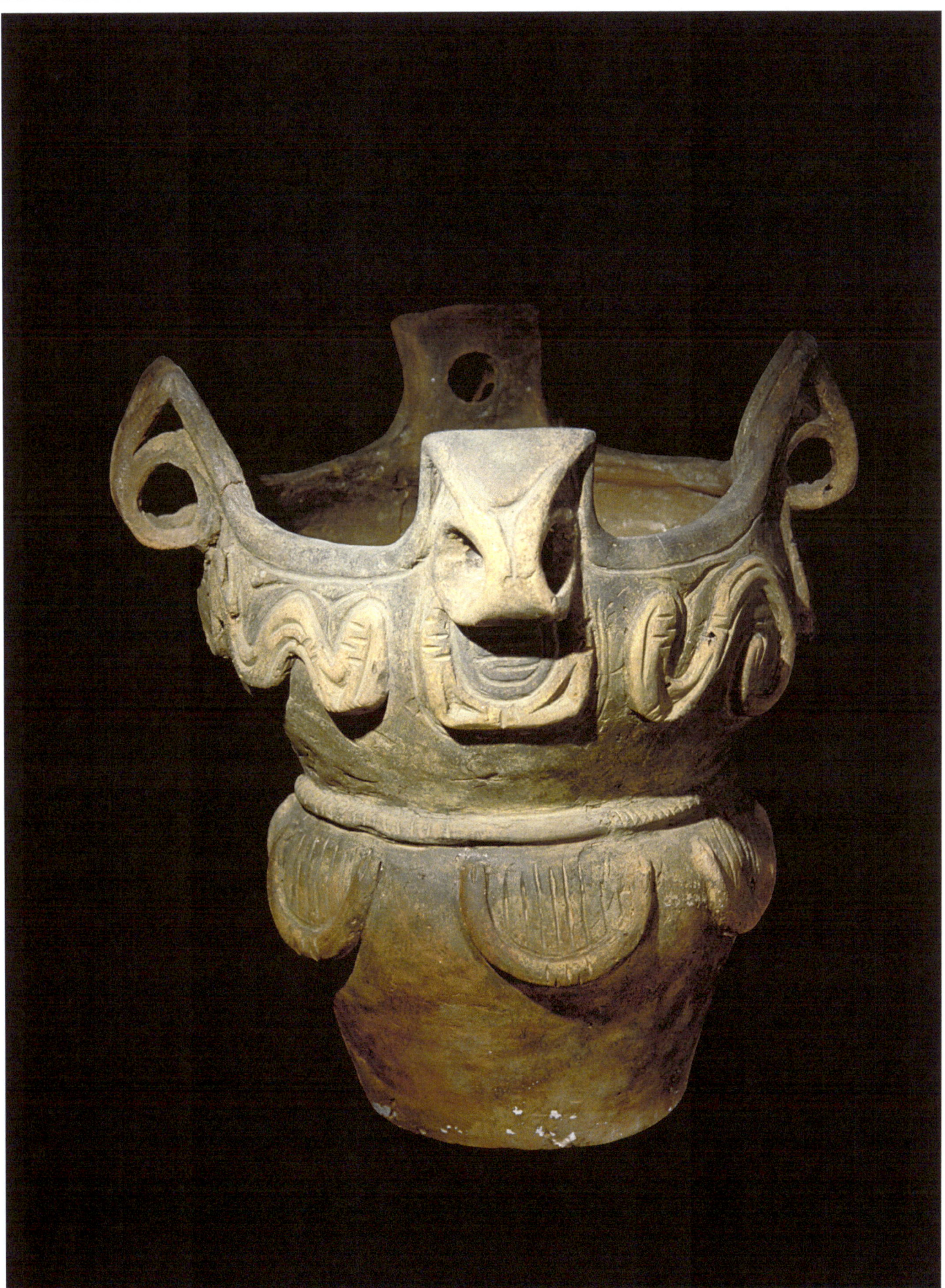

Liquor pot with snake pattern
Tounai ruins
Idojiri style I
Dwelling site #9
Excavated in 1962
Middle Jomon, Middle
4,500 years B.P.
12.2cm(H), 11.0cm(D)
"Idojiri Report" P97, No.318;
"Tounai Report" P.315, No.224
ID-049

This is a small sized perforated flanged earthenware. A pair of coiling snake with a triangle head can be seen on the body. Upper snout end is made a little higher. The number of holes is 14. On the Shoulder can be seen a relief of waves or snake-patterns.

On the inner and outer surface remains slightly a black colored layer that is assumed to be Japanese lacquer. The outer edge of the bottom is rubbed in 5 mm width.

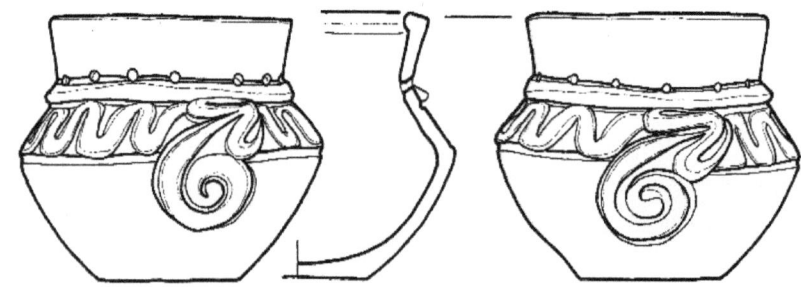

Liquor pot with snake pattern

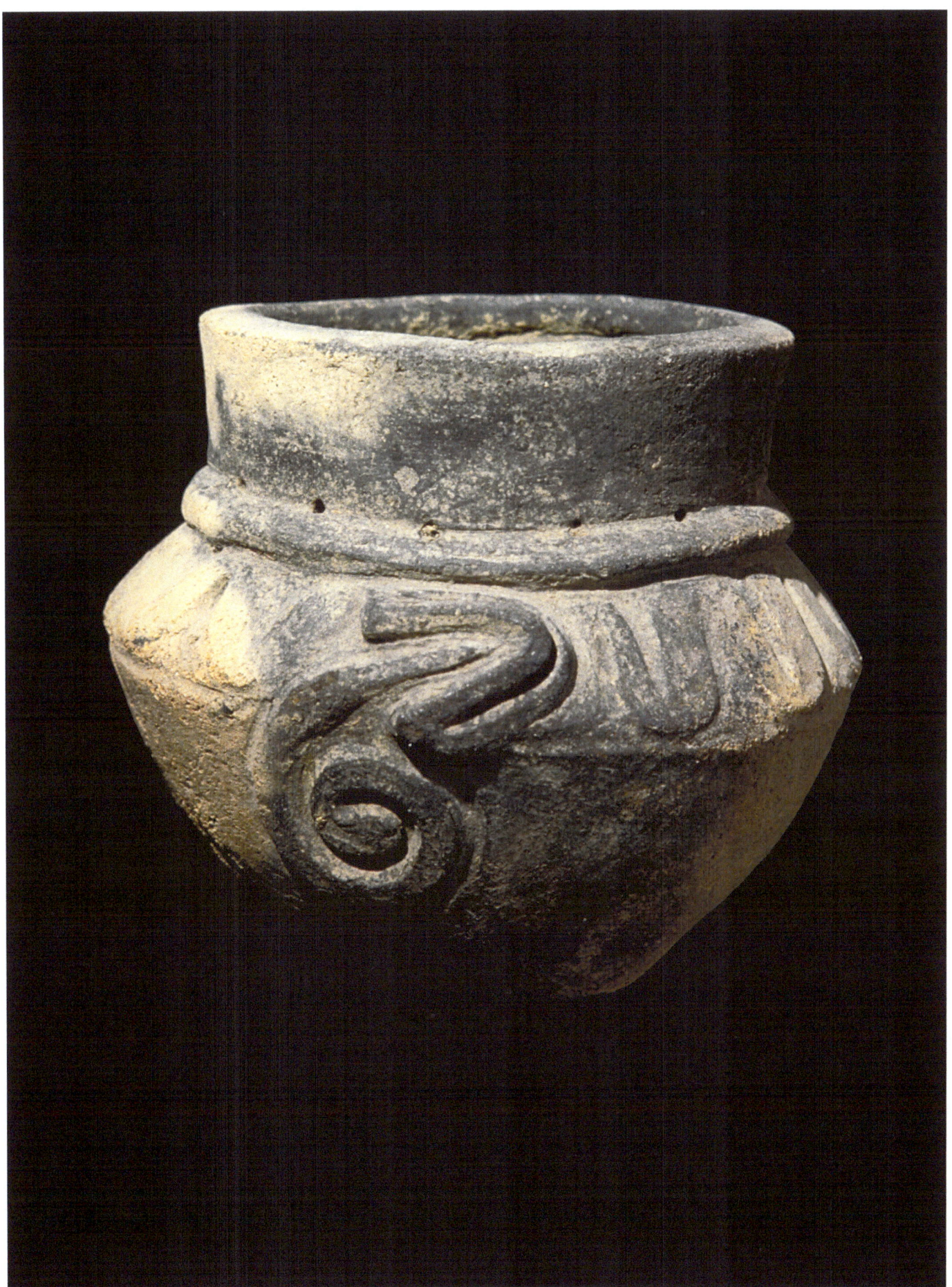

Liquor pot with snake pattern

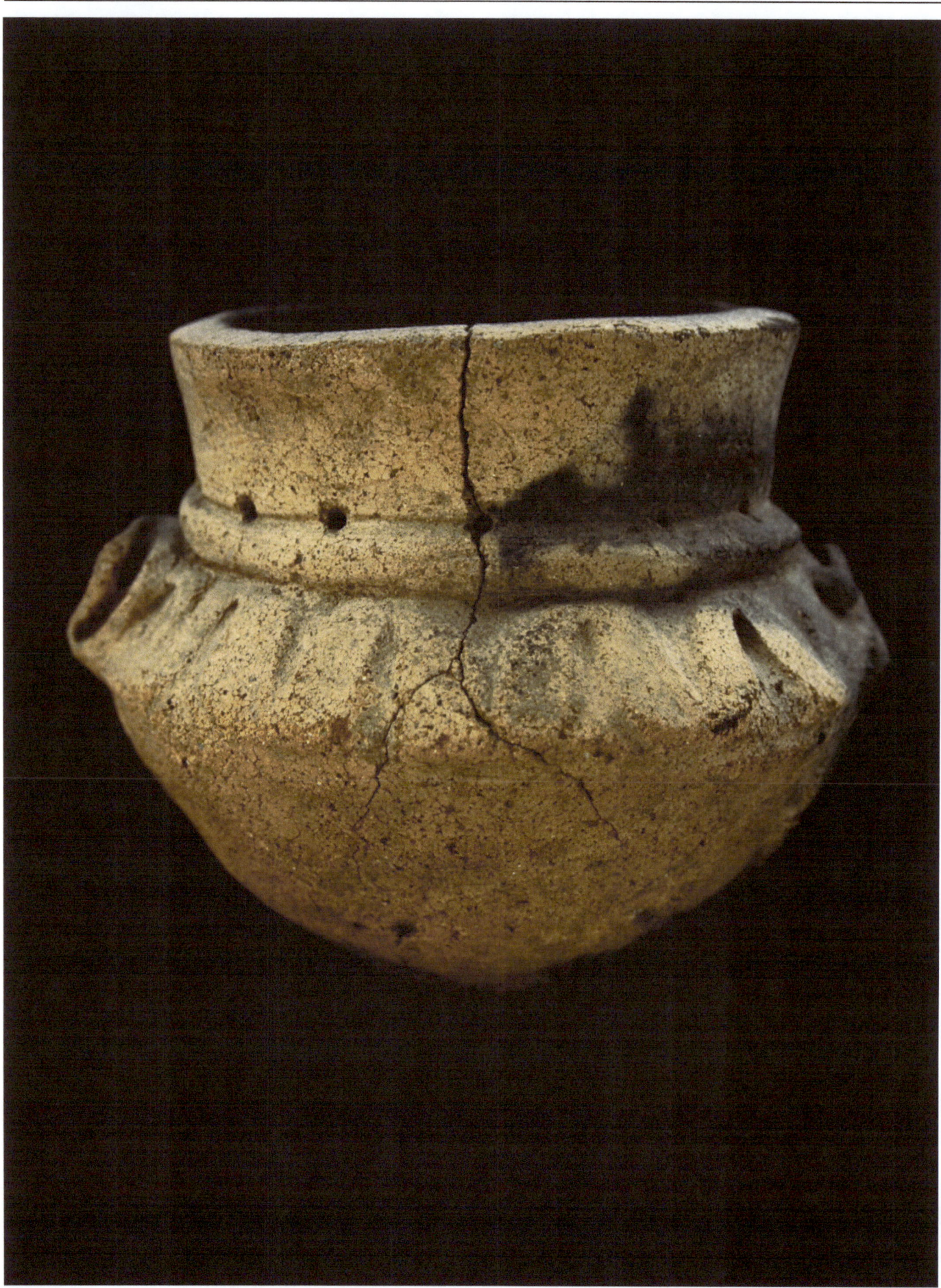

Liquor pot with snake pattern

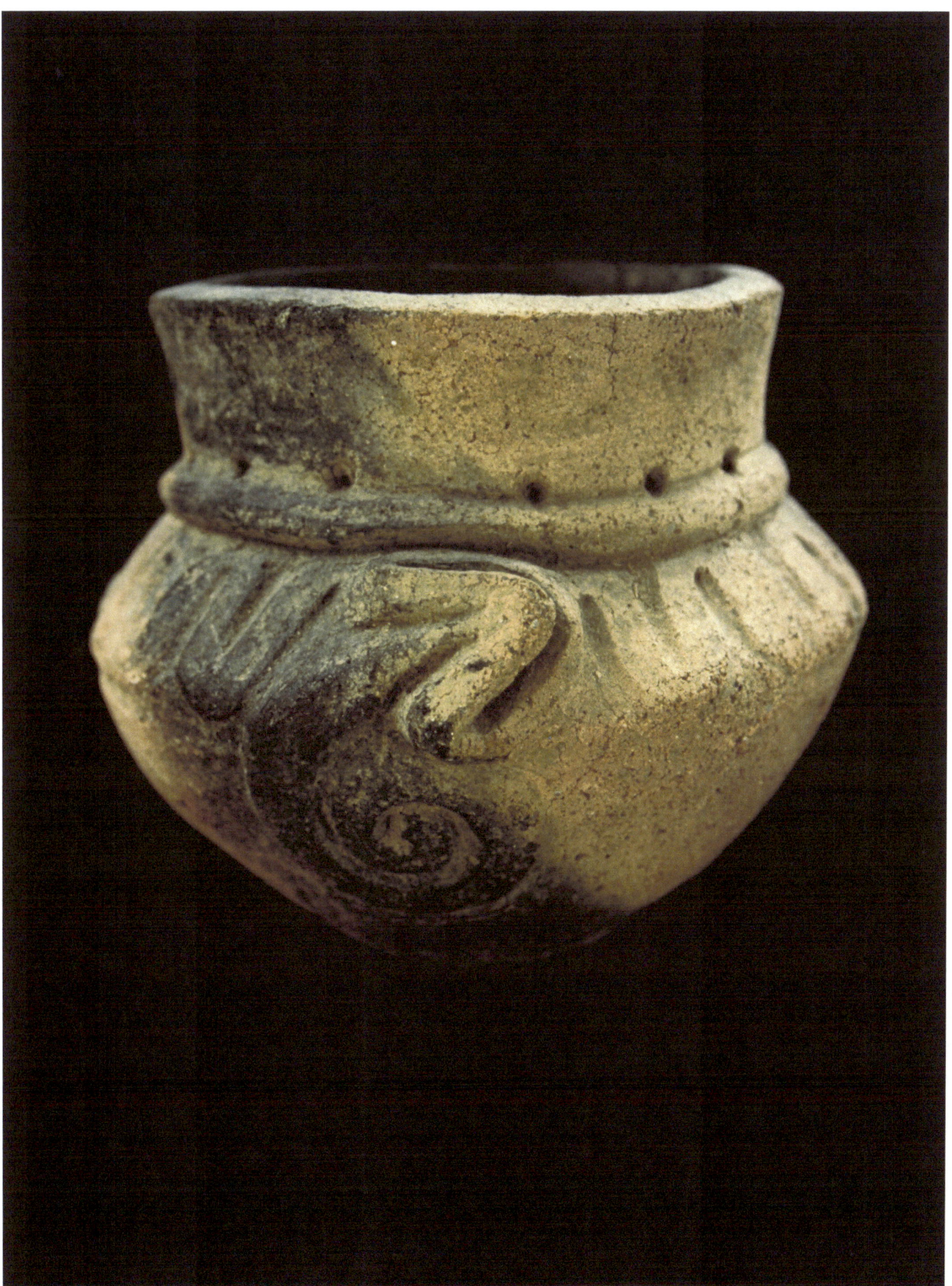

Both ears bowl
Tounai ruins
Idojiri style I
Dwelling site #9
Excavated in 1962
Middle Jomon, Middle
4,500 years B.P.
8.0cm(H), 10.5cm(D)
"Idojiri Report" P97, No.316;
"Tounai Report" P.315, No.226
ID-068

The outer surface of this Both Ears Bowl is made slightly uneven. On the half bottom and body can be seen an arched tar-like accretion of 15mm width.

On the inner surface, accretions such as scorching in 30mm width can be seen along the lip.

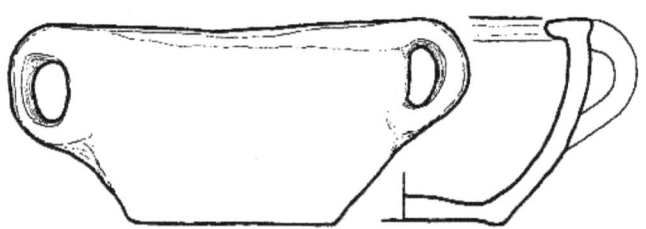

Both ears bowl

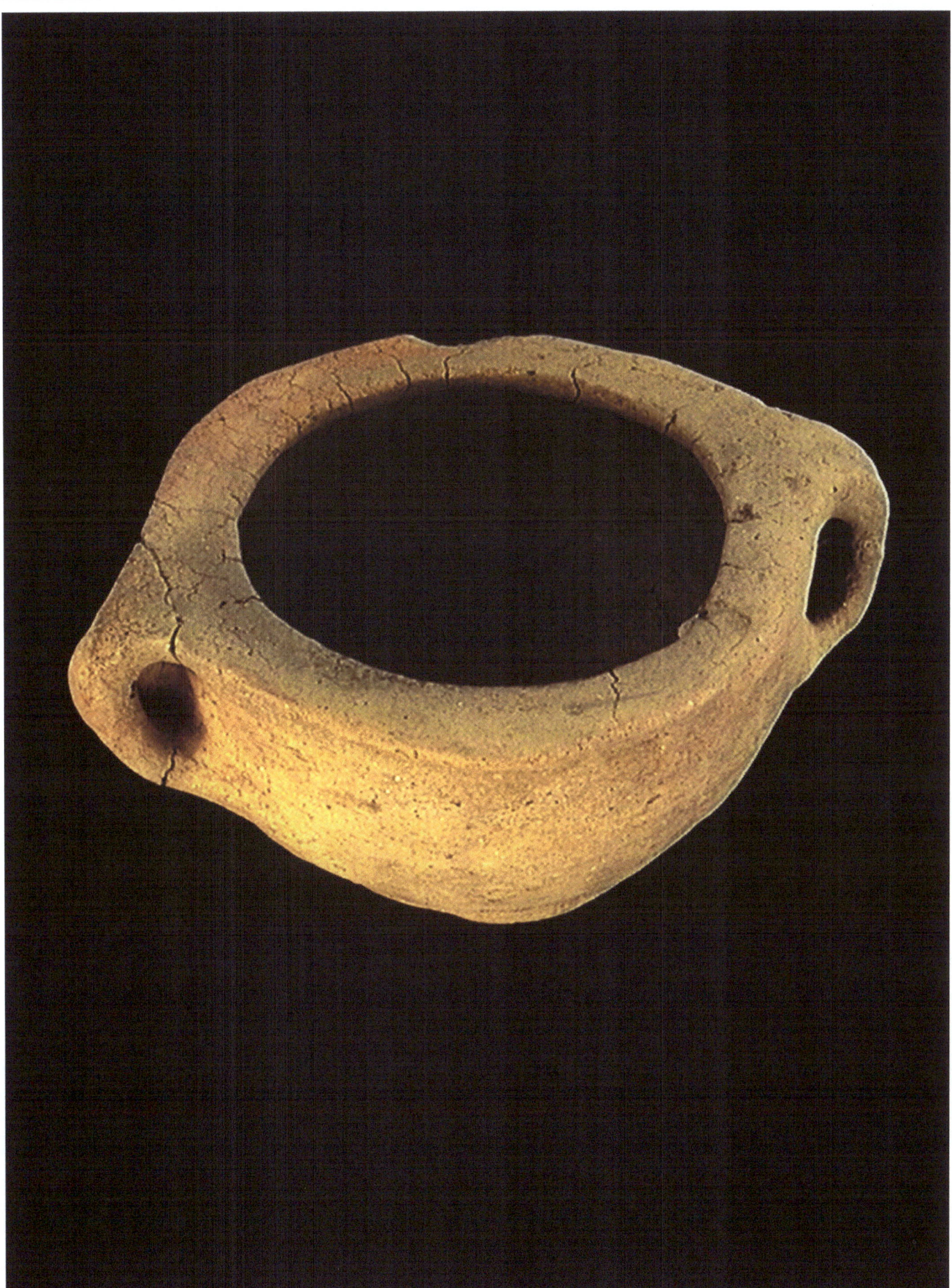

Both ears bowl

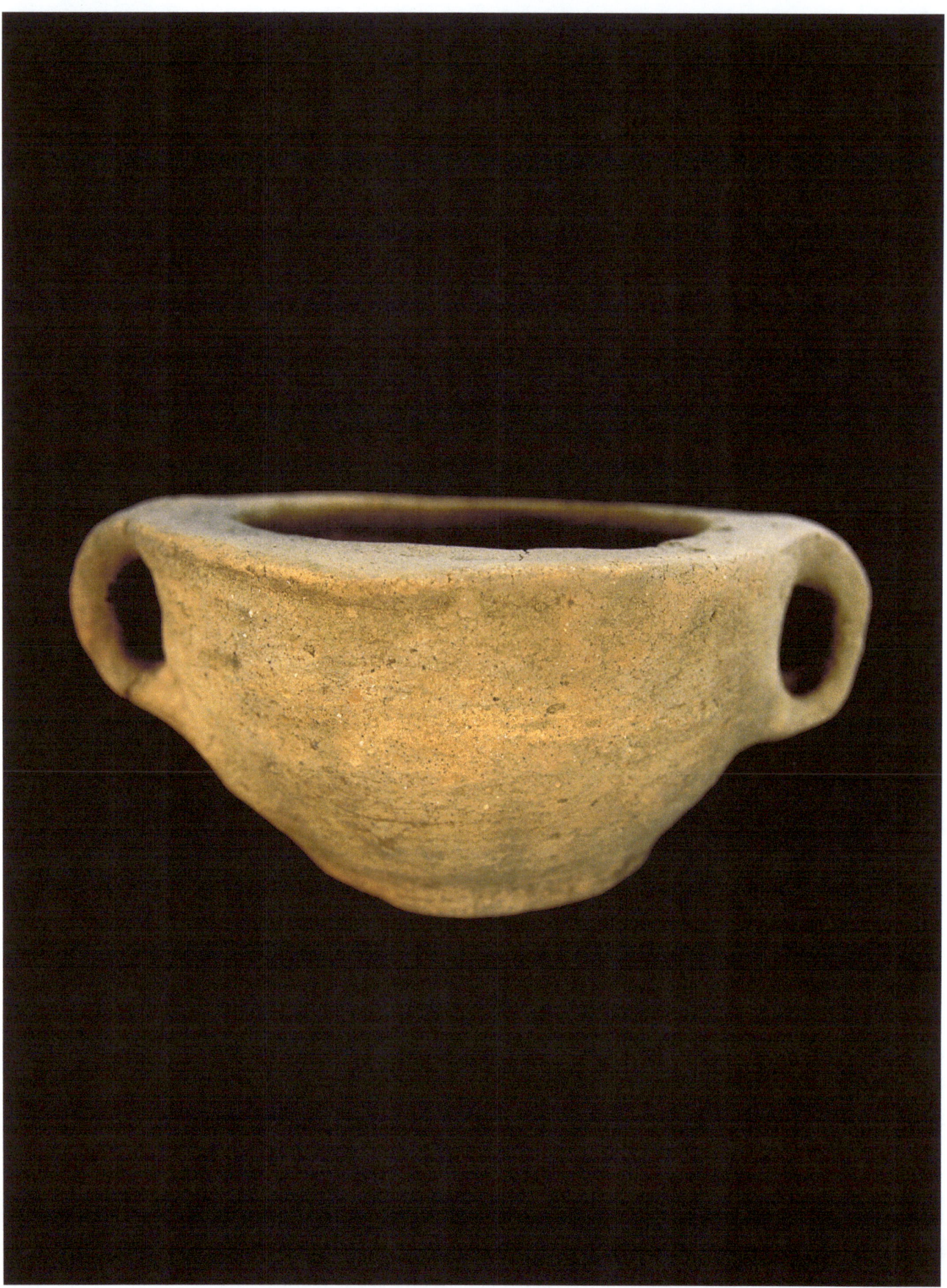

Both ears bowl

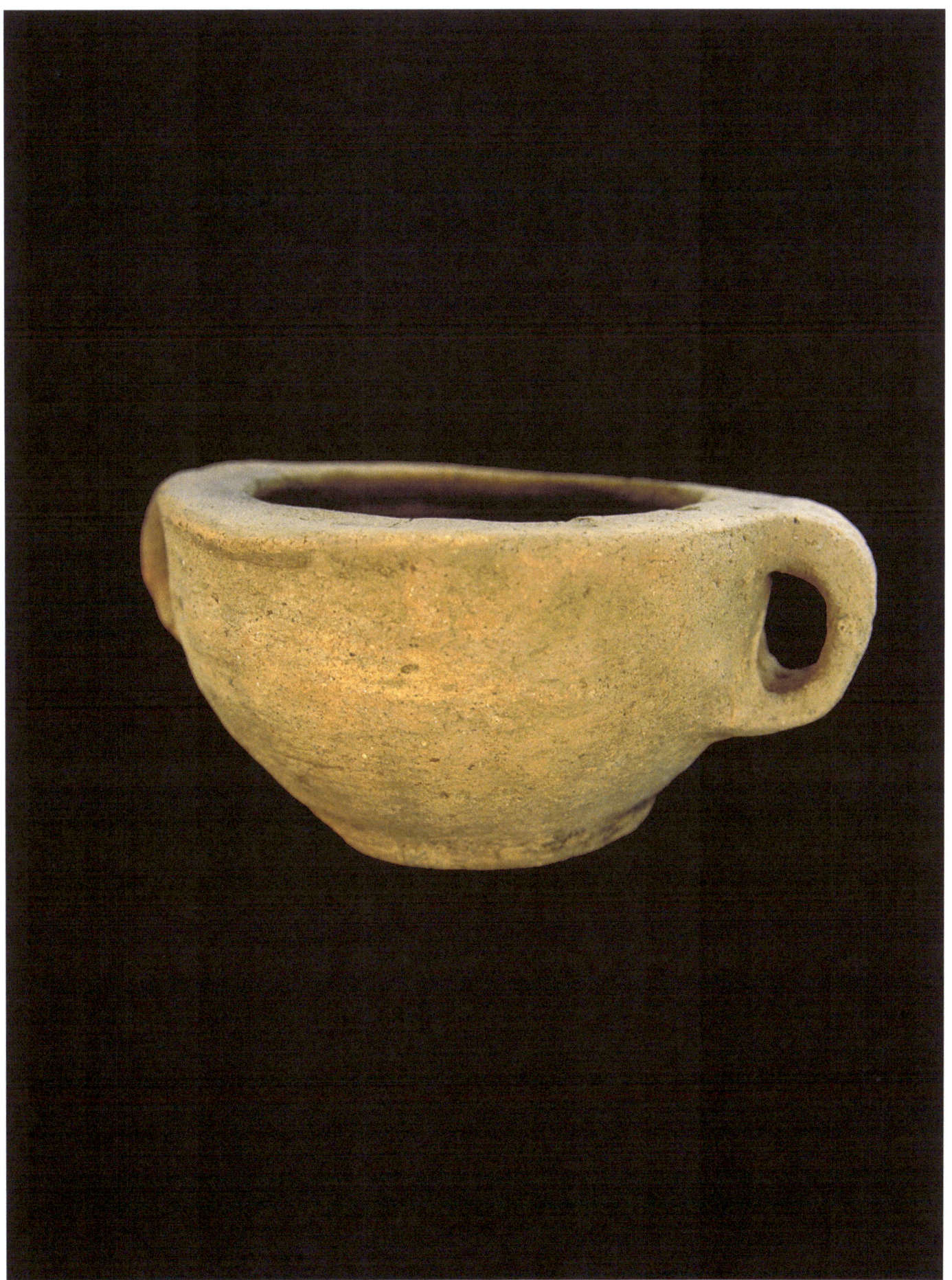

God statue type deep bowl
Tounai ruins
Idojiri style I
Dwelling site #9
Excavated in 1962
Middle Jomon, Middle
4,500 years B.P.
26.4cm(H), 21.7cm(D)
"Idojiri Report" P97, No.311;
"Tounai Report" P.315, No.216
ID-074

This is a deep bowl with an umbrella-shaped convex band that protrudes all around in the form of inverted triangle. On the body can be seen a pair of J-shaped bulge that is arranged on the front and back. A part of J-shaped hook is made flatter. A short descending line falls in the middle.

The bowl is made carefully and there is a dull luster. The upper half of the outer surface has soot and the middle of inner wall has a rough skin in 4cm width.

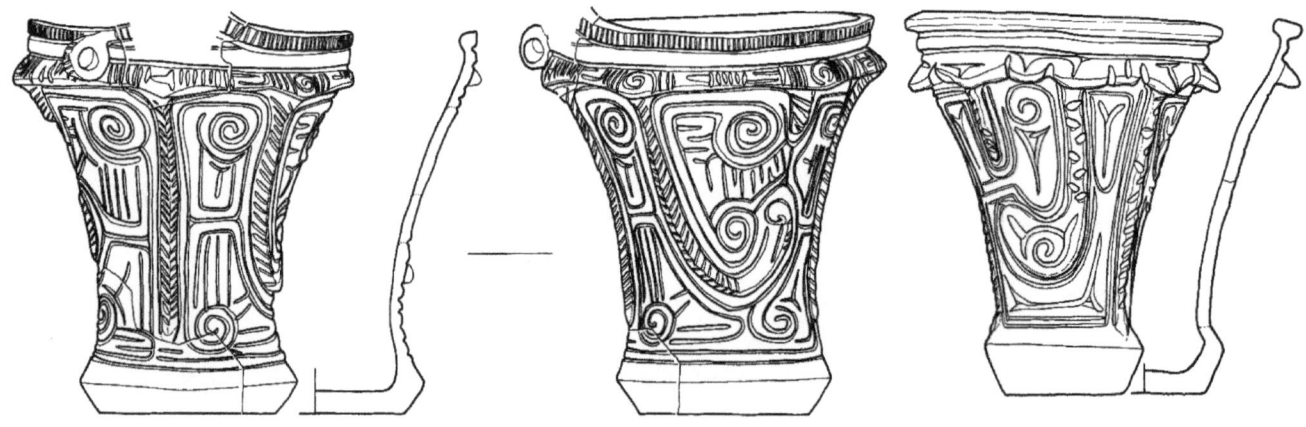

God statue type deep bowl

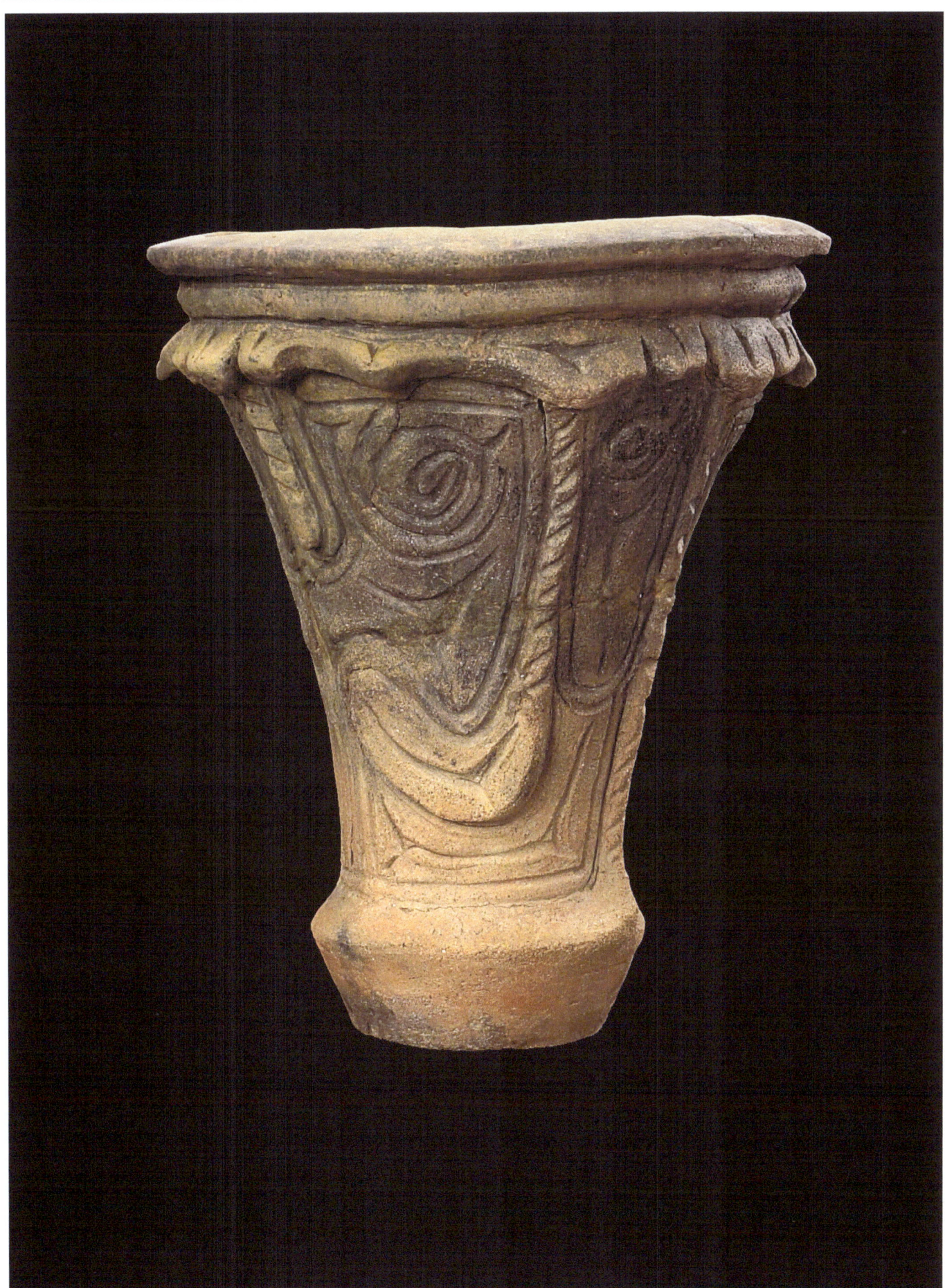

God statue type deep bowl

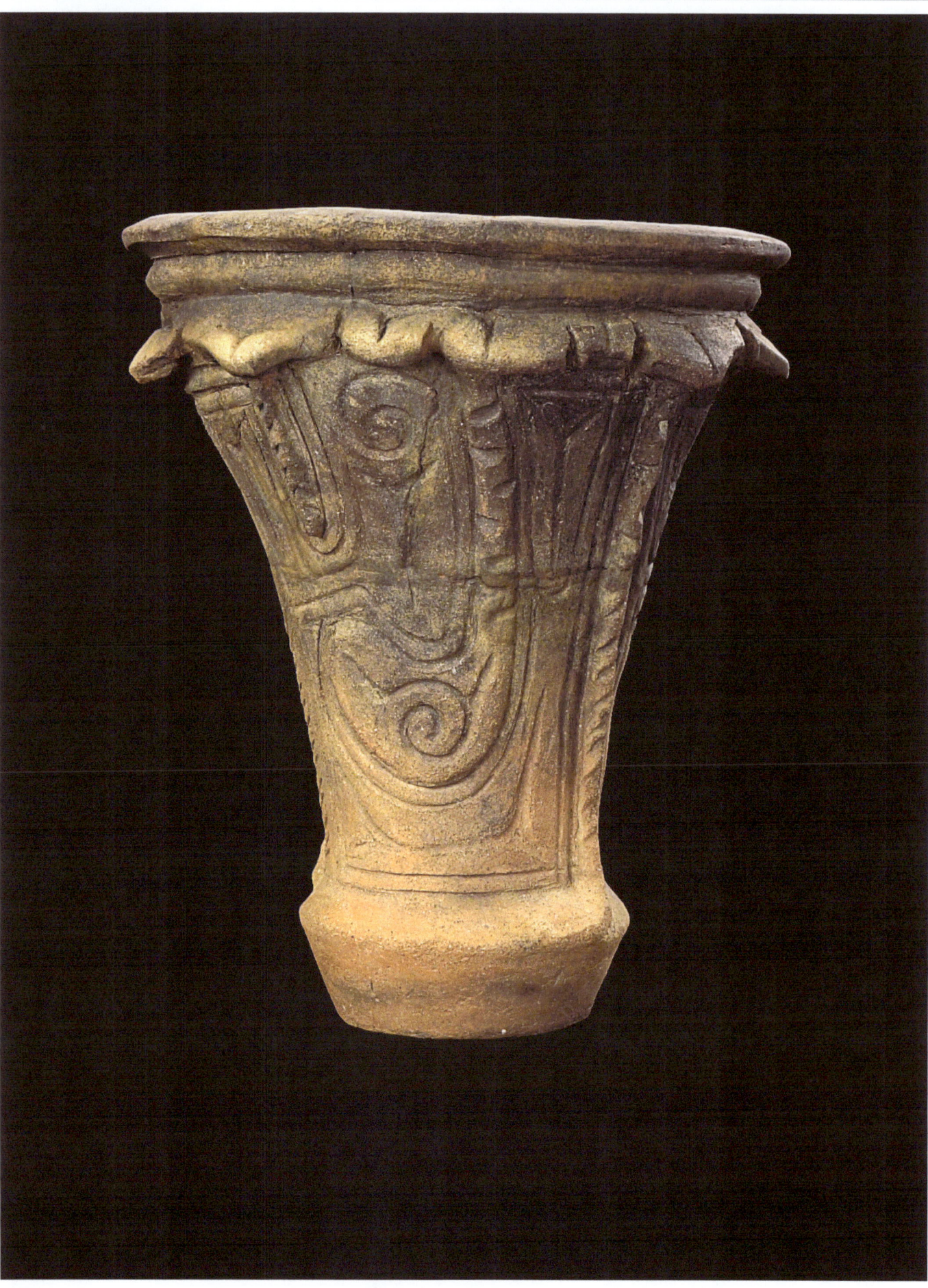

God statue type deep bowl

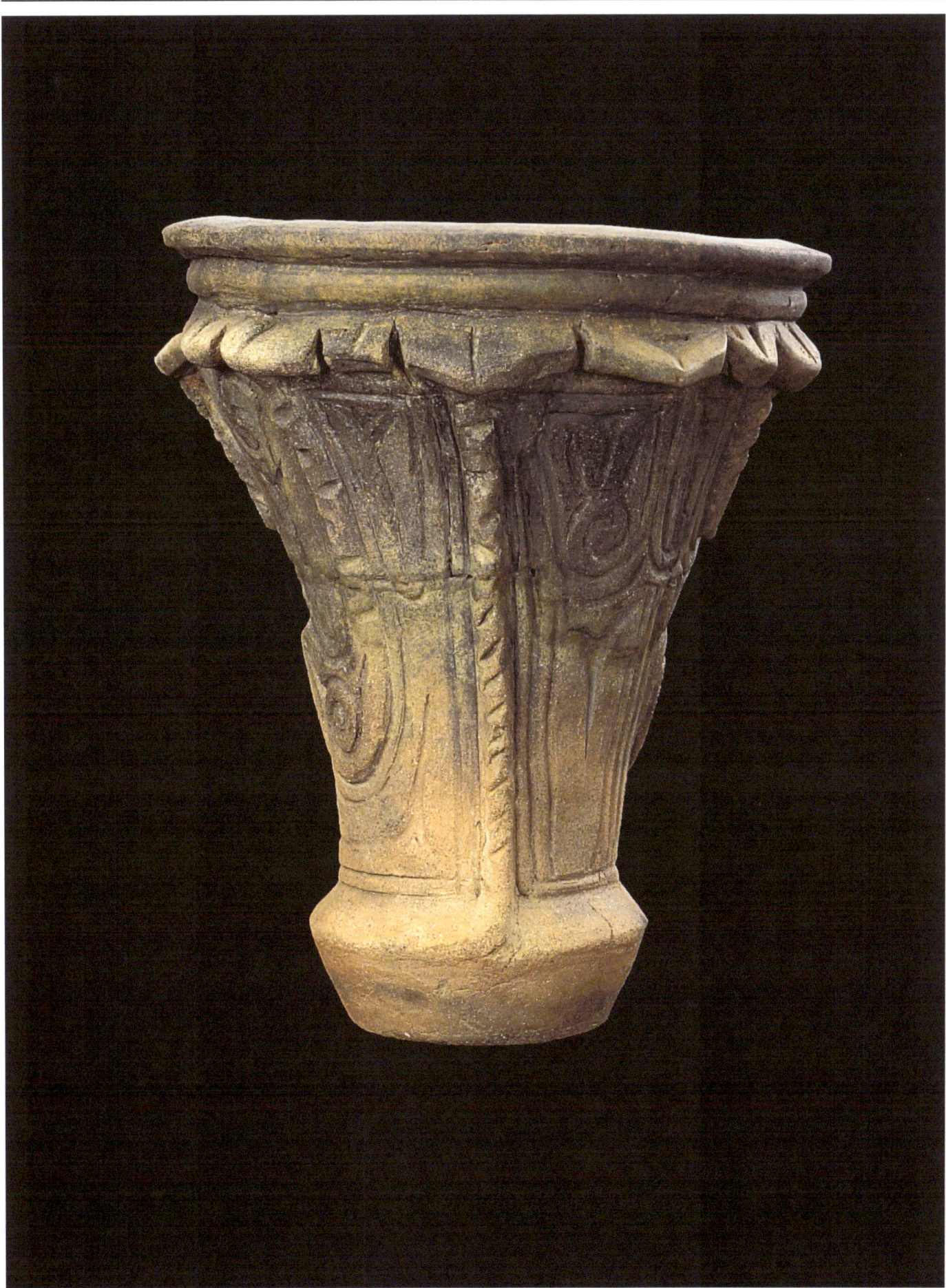

Diamond shaped deep bowl with frog patterns
Tounai ruins
Idojiri styel I
Dwelling site #9
Excavated in 1962
Middle Jomon, Middle
4,500 years B.P.
27.3cm(H), 18.5cm(D)
"Idojiri Report" P.97, No.312;
"Tounai Report" P.315, No.223
ID-075

This deep bowl has a pair of protrusion on each other side of the lip. A narrow ridge with twill cedar pattern drips down from that portion. On each other side of the body are arranged four diamond forms that are made of ridges going up and down. This is a diamond-shaped frog that possesses four limbs. The pair of drooping ridges can be regarded to be the spine. In the upper half-moon shaped part that represents forelimbs are arranged a couple of engraves such as spirals, rings and trigeminal-shaped pattern. The twill cedar pattern on the ridge and the PUSH/PULL point sequence on the both side are quite fine and clear.

On the upper half of the body can be seen an adhesion of soot on the ridge, and on the inner side from the neck to the bottom can be seen some scab-like scorching.

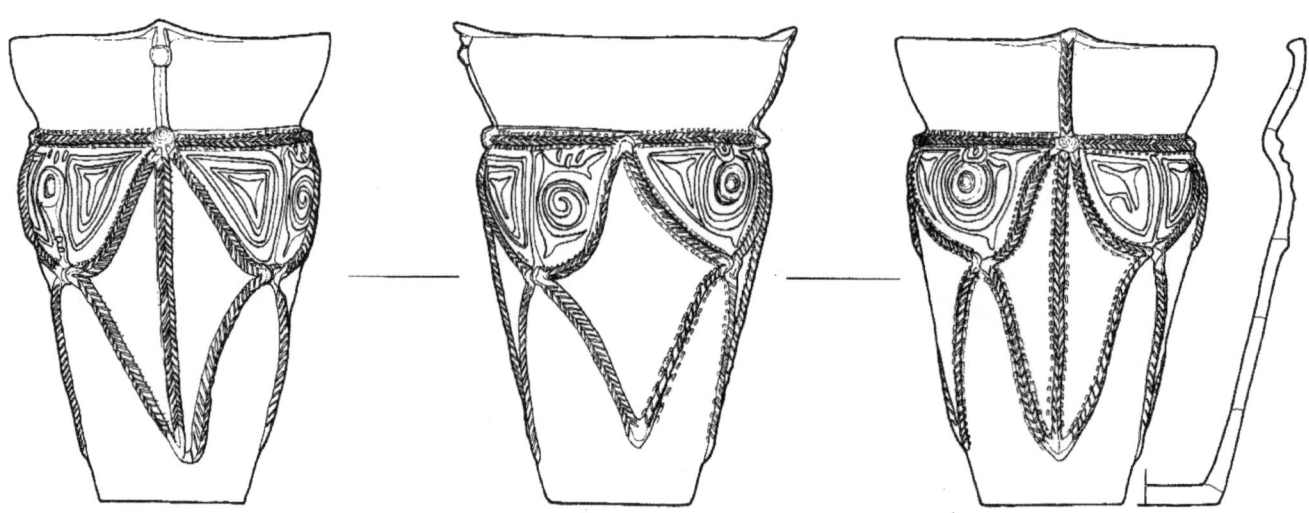

Diampnd shaped deep bowl with frog patterns

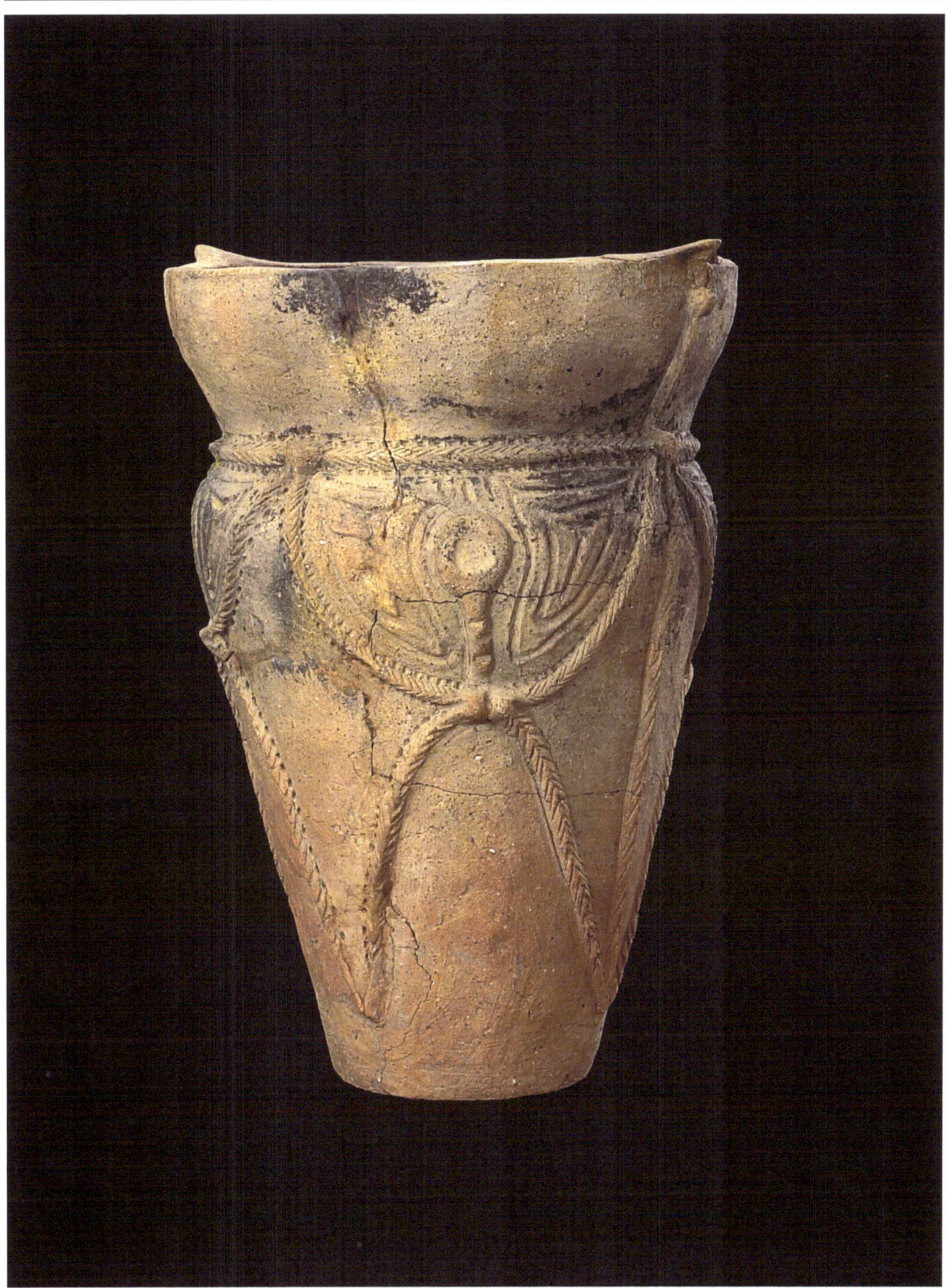

Diampnd shaped deep bowl with frog patterns

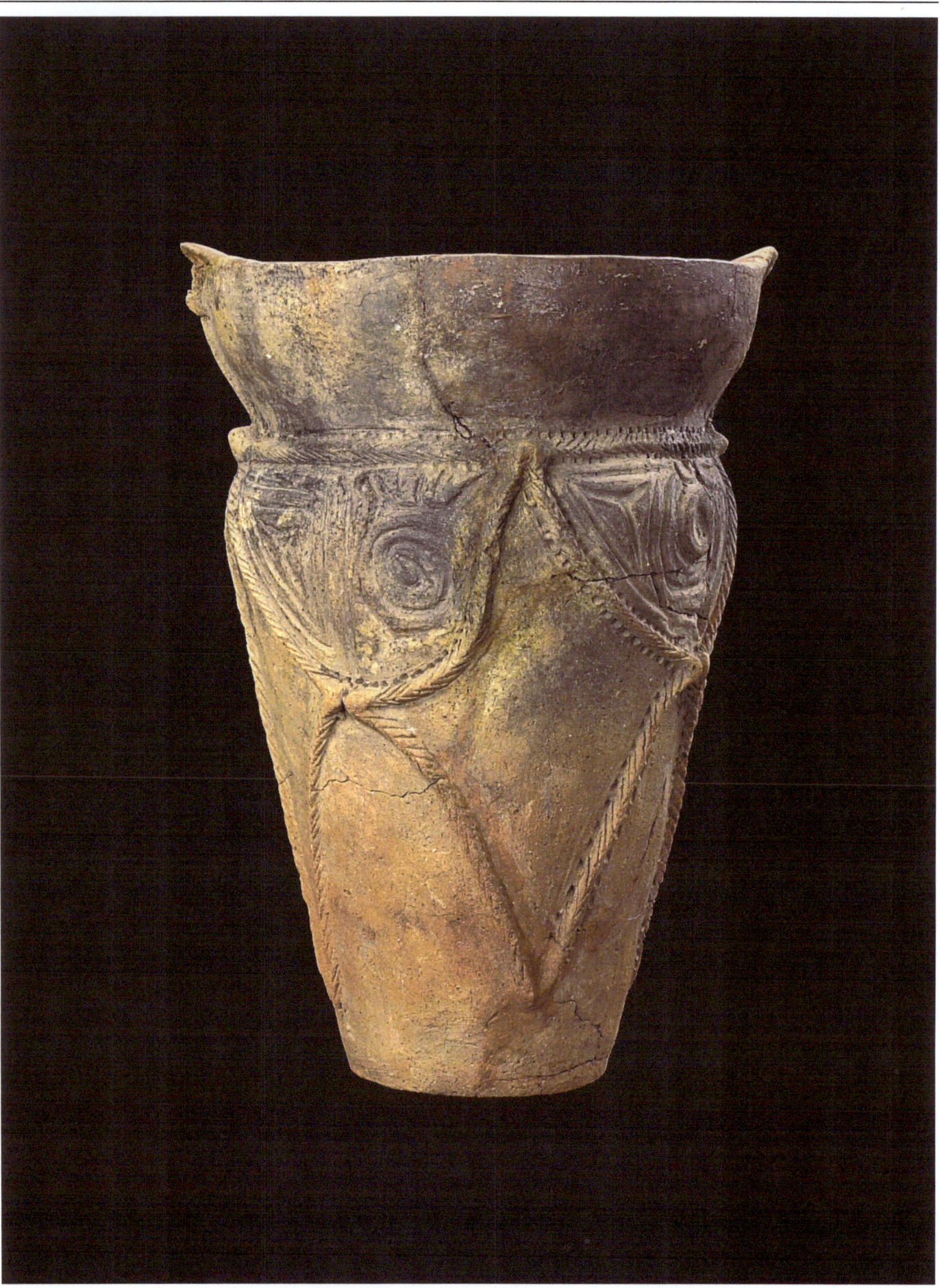

Diampnd shaped deep bowl with frog patterns

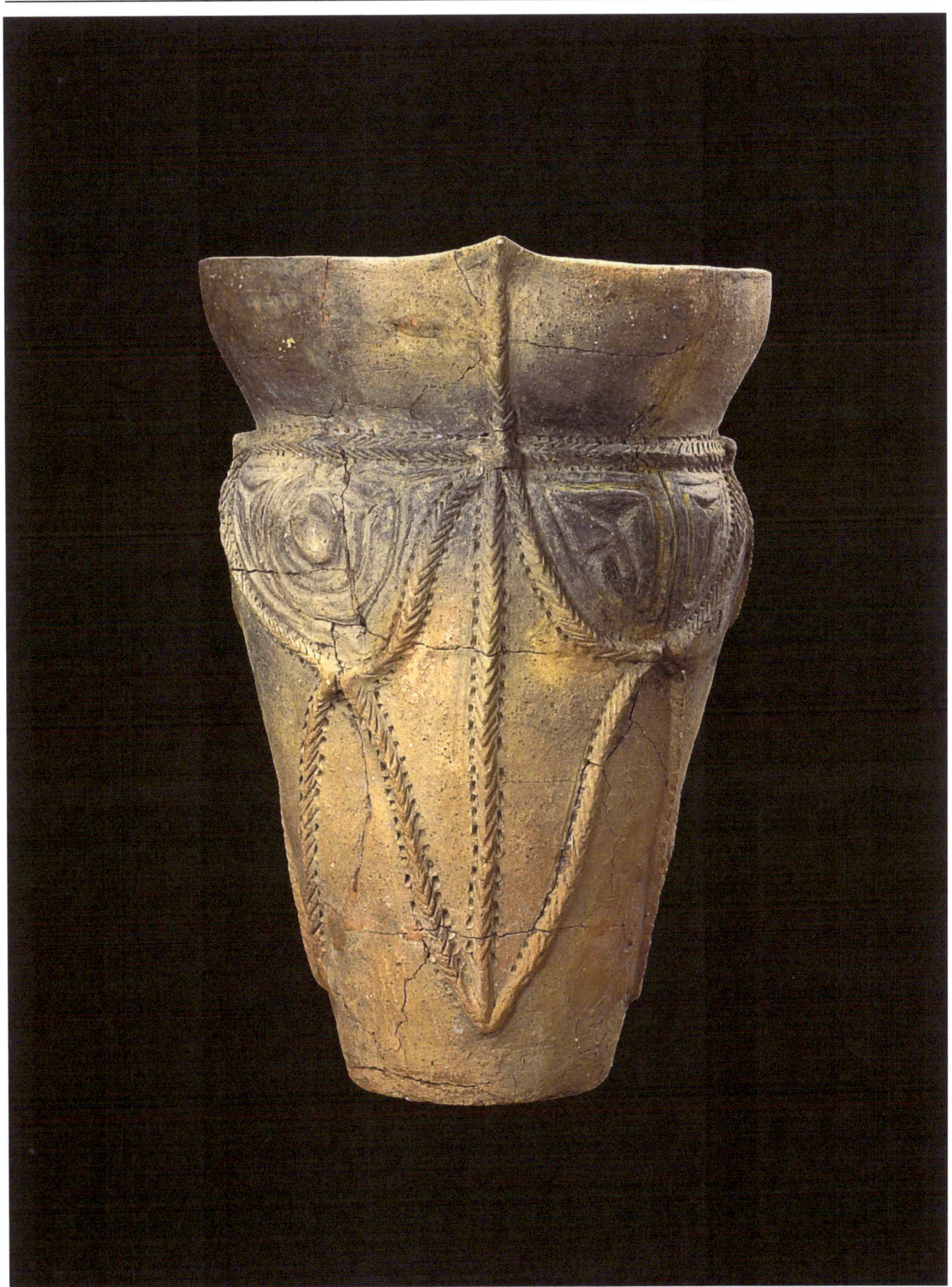

God statue type deep bowl with a frog pattern
Tounai ruins
Idojiri style I
Dwelling site #9
Excavated in 1962
Middle Jomon, Middle
4,500 years B.P.
36.9cm(H), 24.3cm(D)
"Tounai Report" P.313, No.214
ID-080

On the " フ (fu)"-shaped mouth edge of this deep bowl is arranged a pointed protrusion and a snake head can be seen on the top. The pointed protrusion is cavity, and circular holes penetrate from the left to the right and from the front to the back. On the left and right mouth edges is arranged a ring-shaped form.

On the upper half of the body can be seen an inverted triangle back. It will be easily recognized that this back is the same as that of the "cylindrical vessel with a statue of god" uncovered at the dwelling site #32. The back is bisected by the spine and arrow-shaped patterns are represented with a bump between them. On the mouse edge of the other side is arranged a diamond-shaped concave pattern. A flat ridge droops with trigeminal-shaped intaglio, and it curves like a hook placing a bump with increments between them. Most part of bottom is missing, and this bowl is a restoration. The surface is filled with Jomon pattern first, and after that it is effaced by cutting in the form of continuous arc.

On the upper half of the body can be seen an adhesion of soot, and on the lower half of the body can be seen some scorches that look thicker near the bottom.

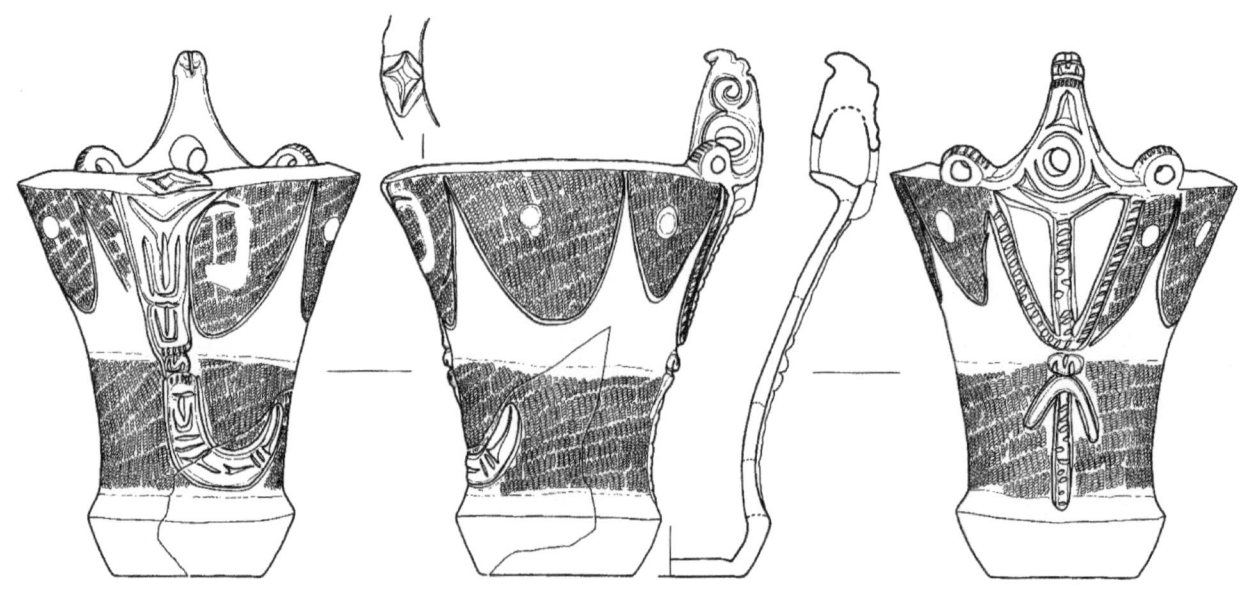

God statue type deep bowl with a frog pattern

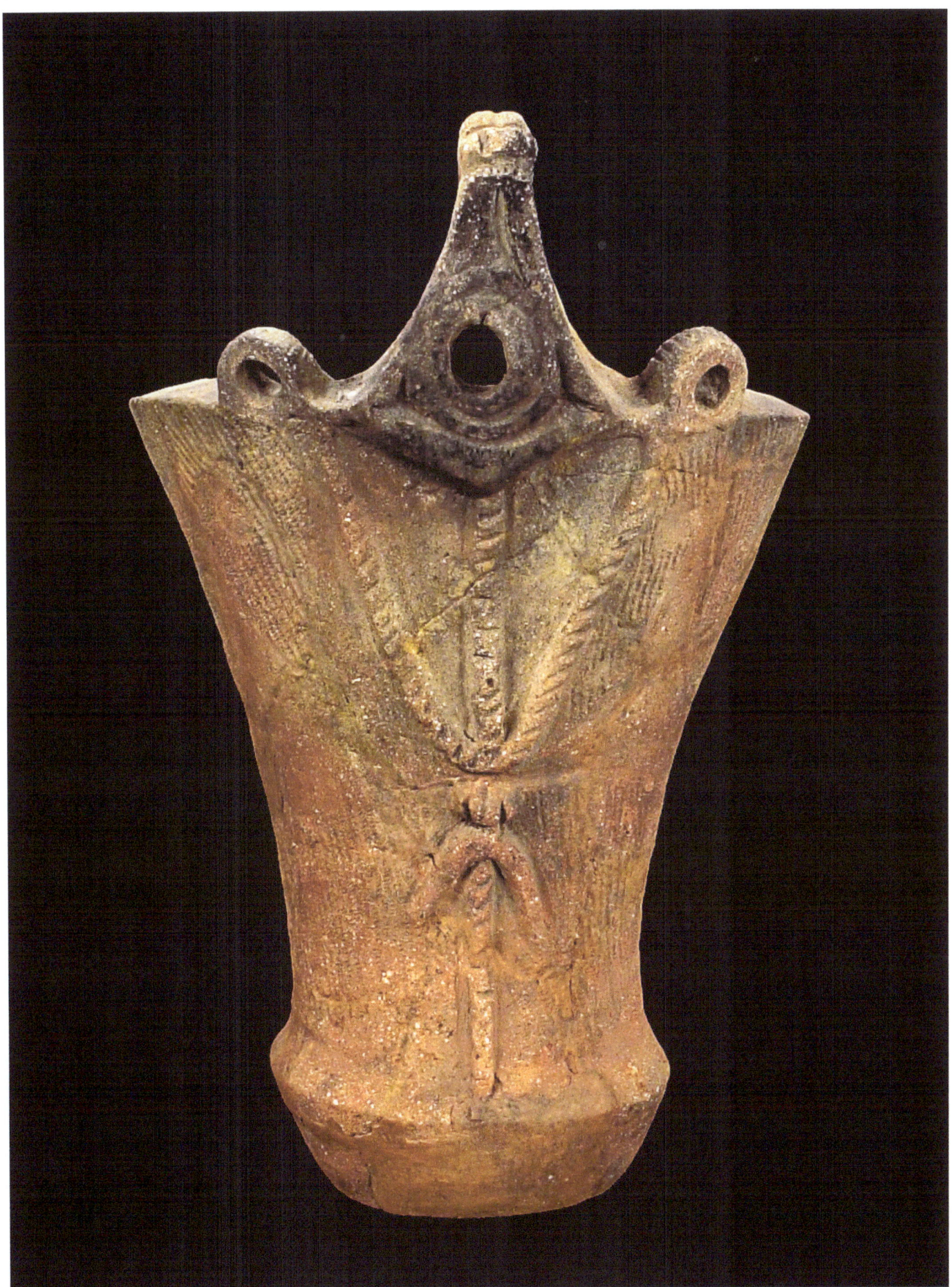

God statue type deep bowl with a frog pattern

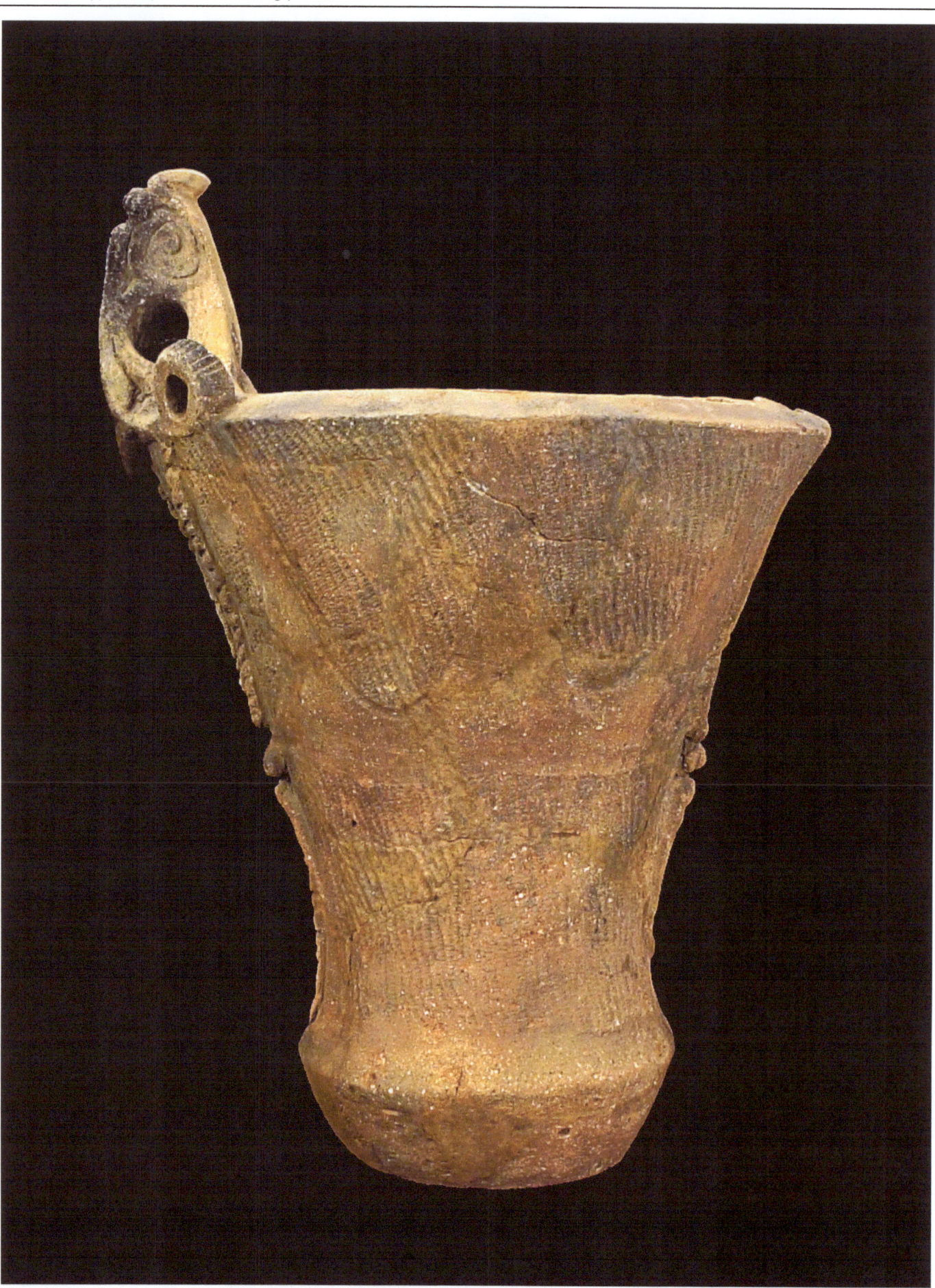

God statue type deep bowl with a frog pattern

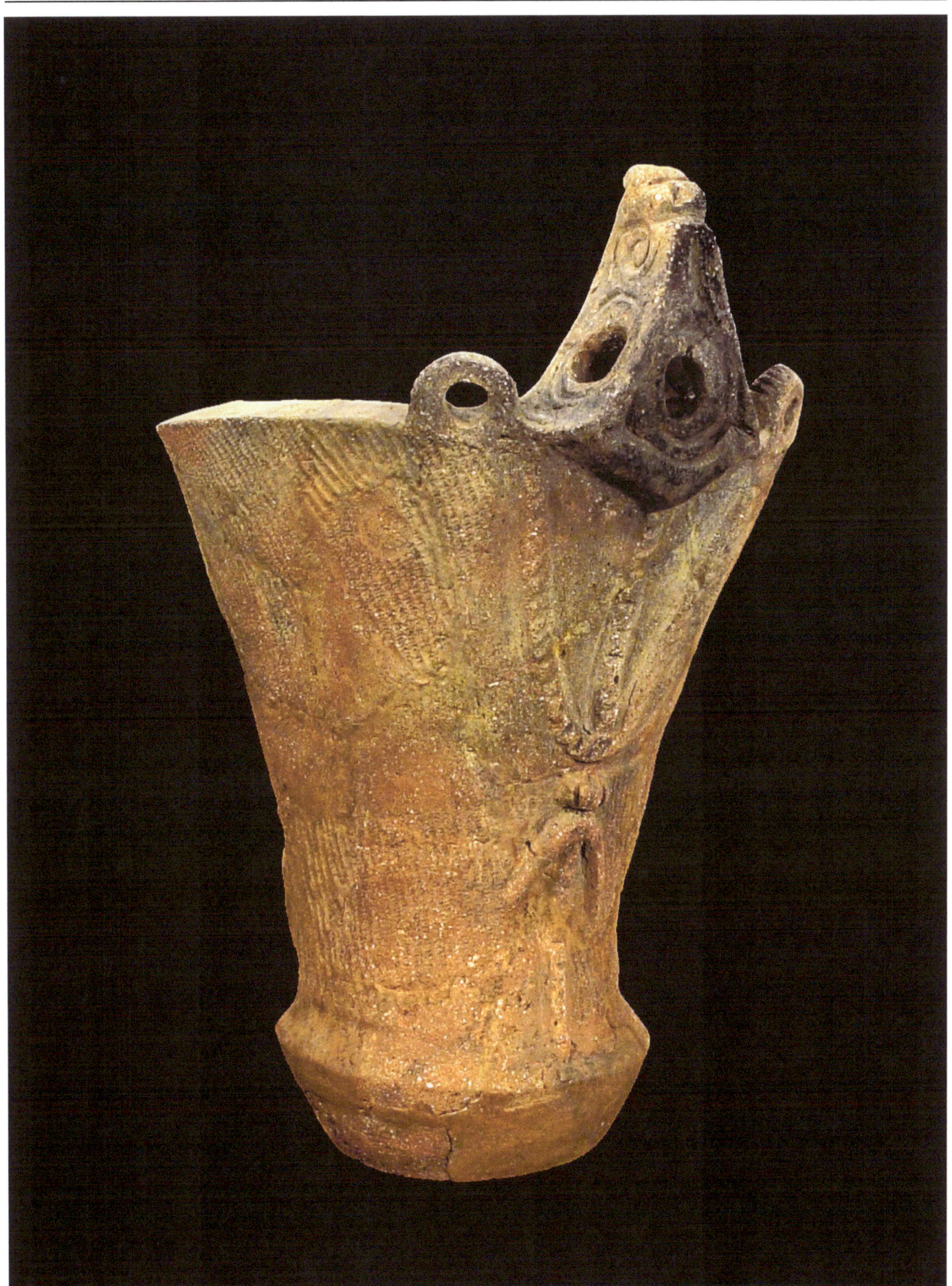

God statue type deep bowl with a frog pattern

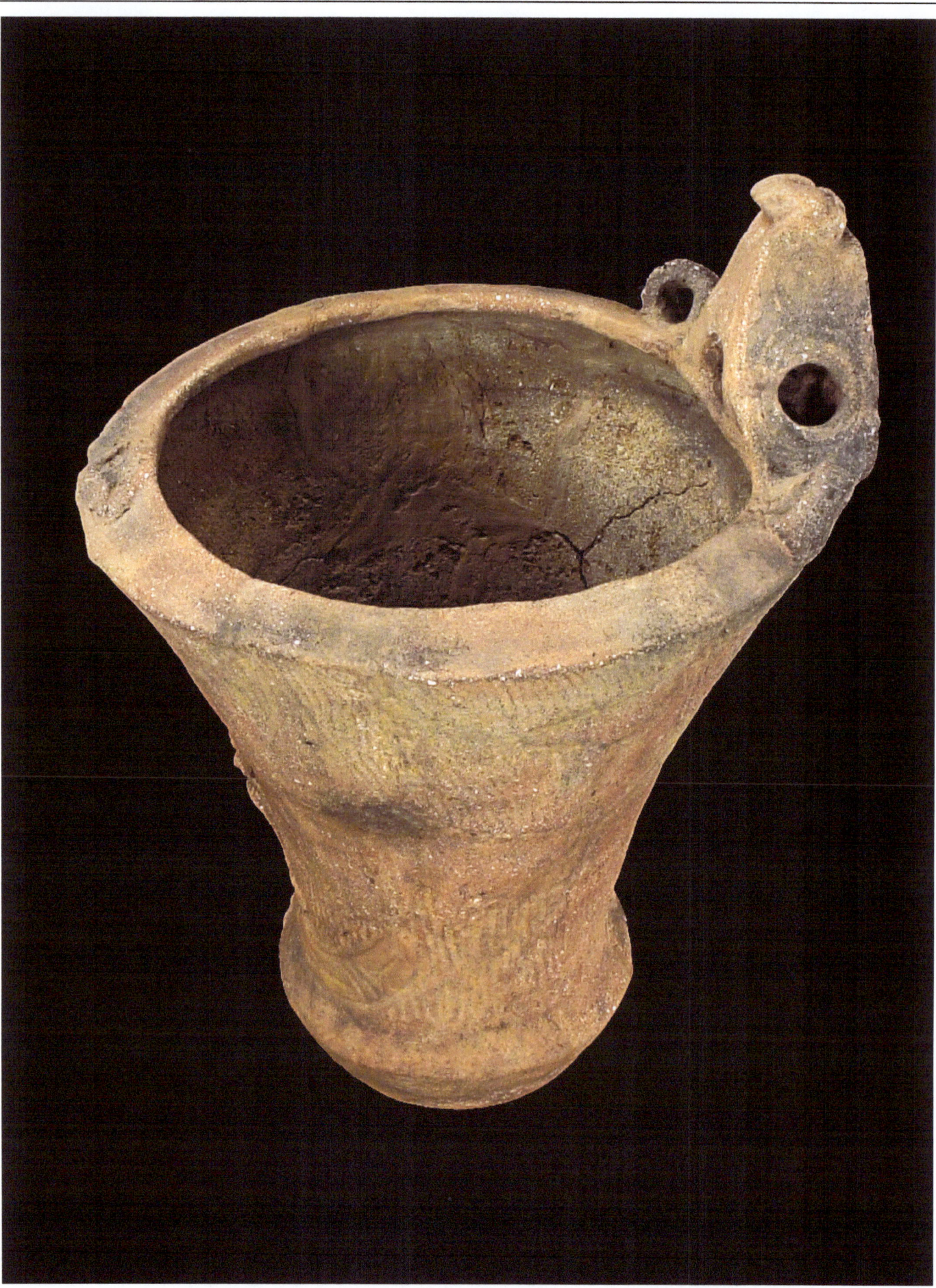

God statue type deep bowl with a frog pattern

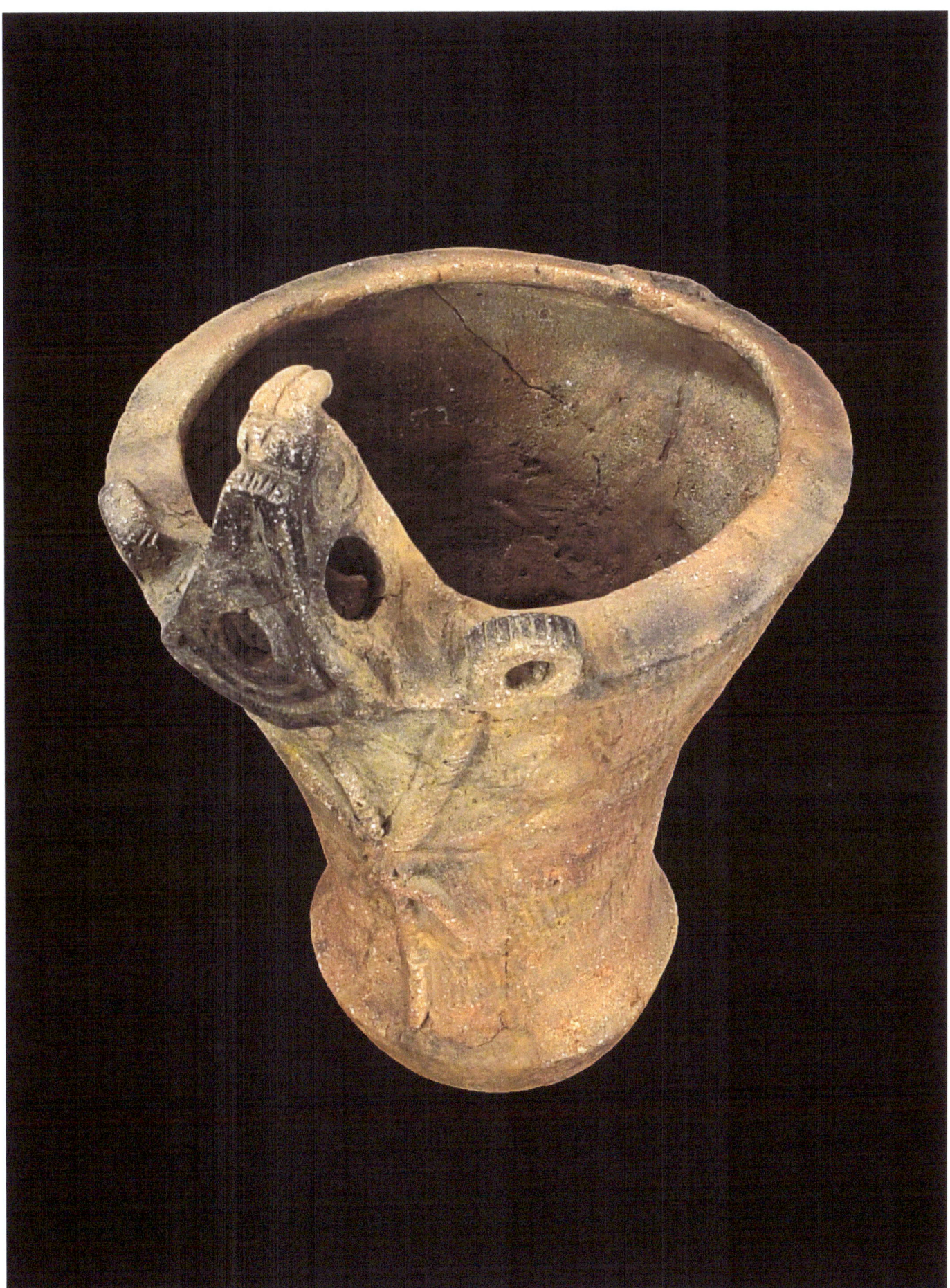

Deep bowl with compartment pattern of vertical stripes
Tounai ruins
Tounai style I
Dwelling site #14
Excavated in 1962
Middle Jomon, Middle
4,700 years B.P.
47.5cm(H), 25.7cm(D)
"Idojiri Report" P.89, No.240;
"Tounai Report" P.331, No.272
ID-039

This deep bowl can be said to be one of the best works of potteries with compartment pattern of vertical stripes. Unfortunately a half of mouth edge is missing. Like 5 consolidated spine, a ridge line droops from the lip. 3 rows of diamond pattern and 2 rows of rectangular compartment pattern are arranged between them and it is filled with thin lines. On the mouth edge of the 2 diamond-shaped compartment patterns are arranged compartment patterns of horizontal stripes. It is the same for another mouth edge, 2 rectangular compartment patterns can be considered to go to the mouth edge as well. Both inside and outside surface are finely finished.

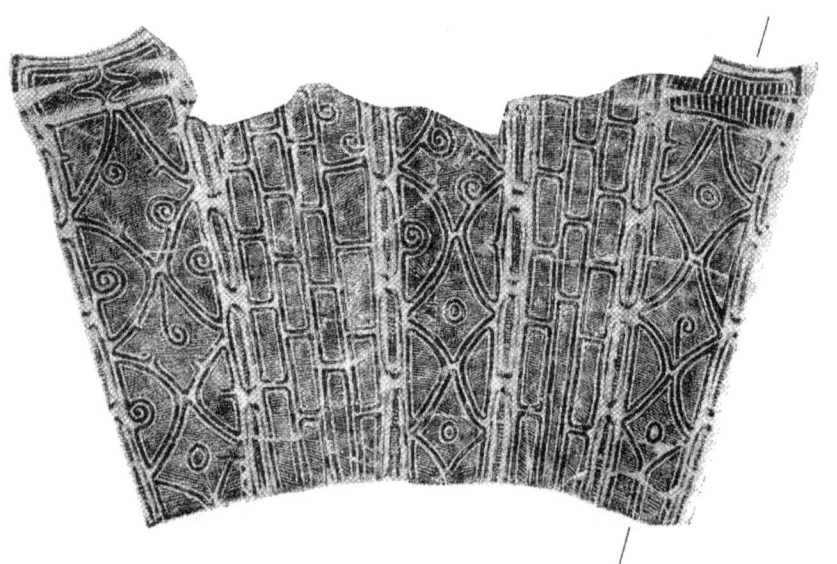
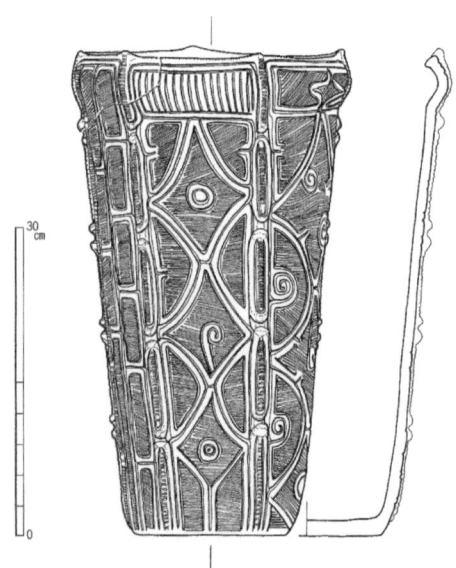

Deep bowl with compartment pattern of vertical stripes

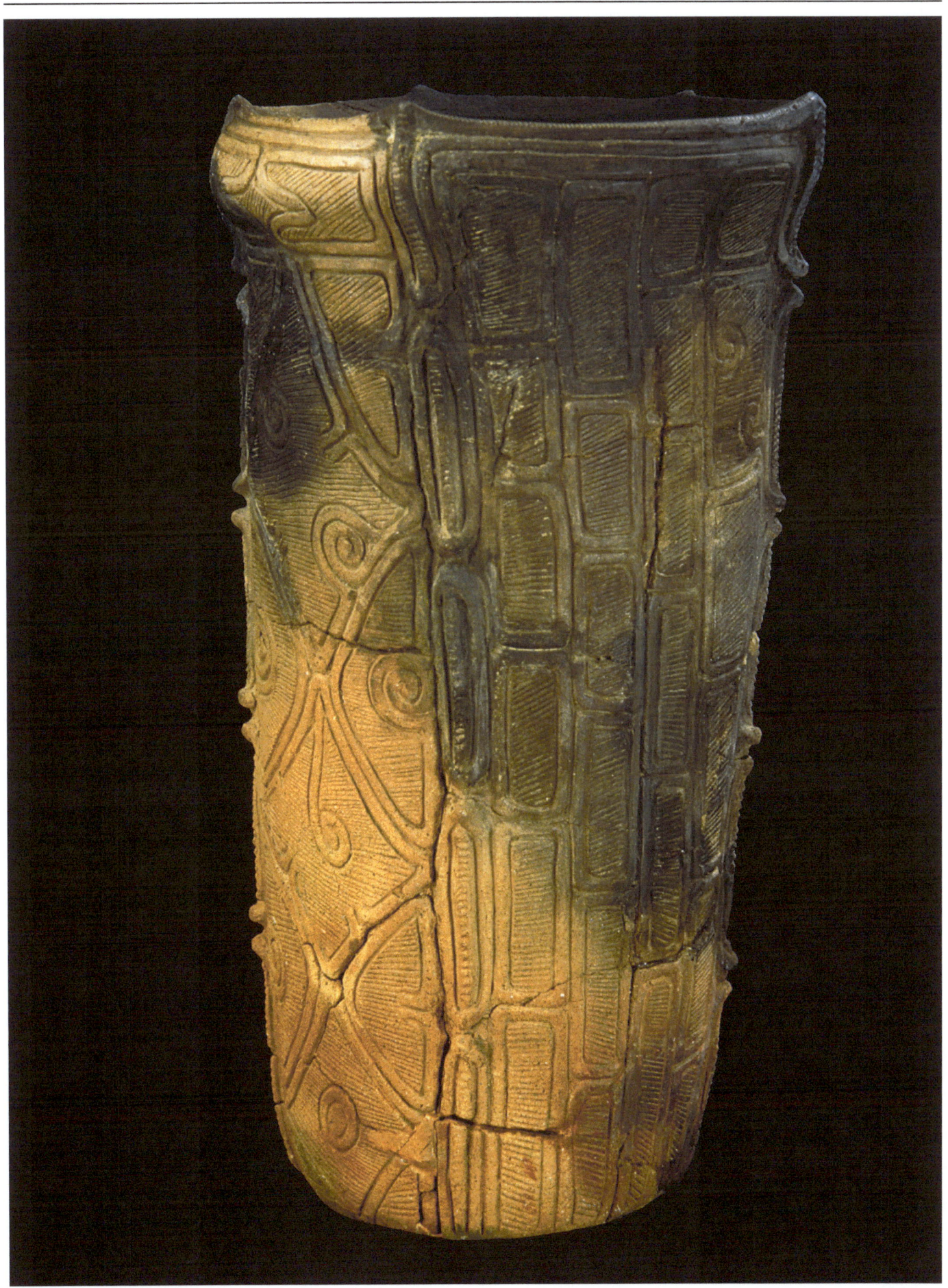

Deep bowl with compartment pattern of vertical stripes

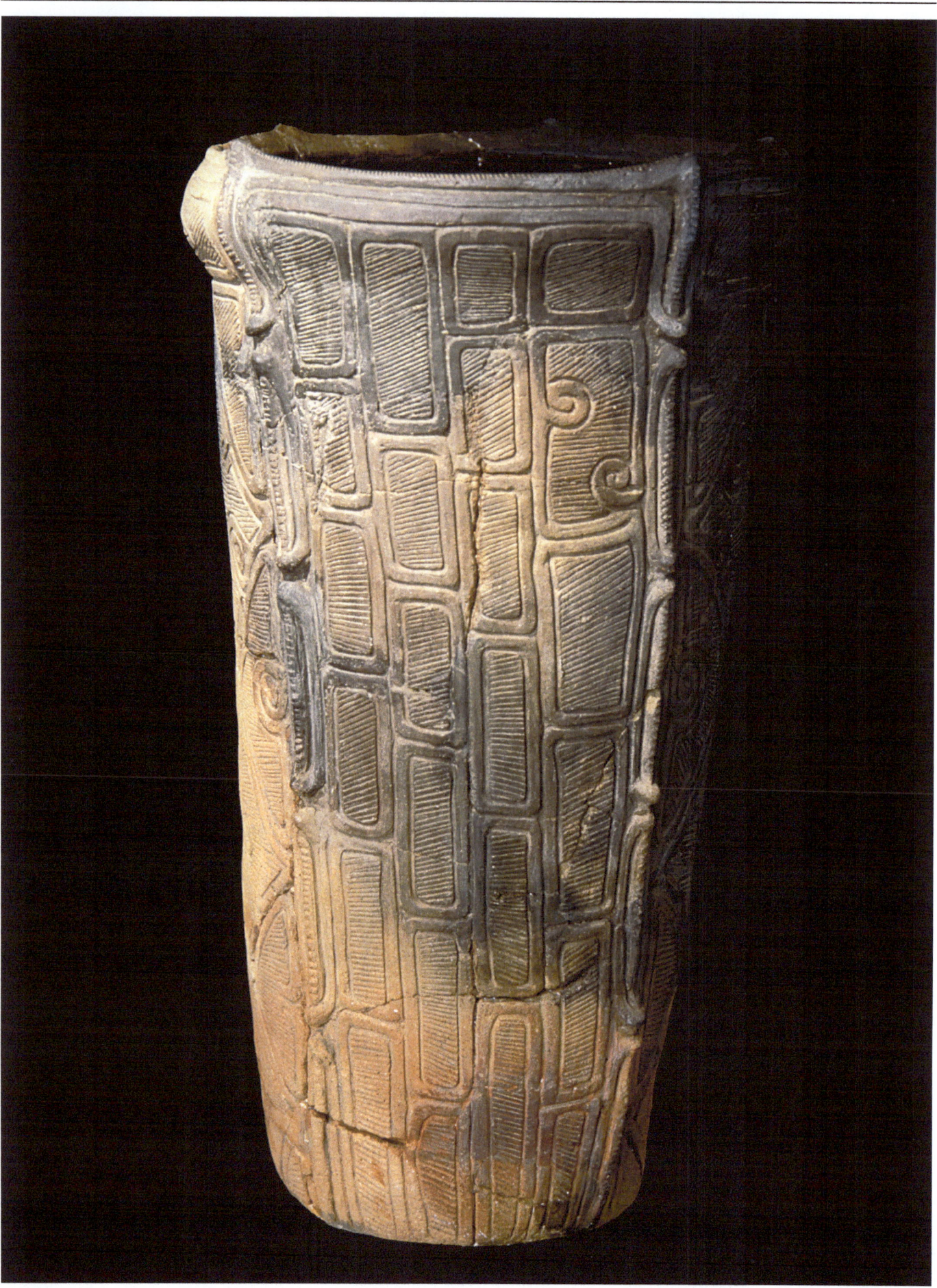

Deep bowl with compartment pattern of vertical stripes

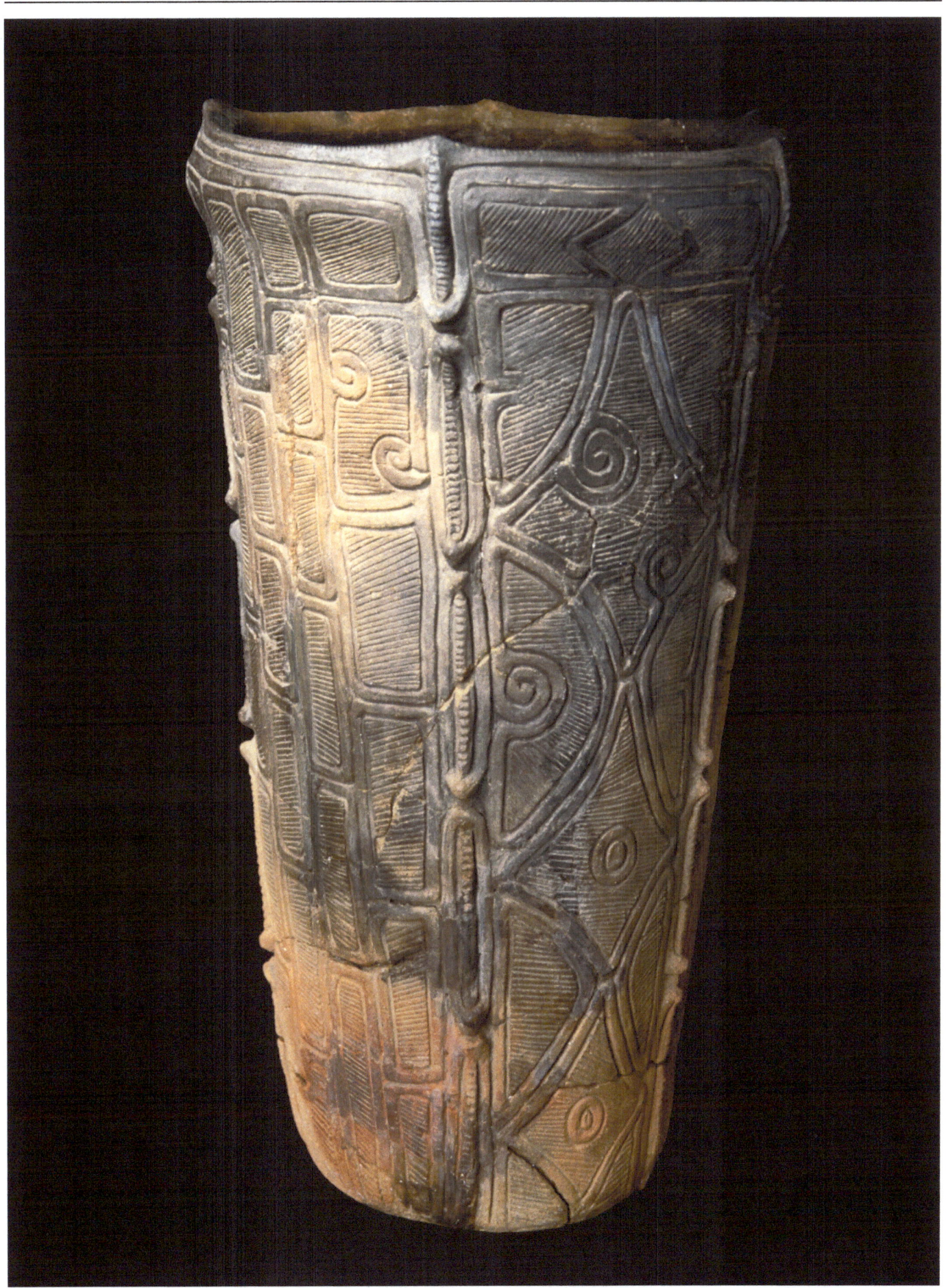

103

Five-stage deep bowl with dual eyes
Tounai ruins
Tounai style I
Dwelling site #14
Excavated in 1962
Middle Jomon, Middle
4,700 years B.P.
57.6cm(H), 37.0cm(D)
"Idojiri Report" P.89, No.240,
"Tounai Report" P.331, No.272
ID-050

This deep bowl is a stately work with an unusual form like 4-tiered rice-cake that stands up from the lower body. On the mouth edge is arranged a form of both eyes. A part of the right eye to the top of the head was missing and restored.

The lip is thick and wide. The outer edge is curled and a form of dual rings is created. On another part, the lip protrudes in triangle shape and another dual ring is created at the lower portion. An image that is assumed to be a diamond-shaped frog can be seen on the back of the dual rings from the top to the second stage. On the second stage are arranged 6 or 7 units of a figure, and on the third stage are arranged 4 patterns that look like a form such as laying the character "大". On the fourth stage can be seen 4 diamond-shaped patterns that bend inside. They give an impression like pictograms. On the top stage are arranged 4 compartment patterns up and down. The bottom had been restored including missing part, but a little less than one third was found during the third excavation.

The surface is finely finished and the upper half is slightly sooty. Some scorches can be seen in 7 cm width near the bottom.

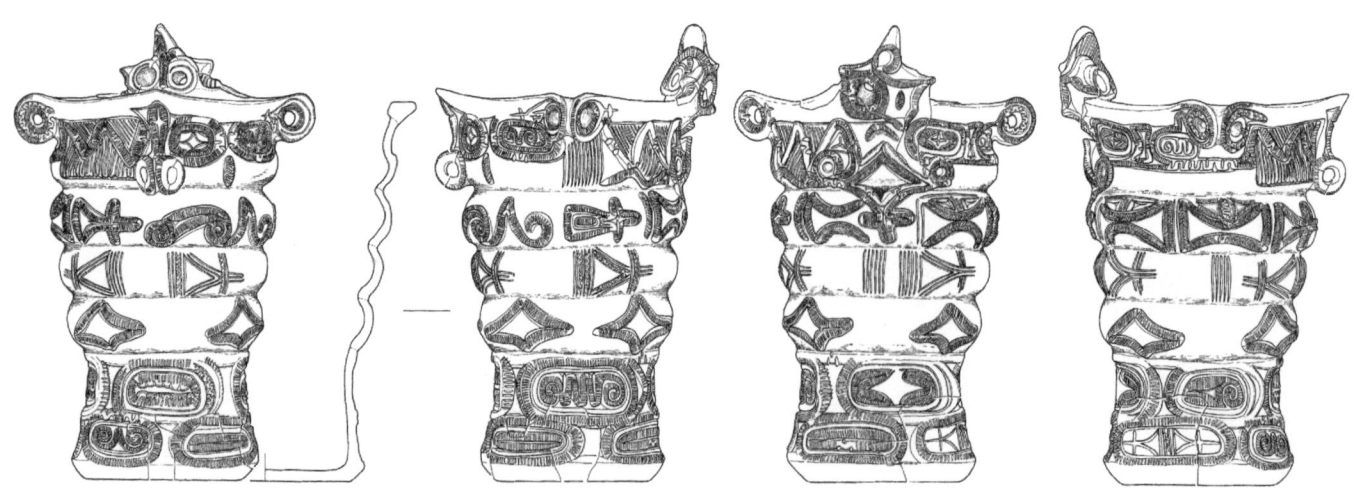

Five-stage deep bowl with dual eyes

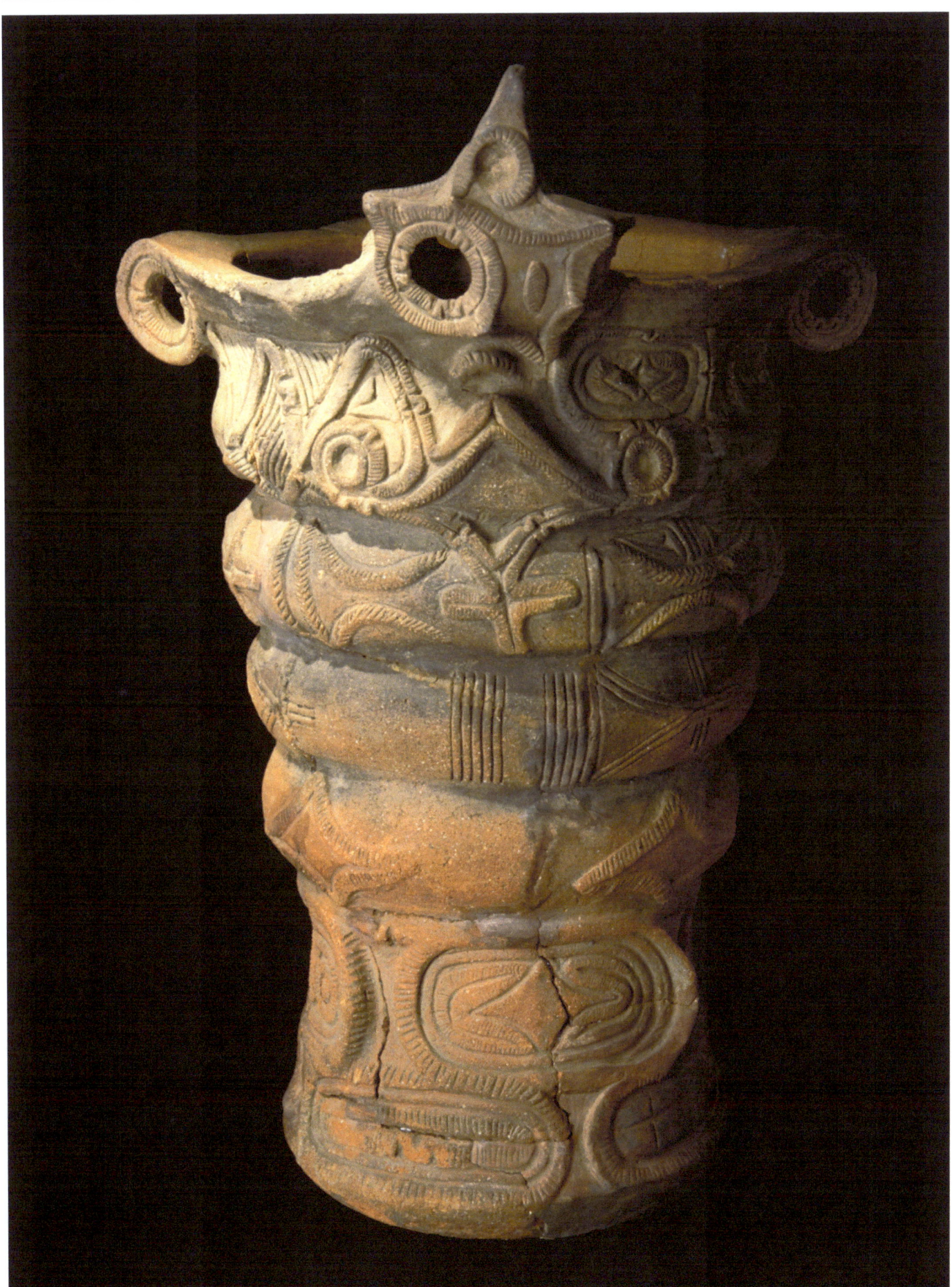

Five-stage deep bowl with dual eyes

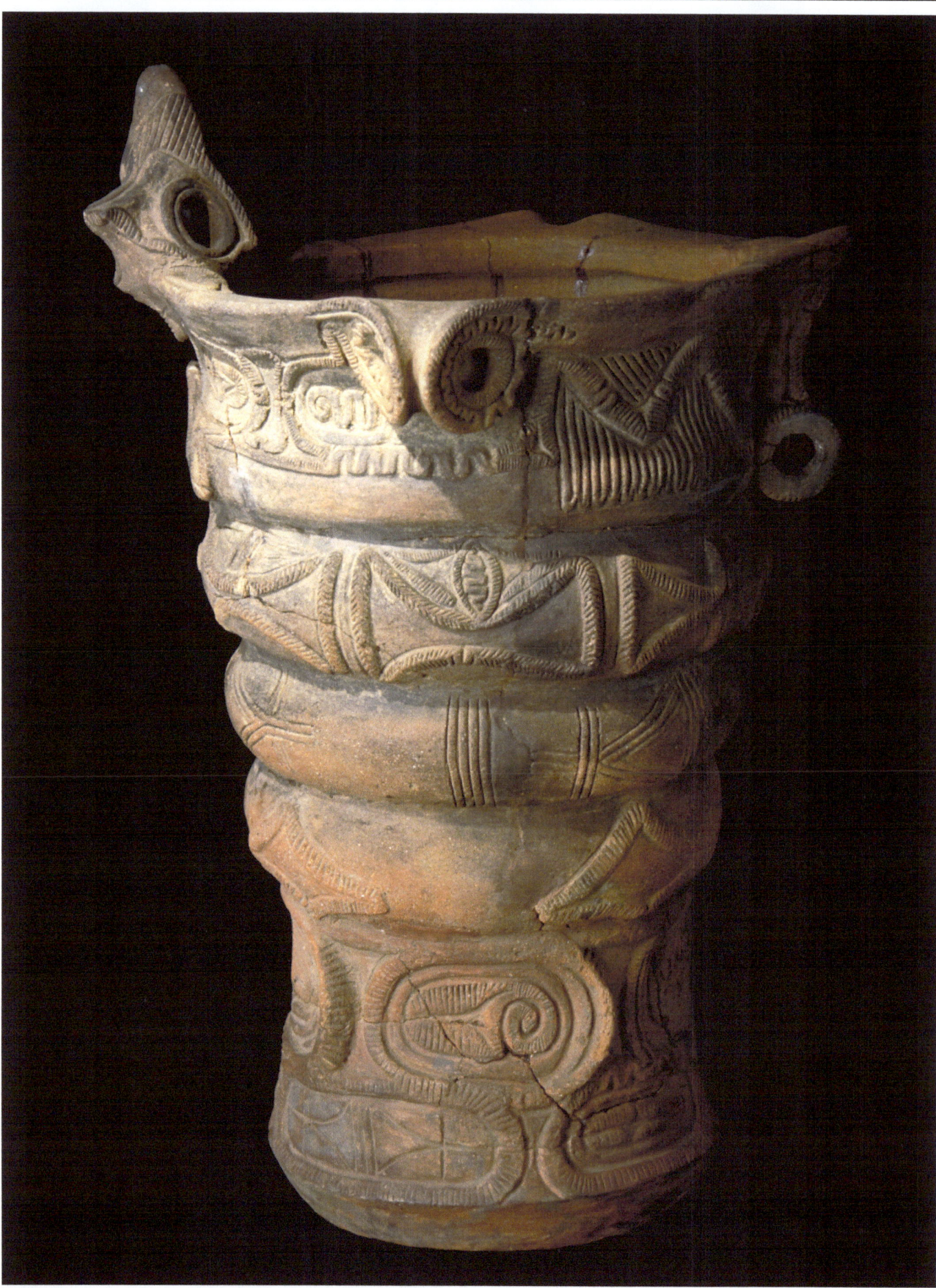

Five-stage deep bowl with dual eyes

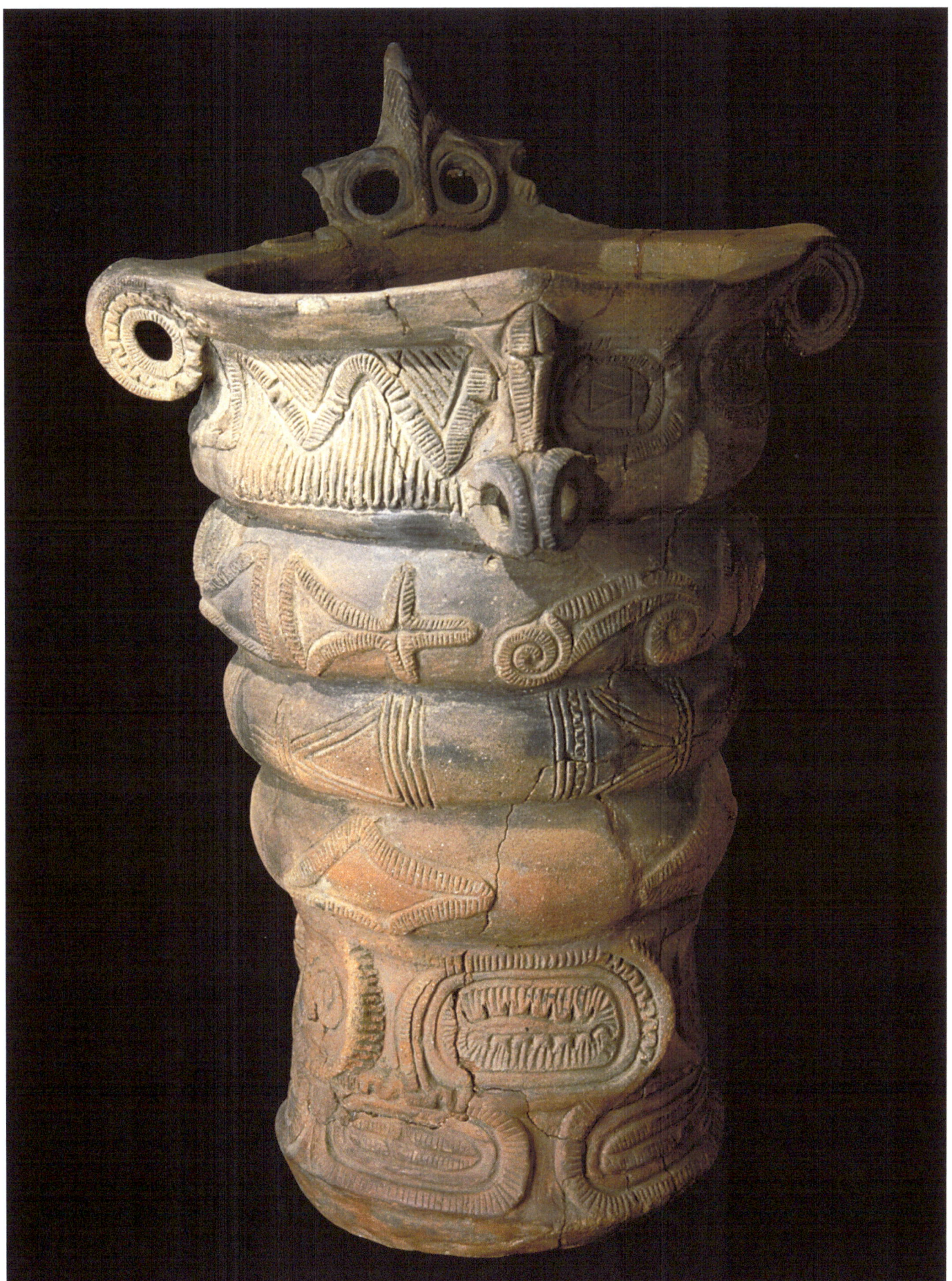

Clay figure with a snake on the head
Tounai ruins
Tounai style I
Dwelling site #16
Excavated in 1962
Middle Jomon, Middle
4,700 years B.P.
10.5cm(H), 9.0cm(D)
"Idojiri Report" P.128, No.197,
"Tounai Report" P.334, No.276
ID-048

The left arm and the lower part from the breast are missing in this clay figure. On the big and flat face are drawn a relatively high nose and eyebrow by ridges, and the glabella is recessed slightly in ginkgo leaf shape. The eyes are thin and sharp like a brush tip with two shallow lines drawn toward the cheek under the left eye. The mouth is so-called "pursy mouth". Arms are short and they expand to right beside. Both of the breasts are represented.

On the top of the head can be seen an object that seems to be a coil of a snake opening the mouth. On the three sides at the skirt of the back of the head and on the top of the head, there are small holes. On the back, a diamond-shaped pattern that bents inside is drawn by a half-cut bamboo tube.

Among the deep bowls with a human face in the Idojiri period, works with a snake on the head are not so rare, but the case of clay figure with a snake on the head is quite exceptional.

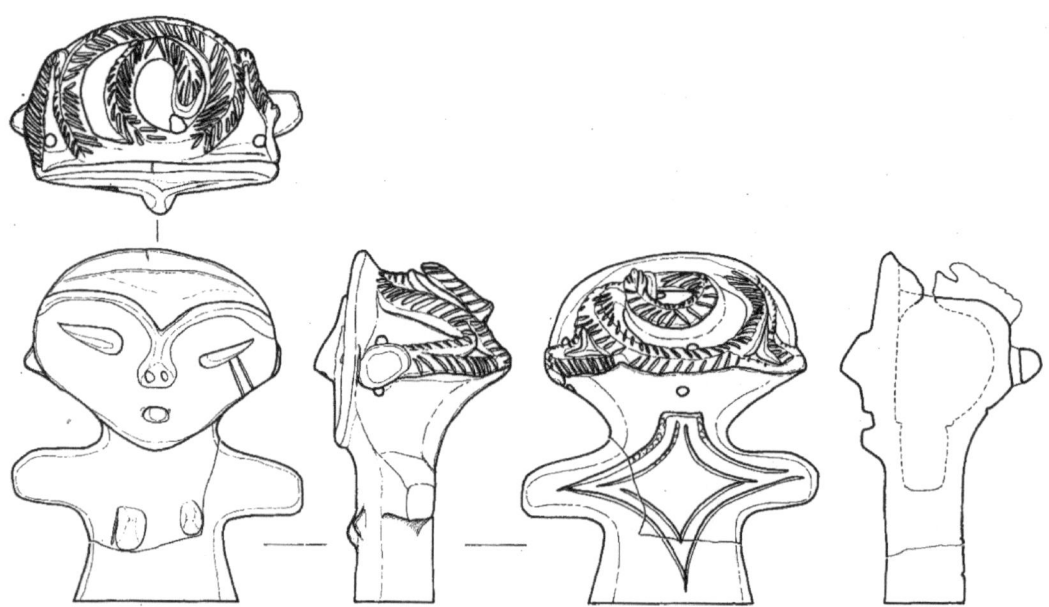

Clay figure with a snake on the head

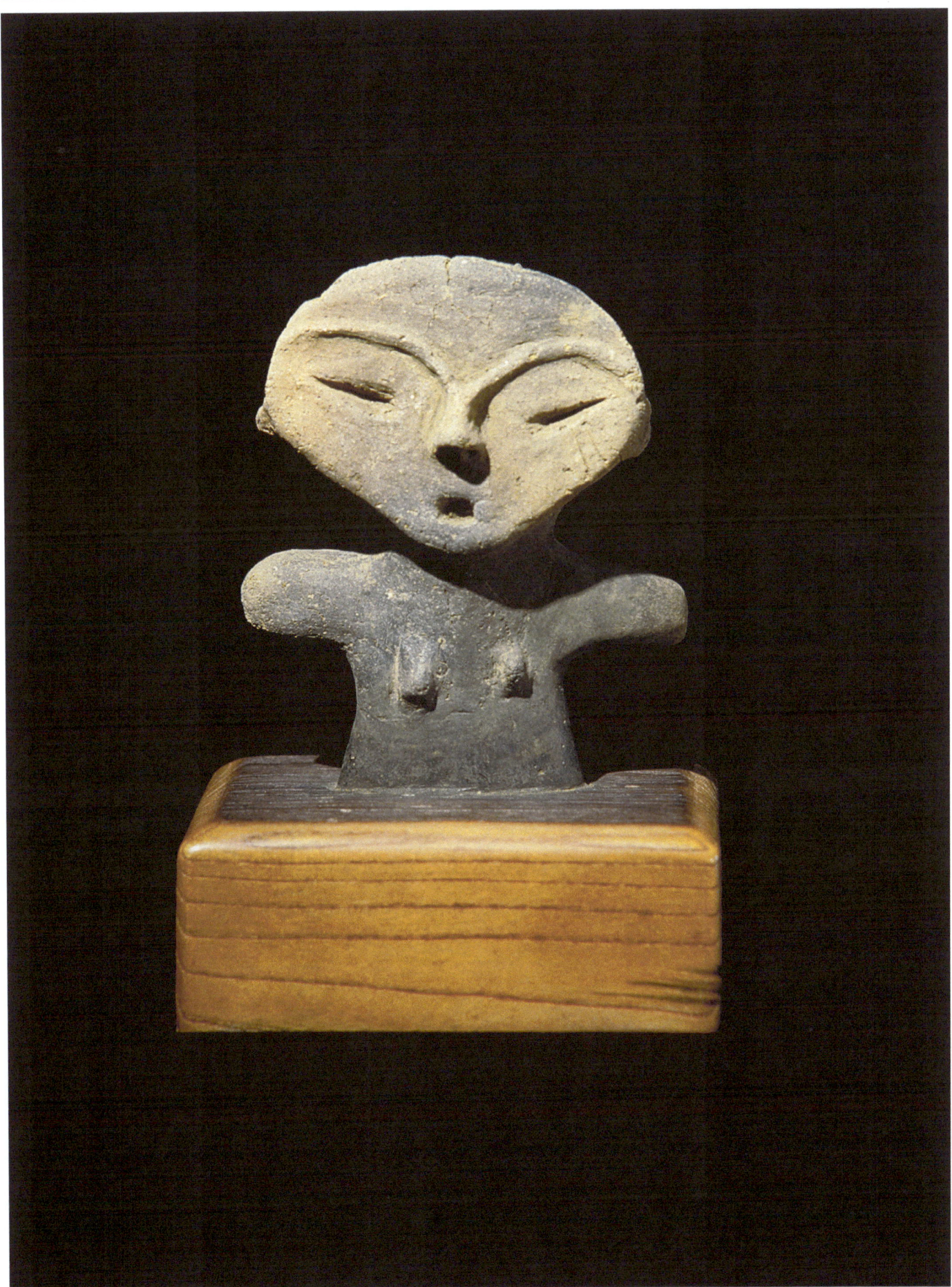

Clay figure with a snake on the head

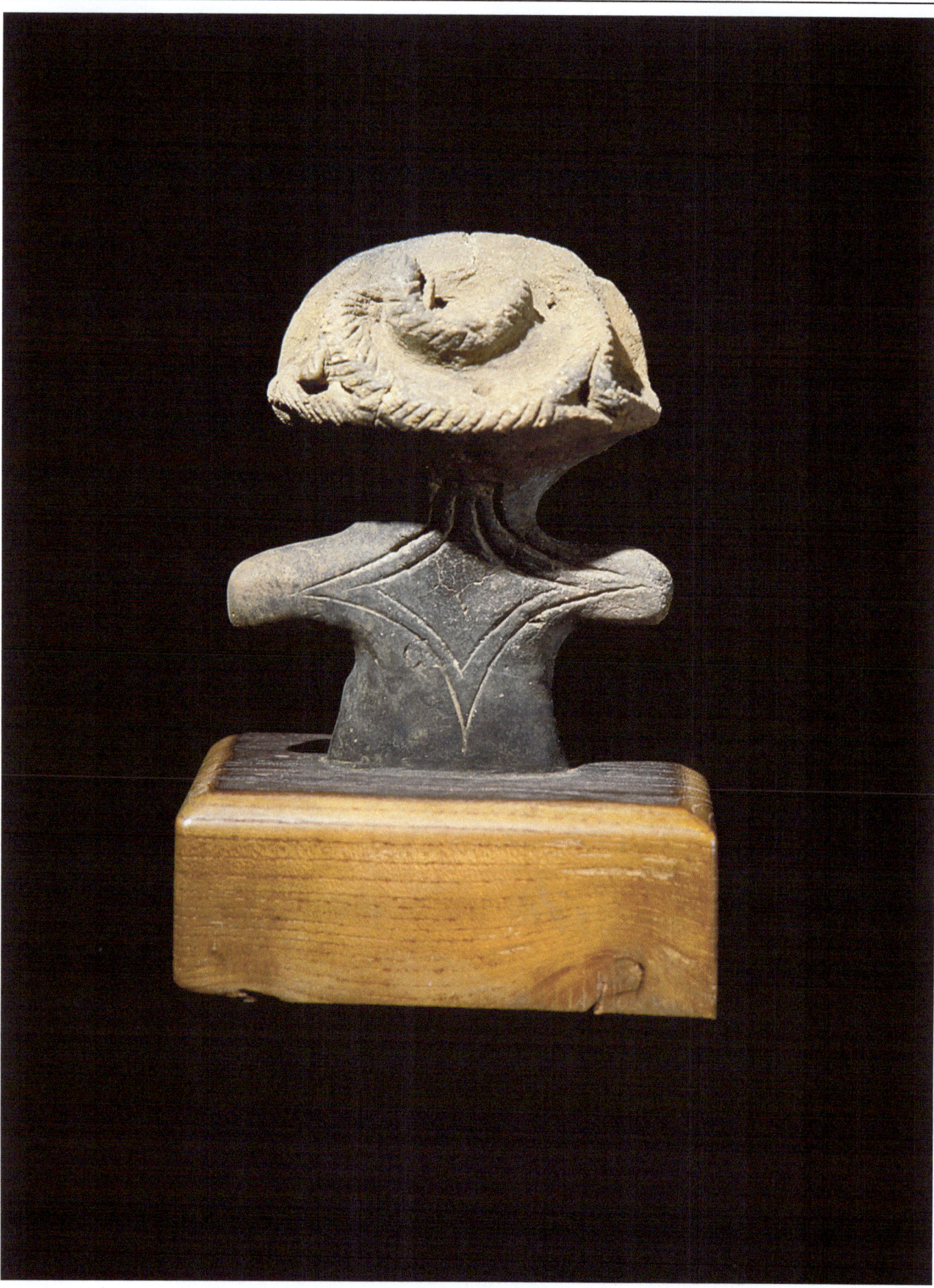

Clay figure with a snake on the head

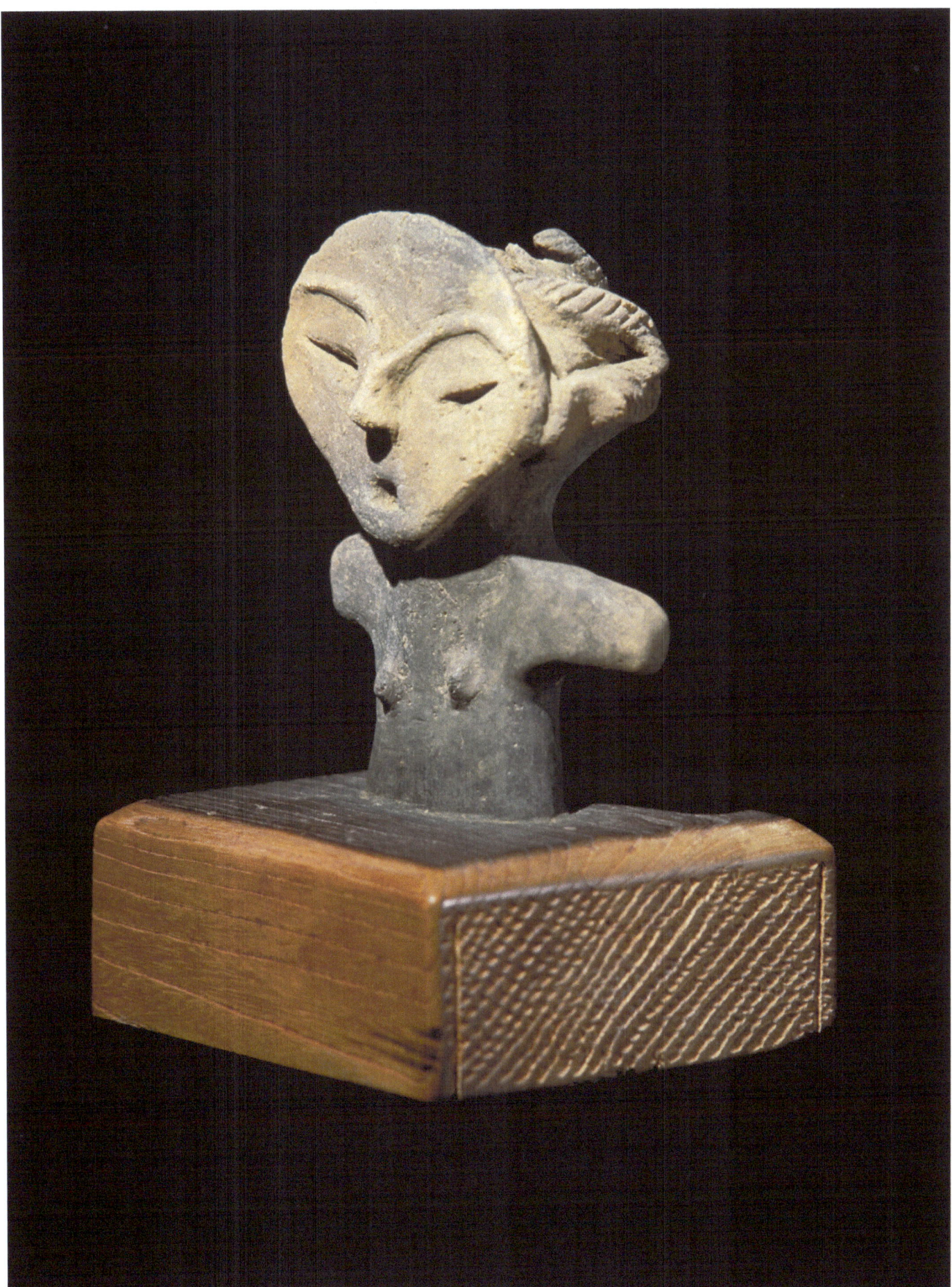

111

Large bowl with breast-shaped rim
Tounai ruins
Tounai style I
Special remains
Excavated in 1962
Middle Jomon, Middle
4,700 years B.P.
60.8cm(H), 34.0cm(D)
"Tounai Report" P.319, No.236
ID-055

This is a large bowl with breast-shaped rim and very heavy. Wavy mouth edge is thick and bends toward the inside. The number of the breast-shaped bulge is 10. Serrated ridge band is arranged between the upper and lower two stages of the horizontal compartment patterns, and lower half of the body is made in Jomon pattern. The serrated ridge band is thick and overhangs from the top, but it is loose at one point and an ellipse-shaped compartment pattern is represented. Trigeminal-shaped patterns and ring-shaped patterns are arranged around it in total 6 inverted triangle patterns including the left and the right.

Upper half of the outer surface is partially sooty. Scorch is not clear, but on the body can be seen some bitter-like stains from the bottom up to the 36cm height.

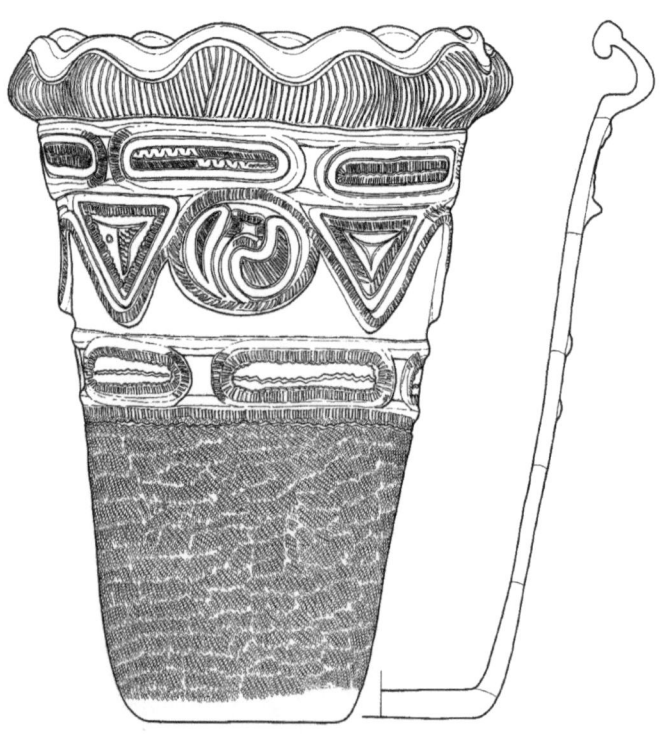

Large bowl with breast-shaped rim

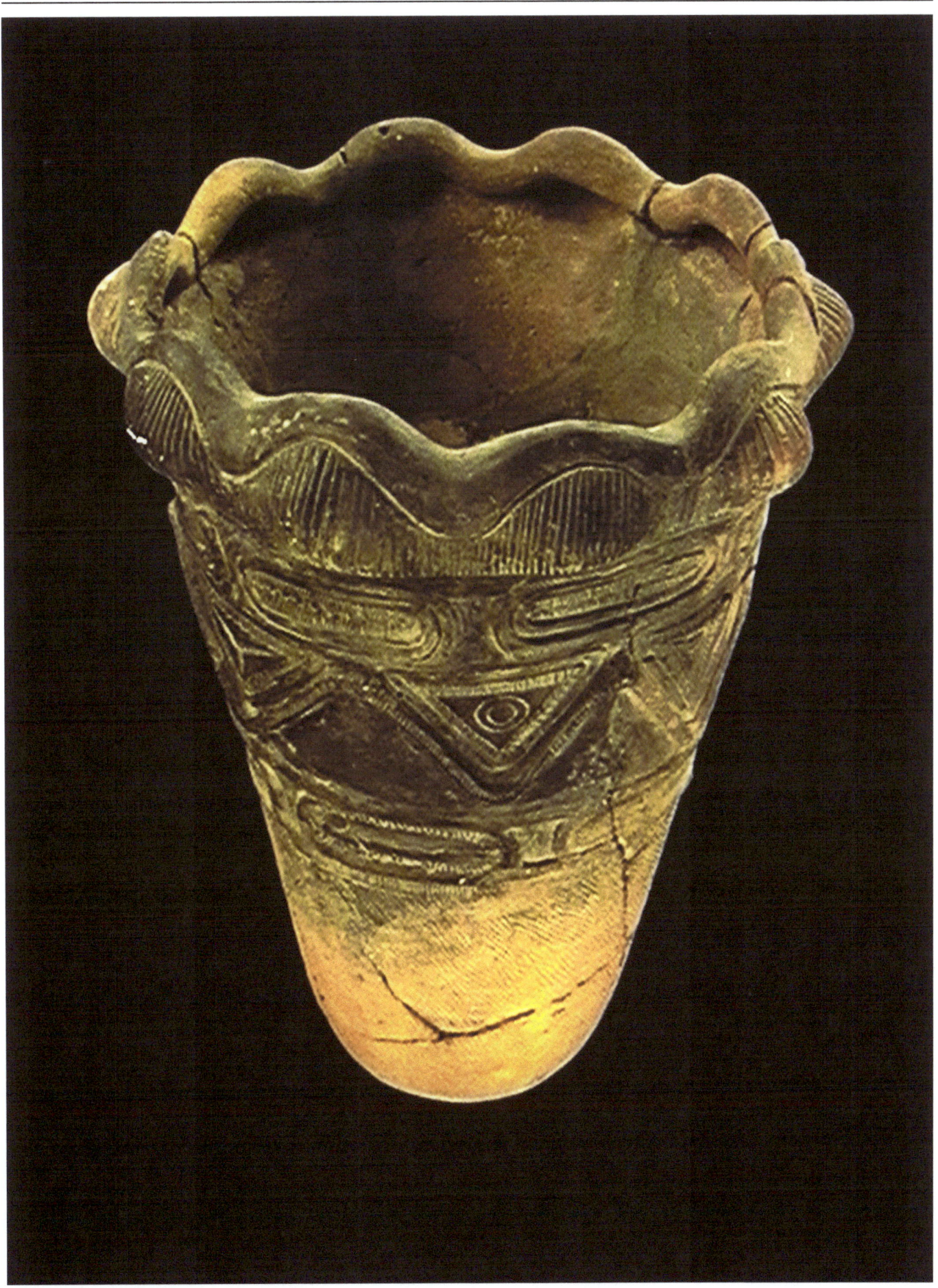

Large bowl with breast-shaped rim

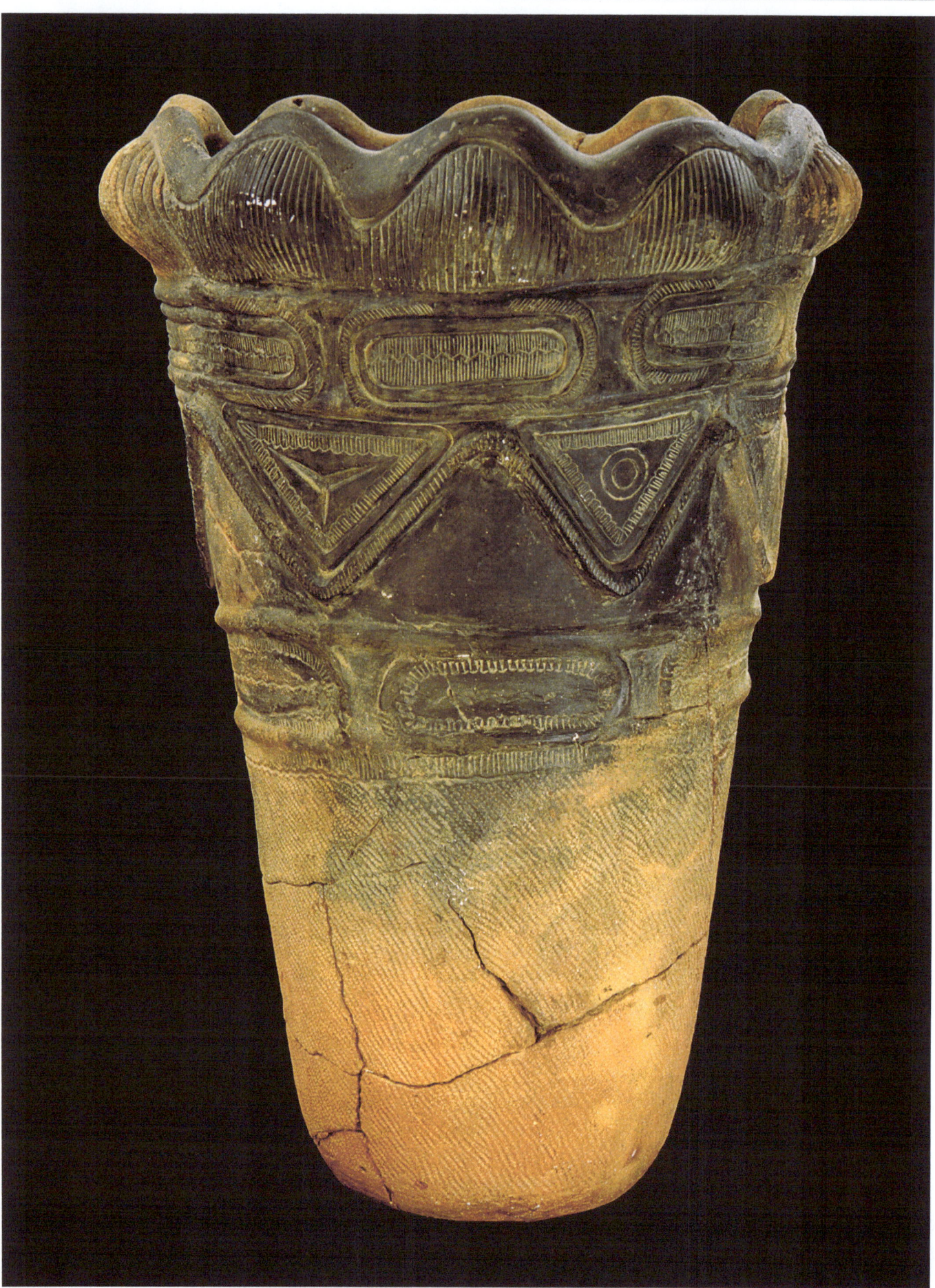

Large bowl with breast-shaped rim

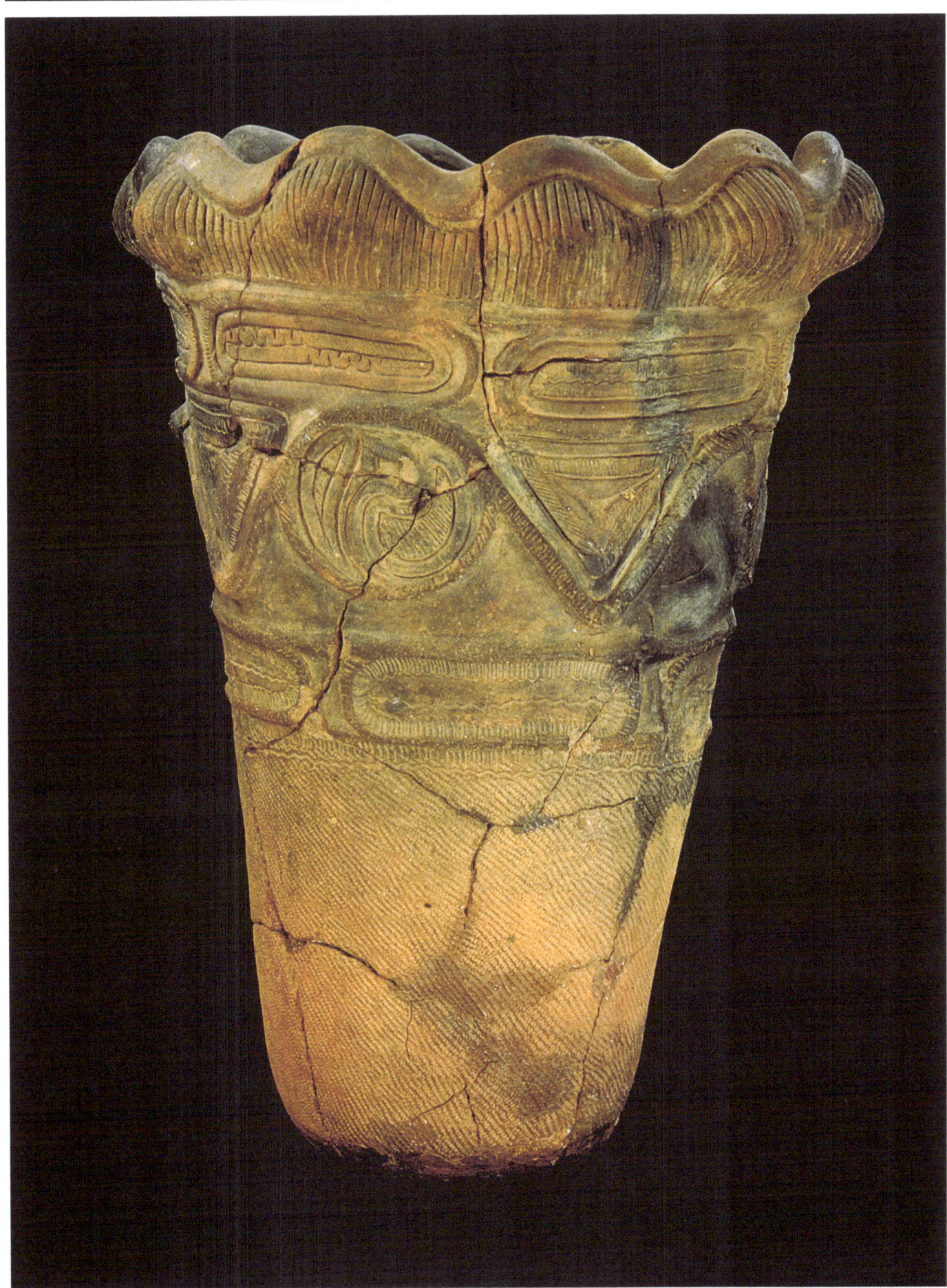

Deep bowl with dual eyes
Tounai ruins
Tounai style II
Special remains
Excavated in 1962
Middle Jomon, Middle
4,600 years B.P.
34.2cm(H), 26.5cm(D)
"Idojiri Report" P.86, No.194,
"Tounai Report" P.324, No.252
ID-012

On this deep bowl are arranged dual eyes and the dual rings at three sides. Those are connected by "W" shaped ridge band. The dual eyes are accompanied with small rings at the left and right side, and the one penetrates. On the front and back of the body are arranged 2 ridges that are opened up and down. On the side of the body is arranged a "J" shaped ridge band.

On the three sides of the bottom are arranged elliptical compartment patterns. It is a pretty bowl. The upper half of the body is partially sooty. Inside is clean without scorch marks.

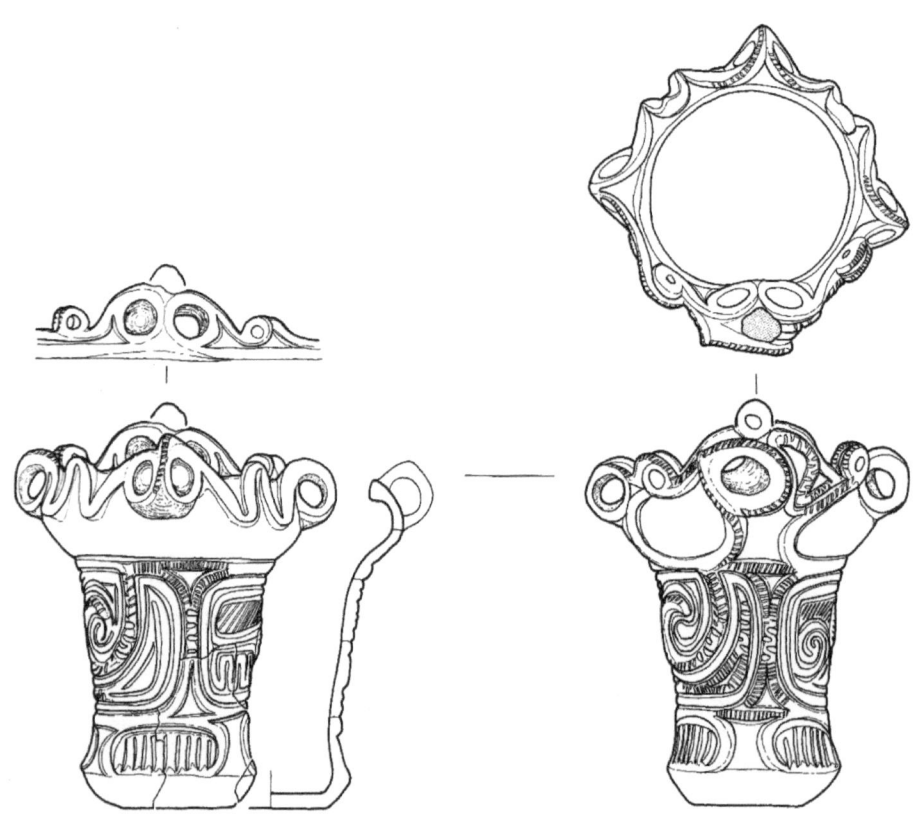

Deep bowl wih dual eyes

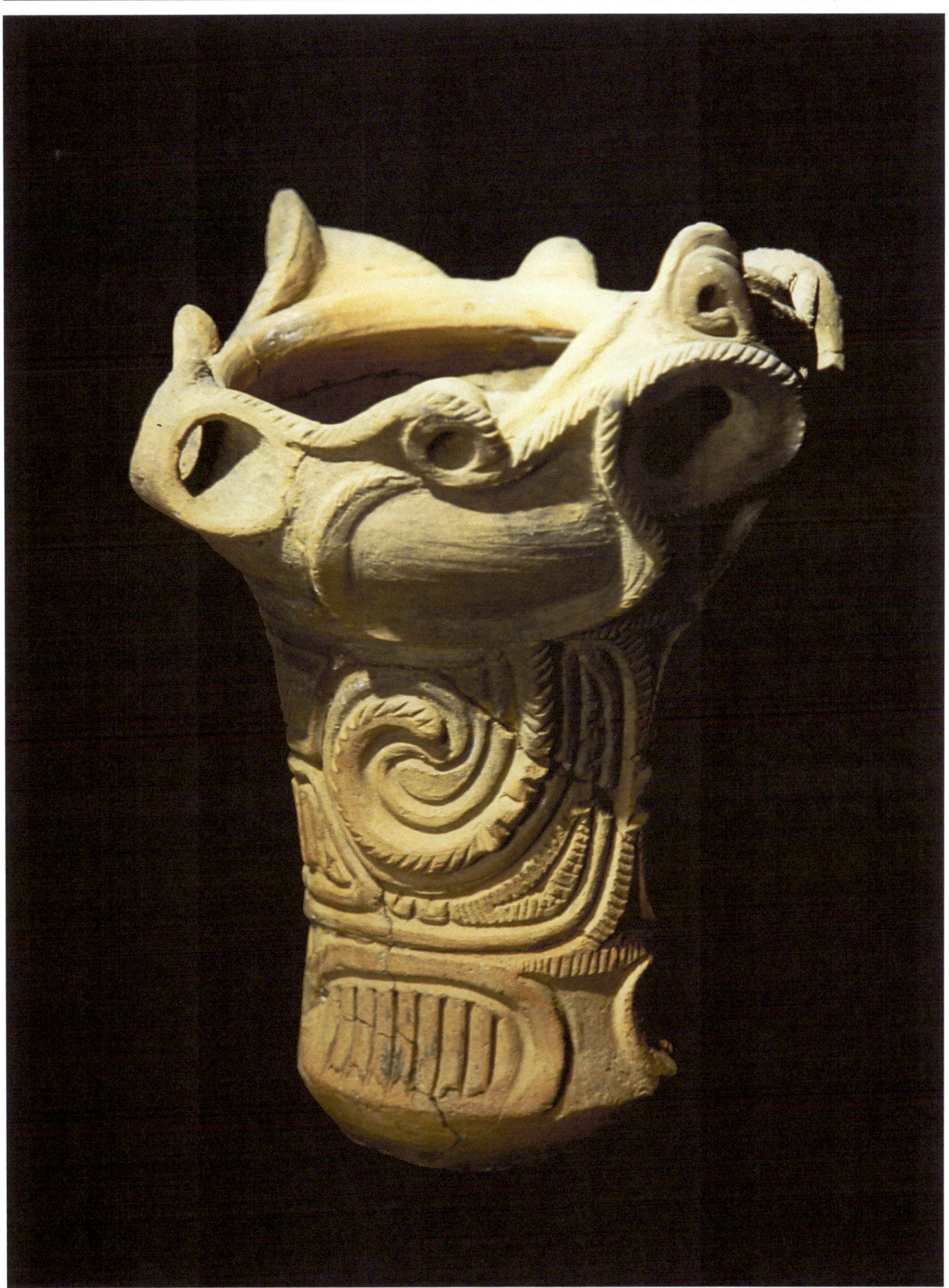

Deep bowl wih dual eyes

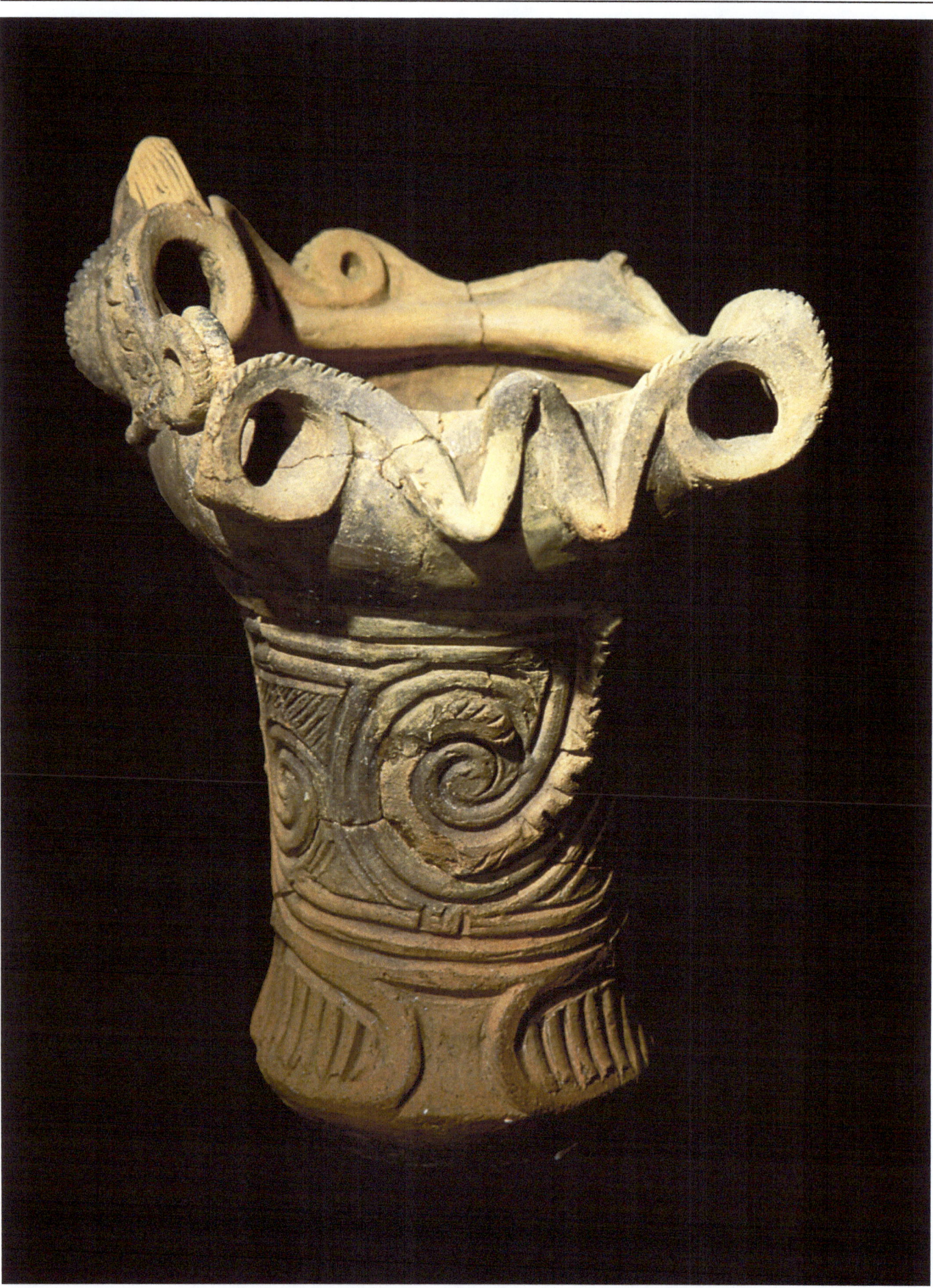

Deep bowl wih dual eyes

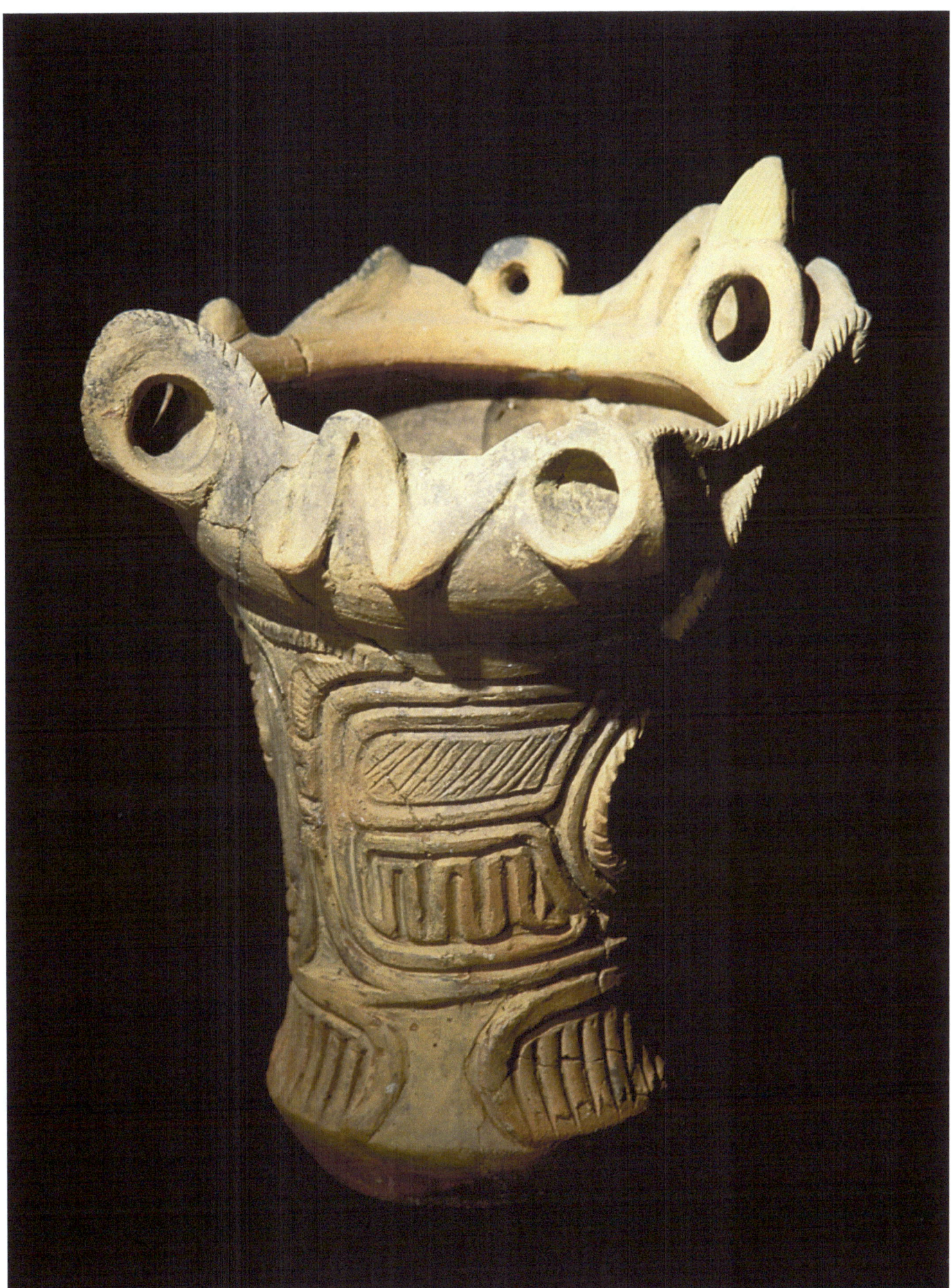

119

Perforated flanged earthenware with half-man half-frog pattern
Tounai ruins
Tounai style I
Special remains
Excavated in 1962
Middle Jomon, Middle
4,700 years B.P.
51.7cm(H), 24.0cm(D)
"Idojiri Report" P.86, No.192,
"Tounai Report" P.322, No.242
ID-051

This perforated flanged earthenware is one of the most representative wares in the artifacts uncovered in Tounai ruins. 30 percent are missing, but important part is extant. It is created very carefully and many glossy parts are remaining. On the body is arranged a pair of dual rings, and on the other side is drawn a half-man half-frog pattern.

That consists of a round head and the semi-spindle body. The legs seem to be withered from the joint to inner thigh. Parallel lines start from the hip, and bend in the form of hook. Upper limbs spread wide diagonally, and another arm that was separated from the middle is bended inside with a big gesture. The instep of three fingers is blistering, and the finger tips are touching the ware body. A bump is arranged on the wrist and a part of joint is constricted.

Opposite side is drawn a strong ring pattern in contact with the dual rings. A convex line surrounds it from the lower part, and it becomes a wide band and bends at the both edges. Needless to say, this is a technique that has coincided with arms on another side. On both sides are arranged up and down a pair of wide ridge bands that are similar to the shape of mortar. On another side, the form of lower part differs slightly.

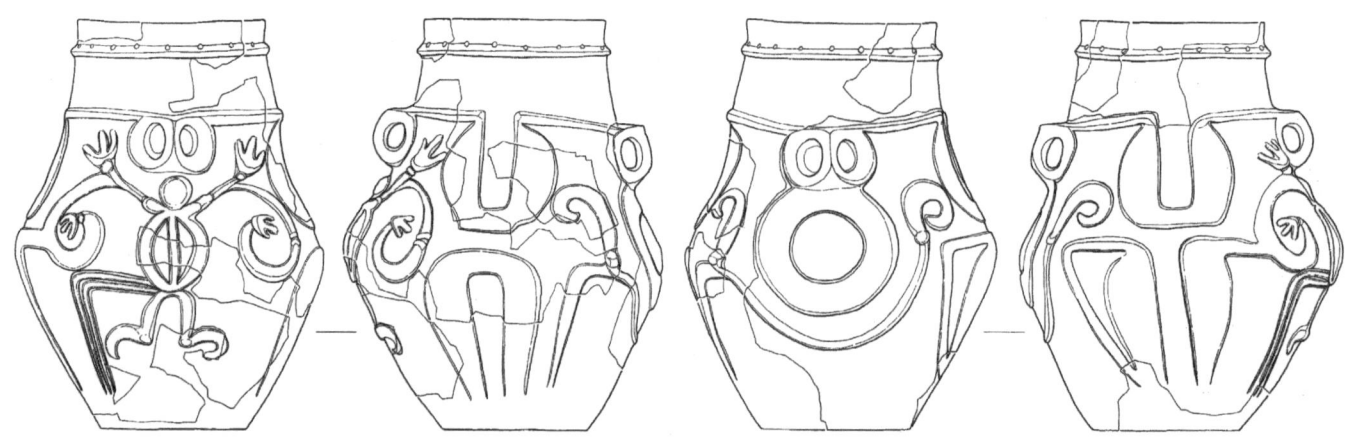

Perforated flanged earthenware with half-man half-frog pattern

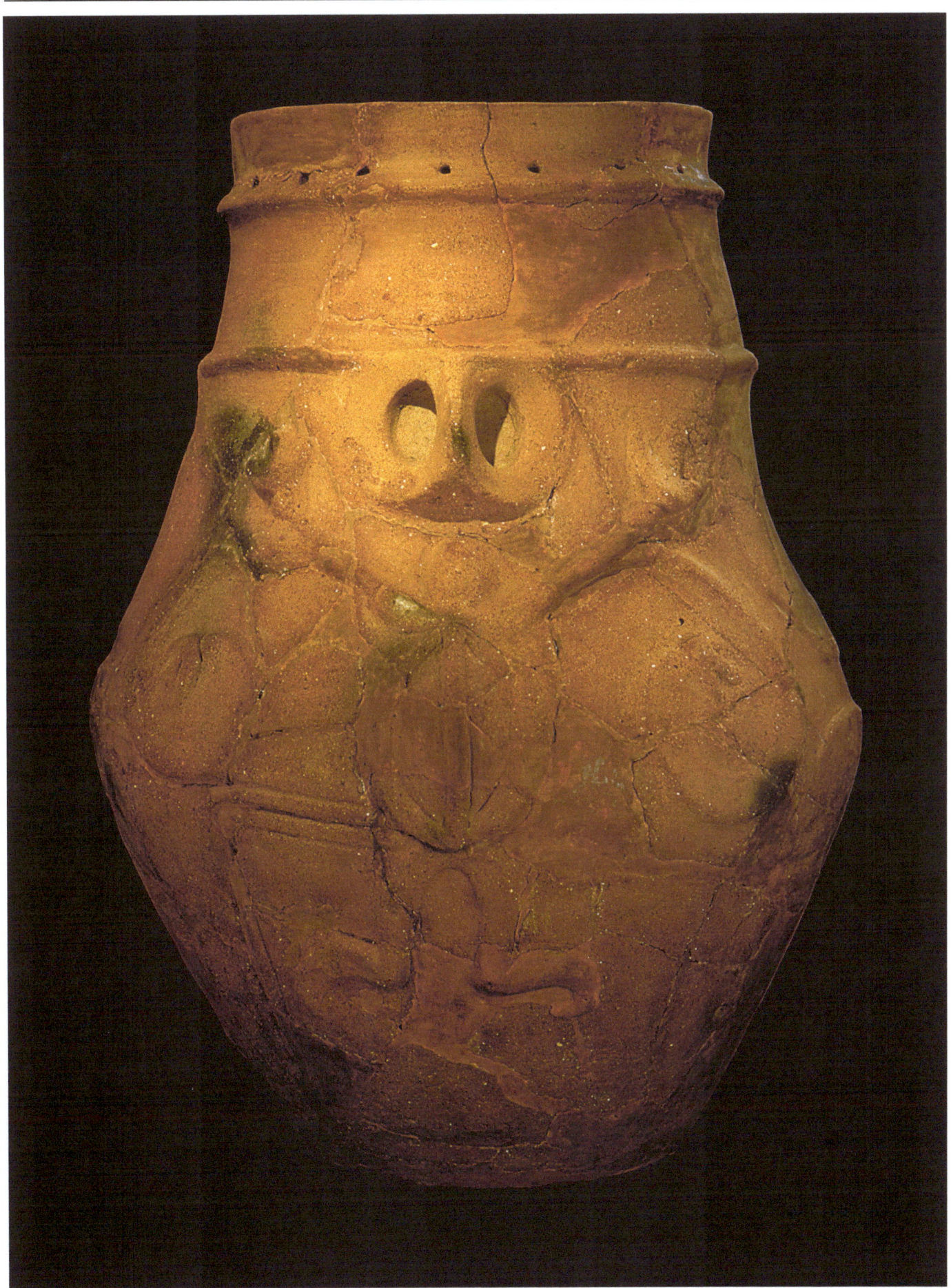

Perforated flanged earthenware with half-man half-frog pattern

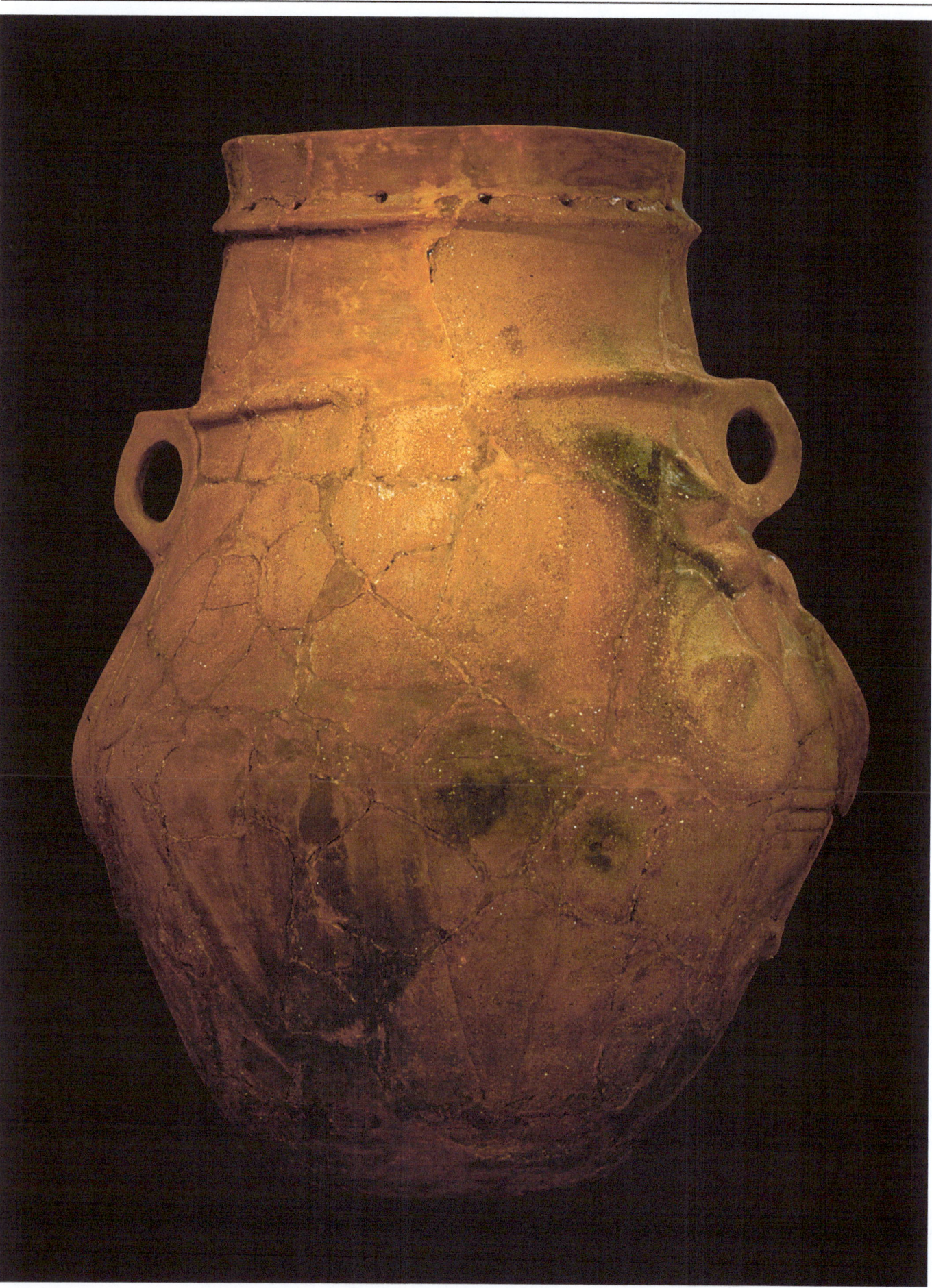

Perforated flanged earthenware with half-man half-frog pattern

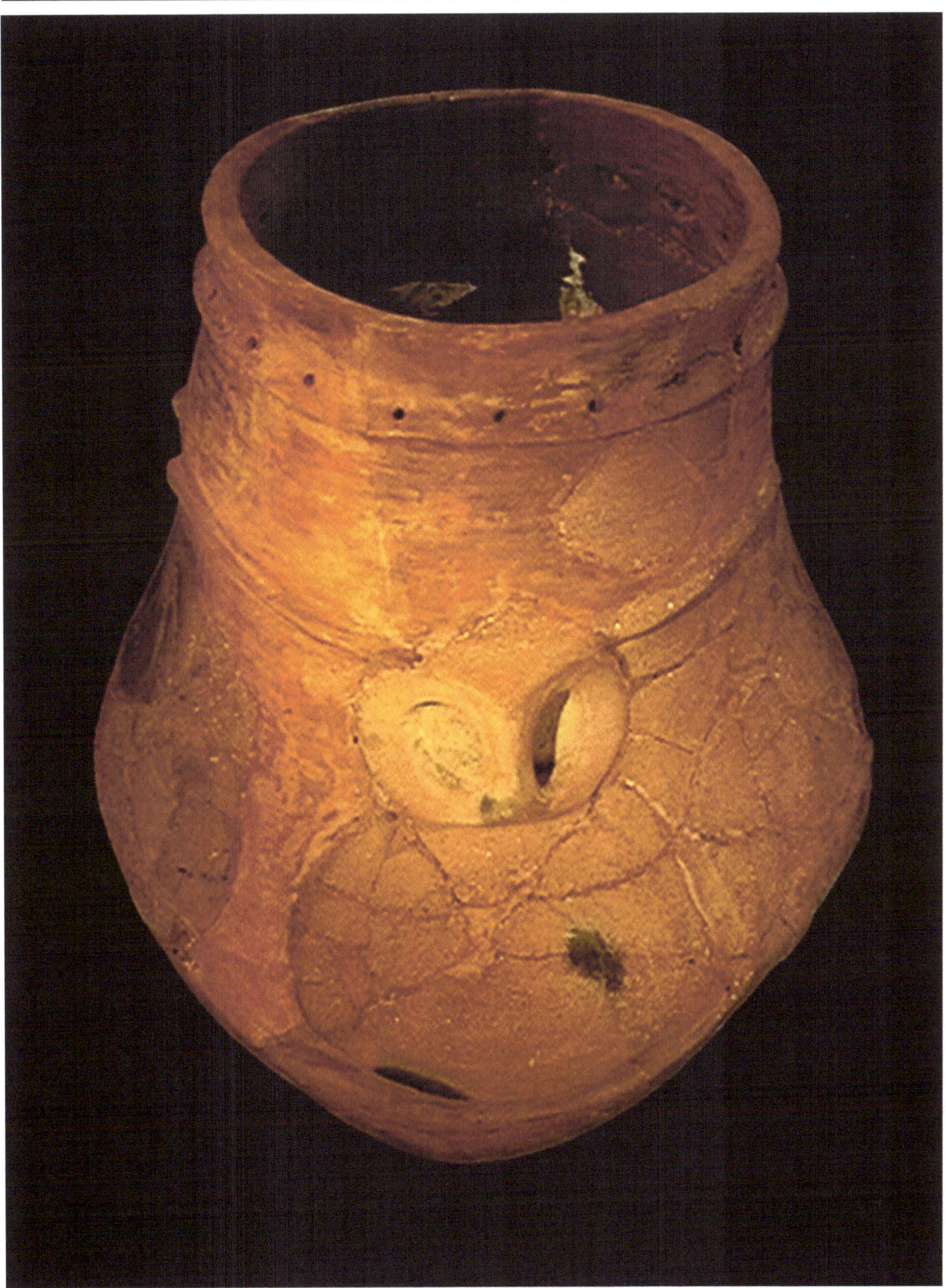

Deep bowl with Mizuchi pattern
Tounai ruins
Tounai style I
Special remains
Excavated in 1962
Middle Jomon, Middle
4,700 years B.P.
46.8cm(H), 29.0cm(D)
"Tounai Report" P.319, No.235
ID-084

This deep bowl is a tub-shaped pottery with a mark of "ring-stacking method" and on the body are arranged a pair of Mizuchi pattern. The shape is the same both front and back, and two elliptical patterns are aligned on the right back side. On the left side of the back, a contact point between the low convex line around the bottom of the rim is twisted.

Upper half of the outer wall is quite sooty. The surface below the border of soot looks rough and some pasty scorch can be seen in 6 cm width from the bottom.

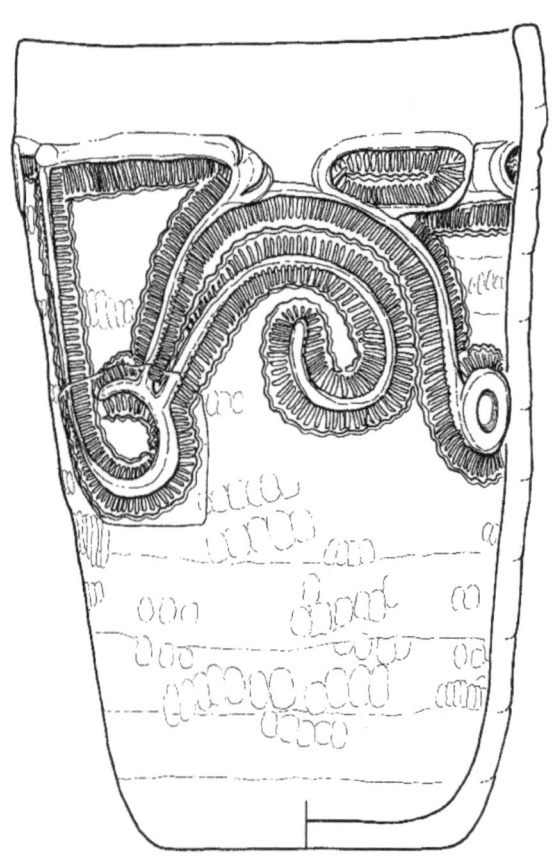

Deep bowl with Mizuchi pattern

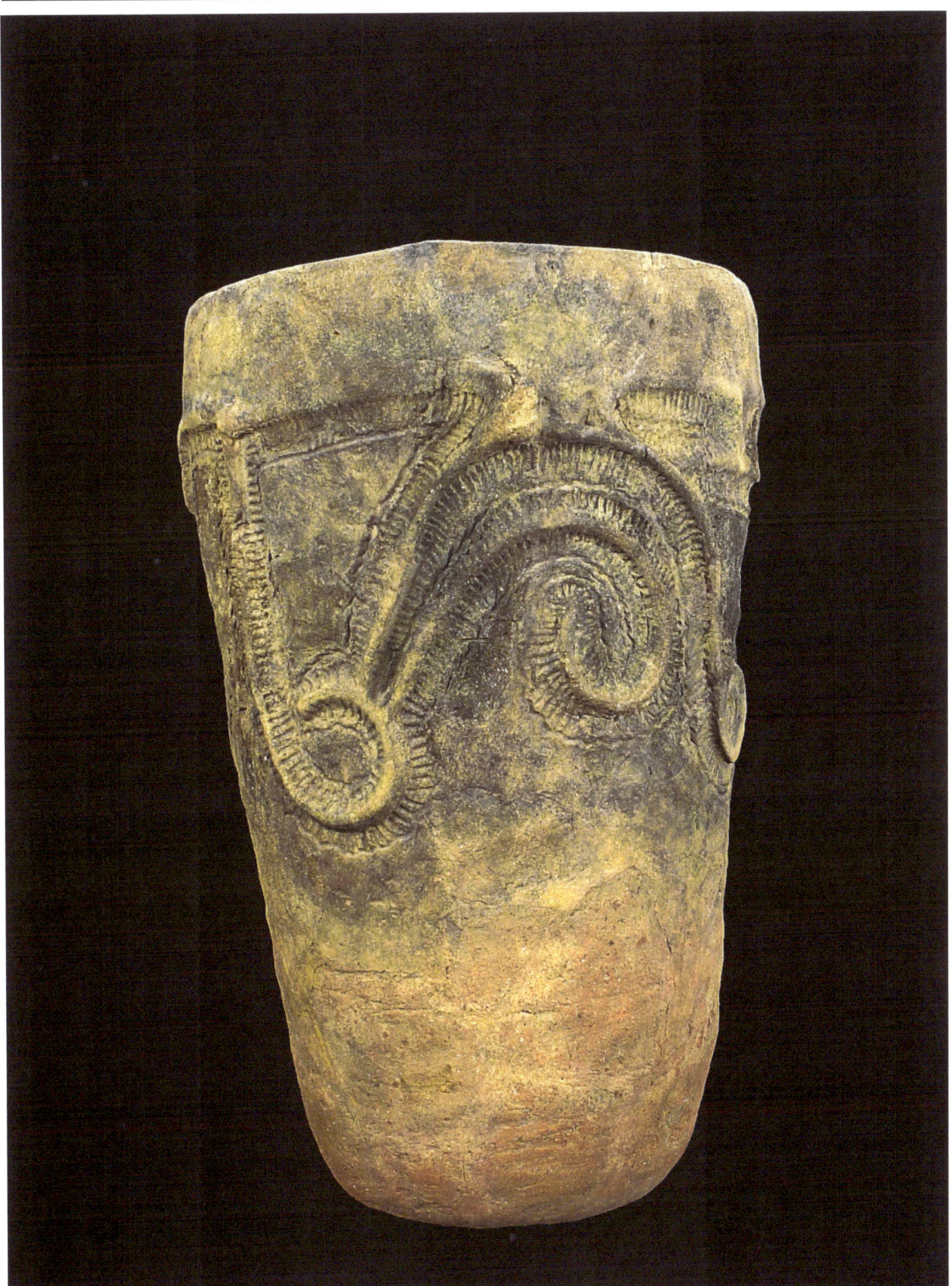

Deep bowl with Mizuchi pattern

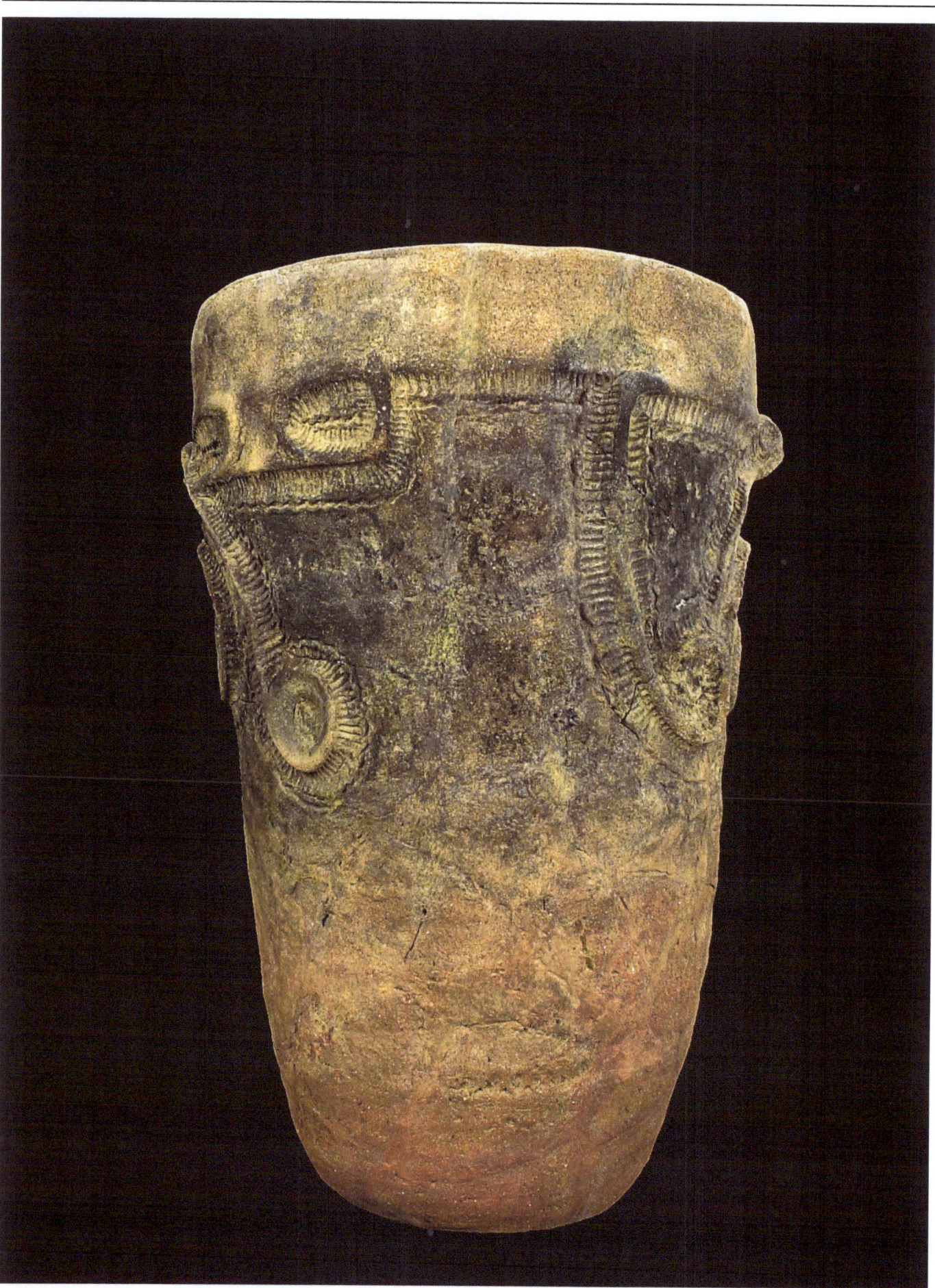

Deep bowl with Mizuchi pattern

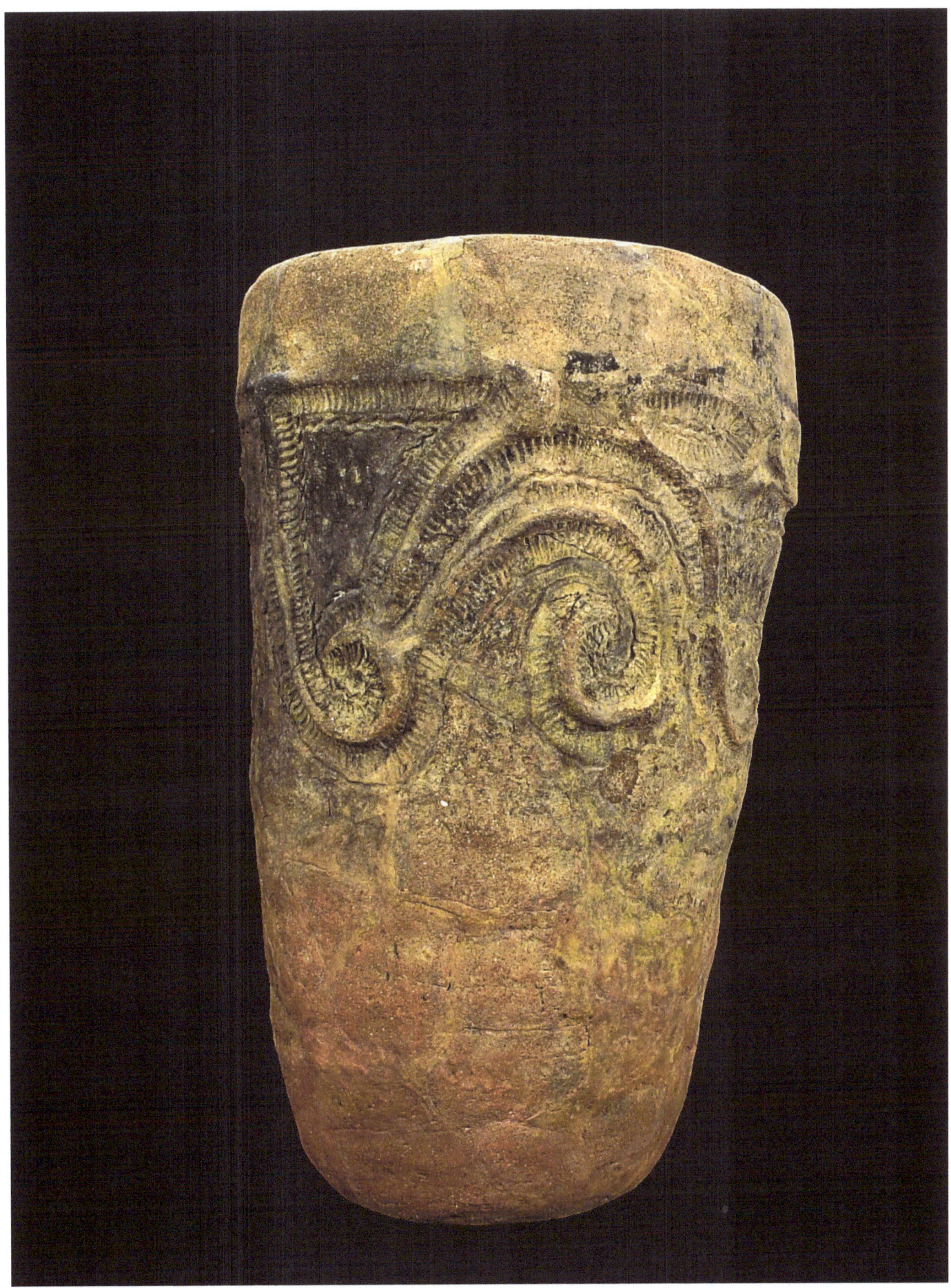

Diamond shaped frog pattern type large bowl
Tounai ruins
Tounai style I
Special remains
Excavated in 1962
Middle Jomon, Middle
4,700 years B.P.
56.5cm(H), 42.5cm(D)
"Tounai Report" P.320, No.241
ID-085

This is a large tub-shaped pottery. The mouth edge forms a thick hoop-shaped. On the rim are arranged two-stage staggered horizontal band compartment patterns. The body in which "ring-stacking marks" remain is divided into four sections by hanging ridge band, and similar patterns are drawn in pair in each section. This ridge band is a combination of Jomon pattern and notches.

The middle of the outer wall is sooty, and on the inner wall slightly remains a scorch in 6 cm width from 3cm above the bottom.

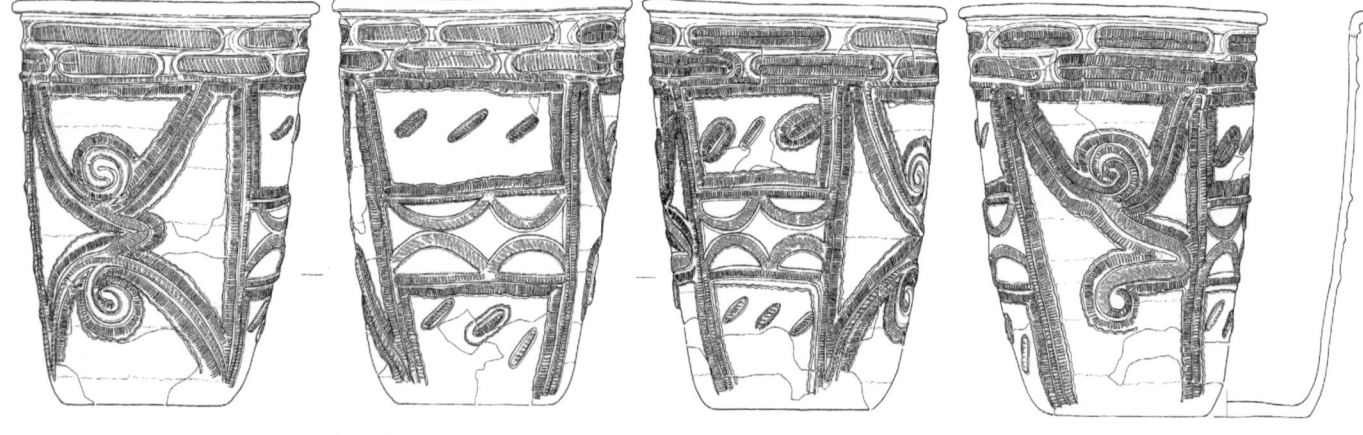

Diamond shaped frog pattern type large bowl

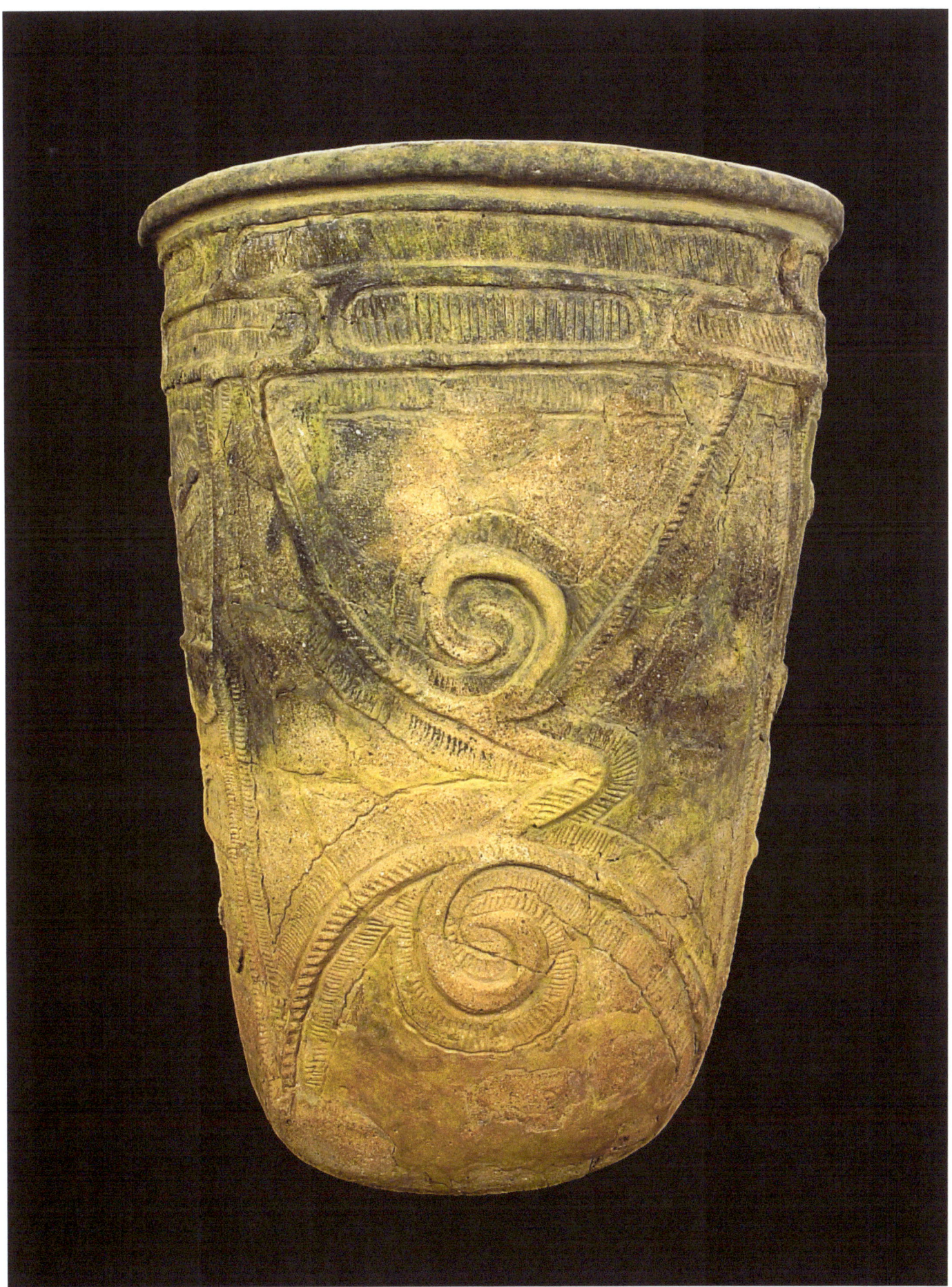

Diamond shaped frog pattern type large bowl

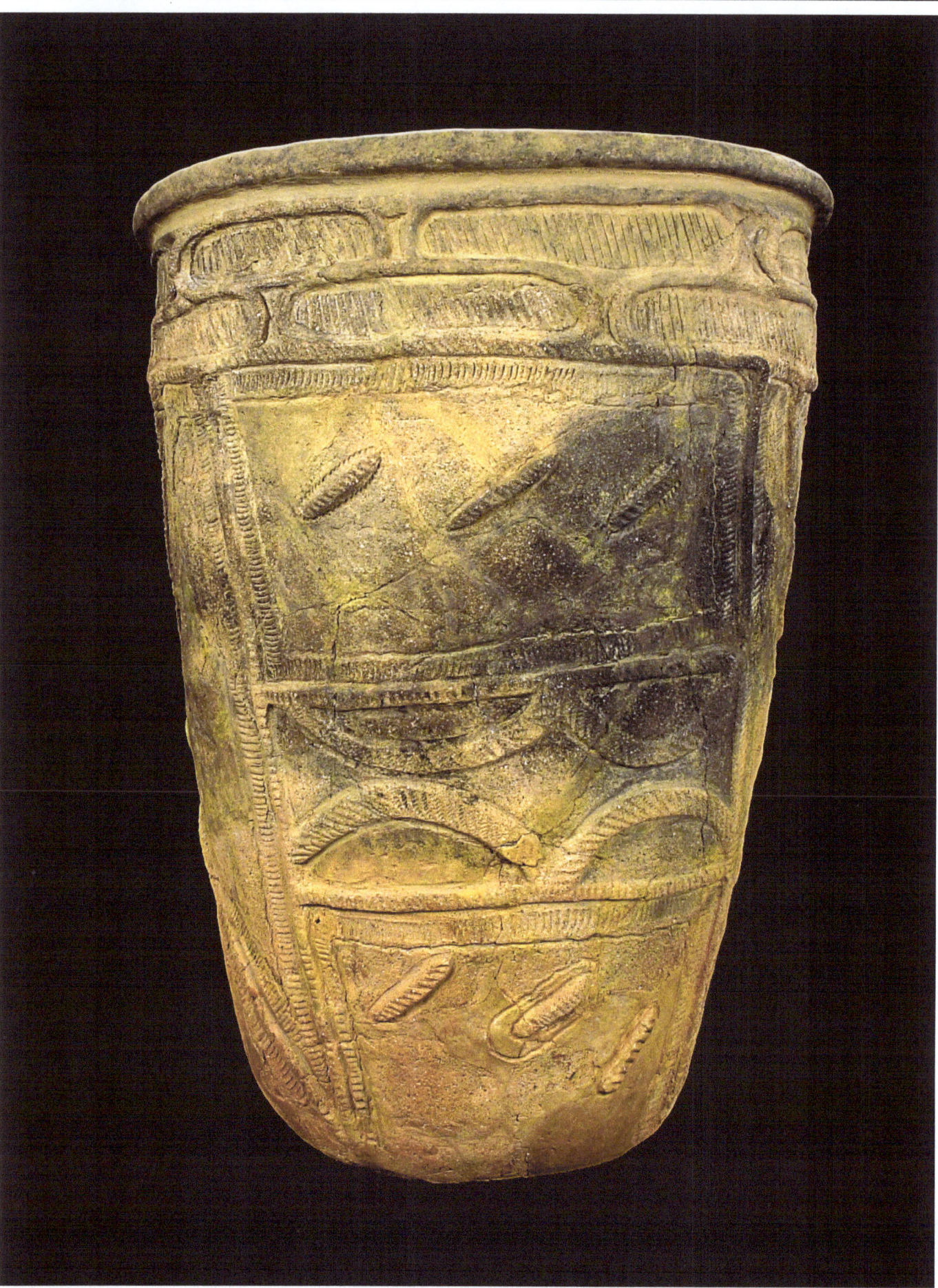

Diamond shaped frog pattern type large bowl

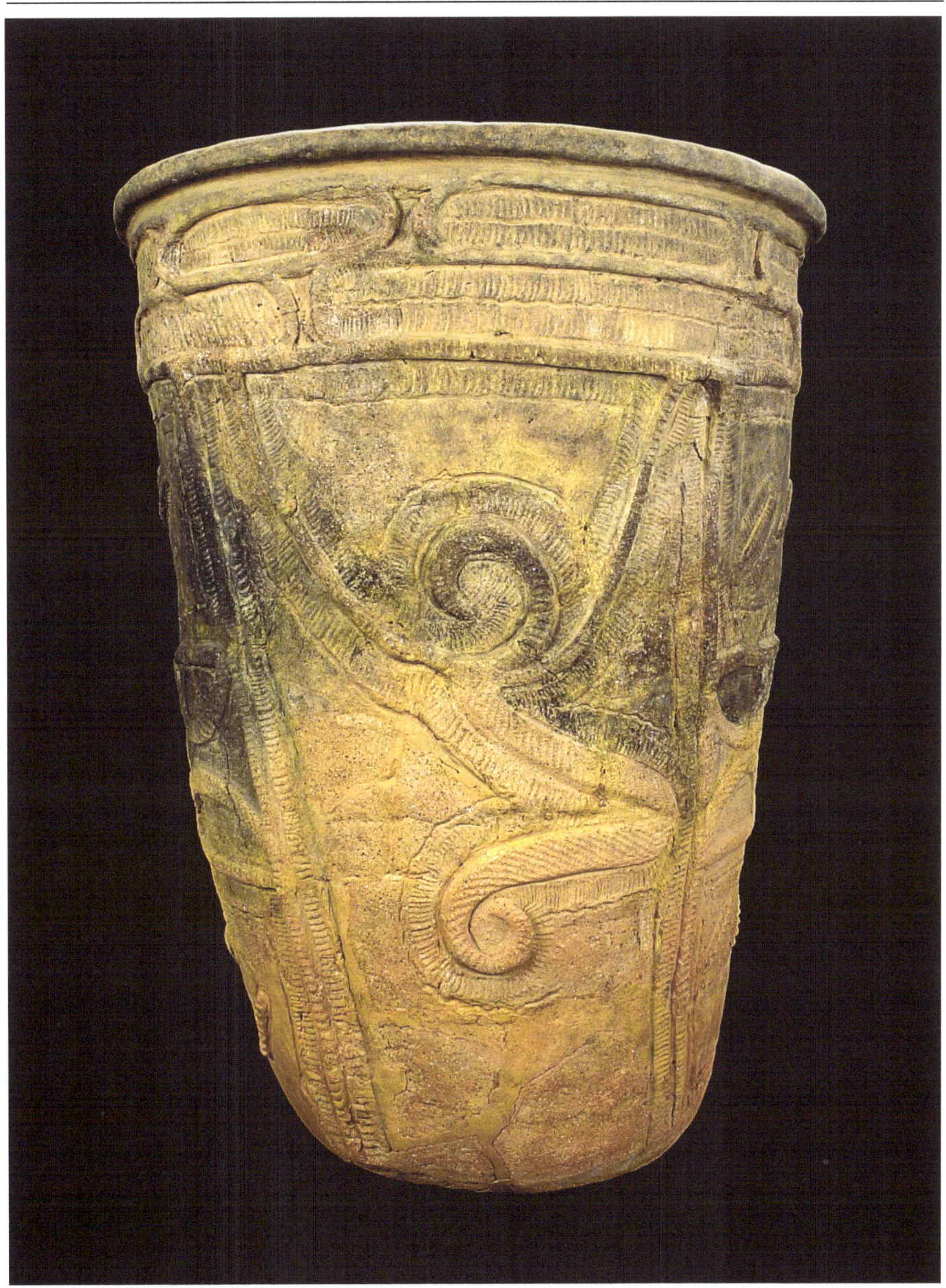

131

Deep bowl
Tounai ruins
Idojiri style I
Dwelling site #19
Excavated in 1962
Middle Jomon, Middle
4,500 years B.P.
37.2cm(H), 30.0cm(D)
"Idojiri Report" P.98, No.353,
"Tounai Report" P.337, No.279
ID-032

On the " く (ku)" shaped mouth of this deep bowl are arranged a pair of box-shaped protrusion and a lower roof-shaped protrusion. One of the box-shaped protrusions is largely damaged and restored in the same way as the side that remains. On the box-shaped protrusion, penetrates circle windows at the left and right, a circular hole is opened on the inside as well. Ring-shaped form that penetrates front and rear is arranged on the top of the head as well, and a snake head is drawn to the right down as it wraps around it. The part corresponding to the body is divided into two as it pinches the left circle window, and reaches to the inner and outer edges of the mouth edge. From the ring-shaped form of the top of the head hangs down a ridge line that forms a shape of upturned bracken at the top, and it folds back and rolls at the ridge band that is wound around the neck.

Lower roof-shaped protrusion is made by the outer edge of the mouth edges that roll and meet from the left and right. At this point is arranged a ridge band, and it makes a ring-shaped form by the outer edge, and it forms a shape of a hand of three fingers on the inside of the slope. On one of the pair of protrusions is engraved only a trigeminal-like pattern, but there are similar examples of expression that represent limb toes of a frog or a half-human and half-frog.

On the upper part above the ridge band of the neck some soots can be partially seen. On the inner wall that corresponds to the Jomon base of the body remains some scorch marks.

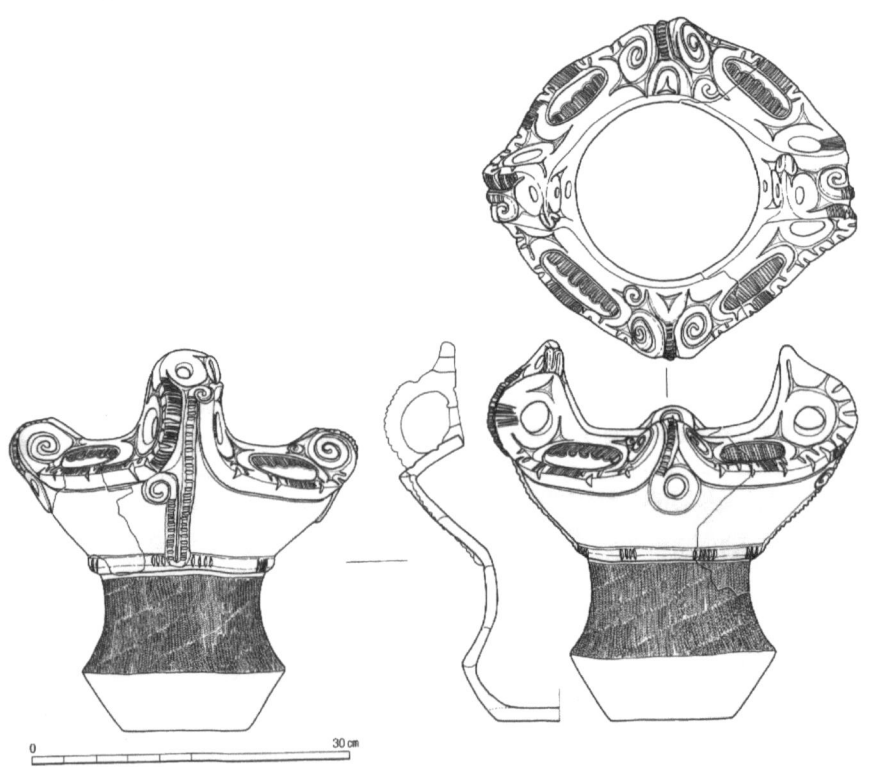

Deep bowl

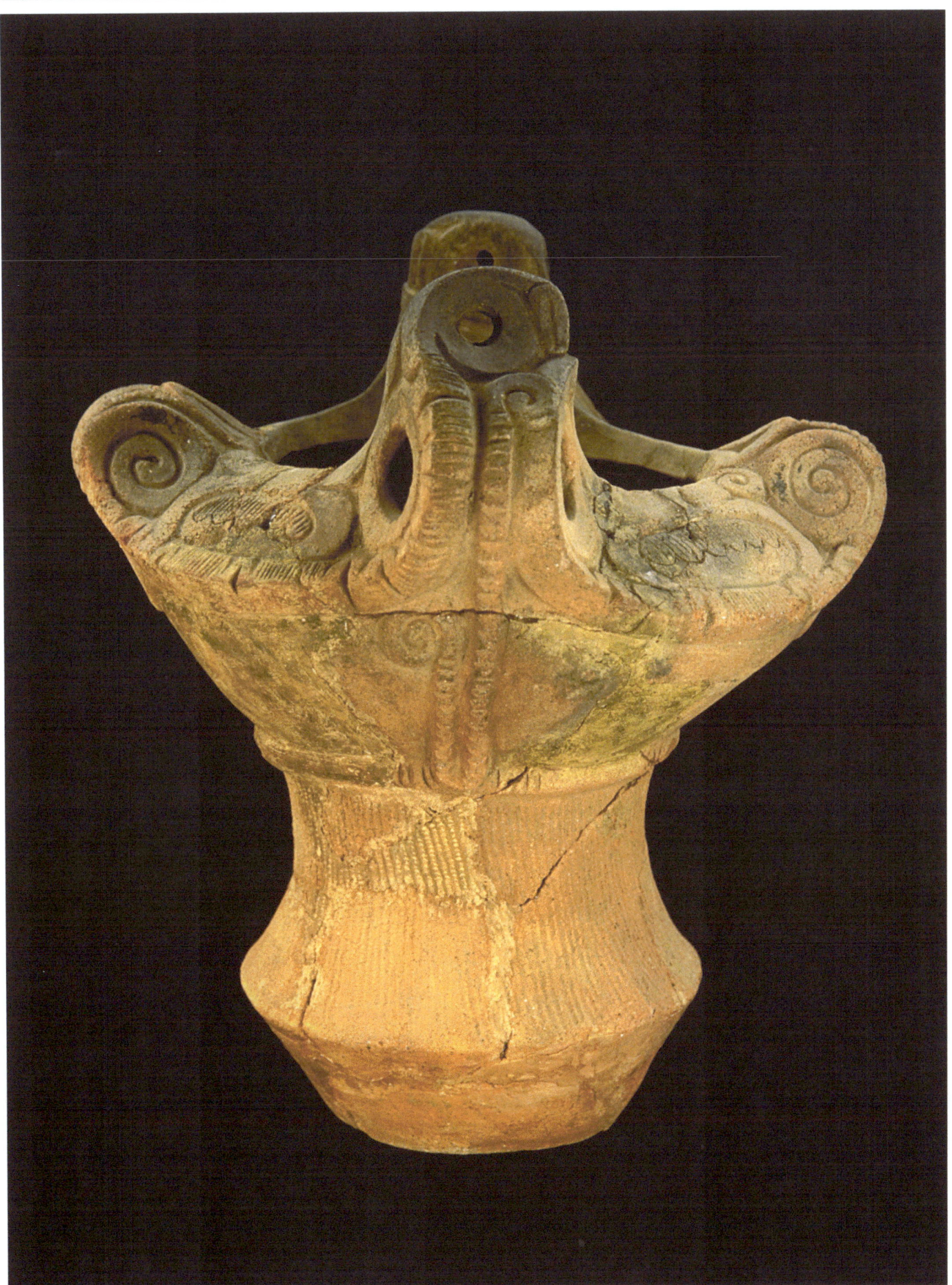

Deep bowl

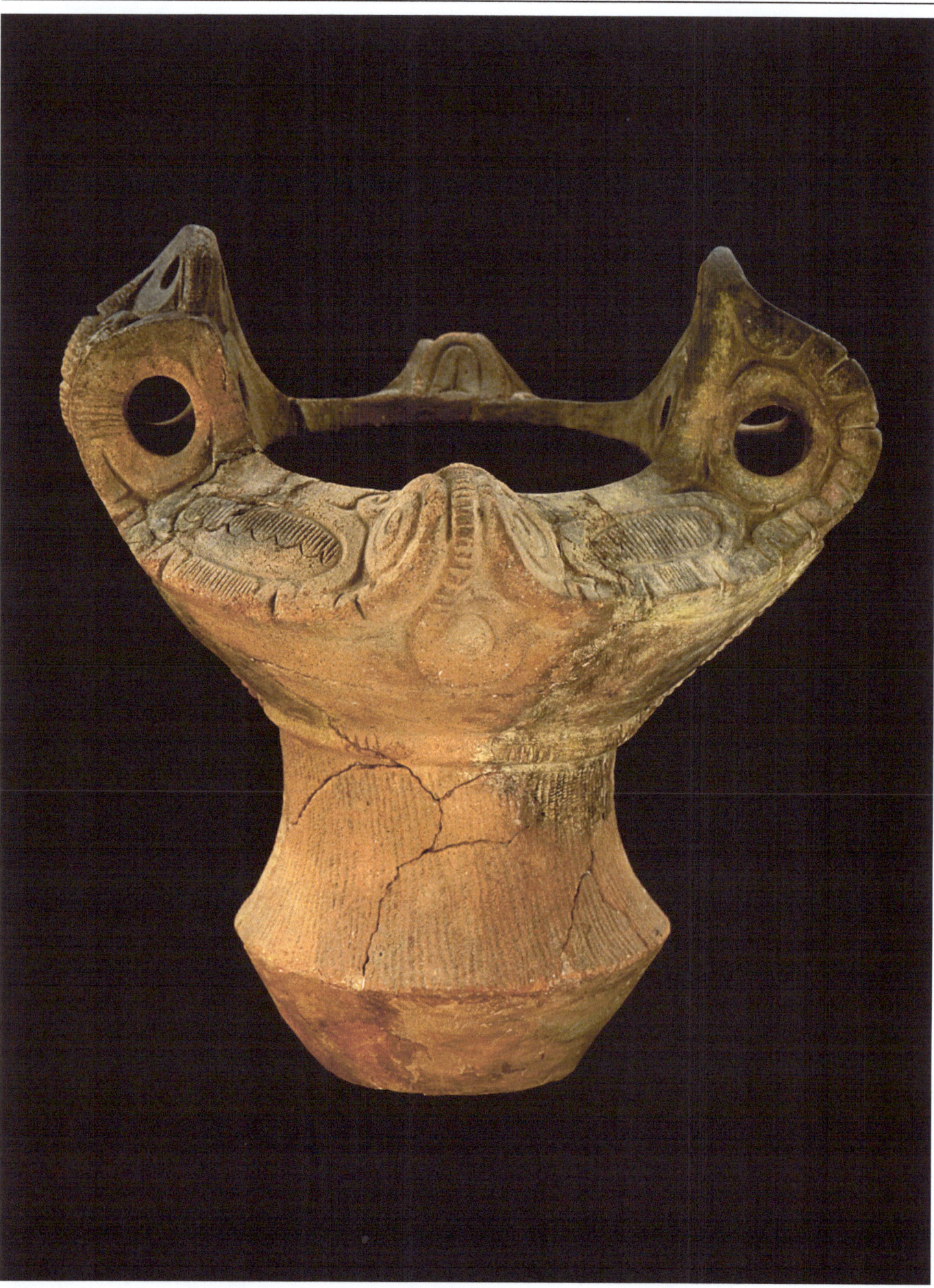

Deep bowl

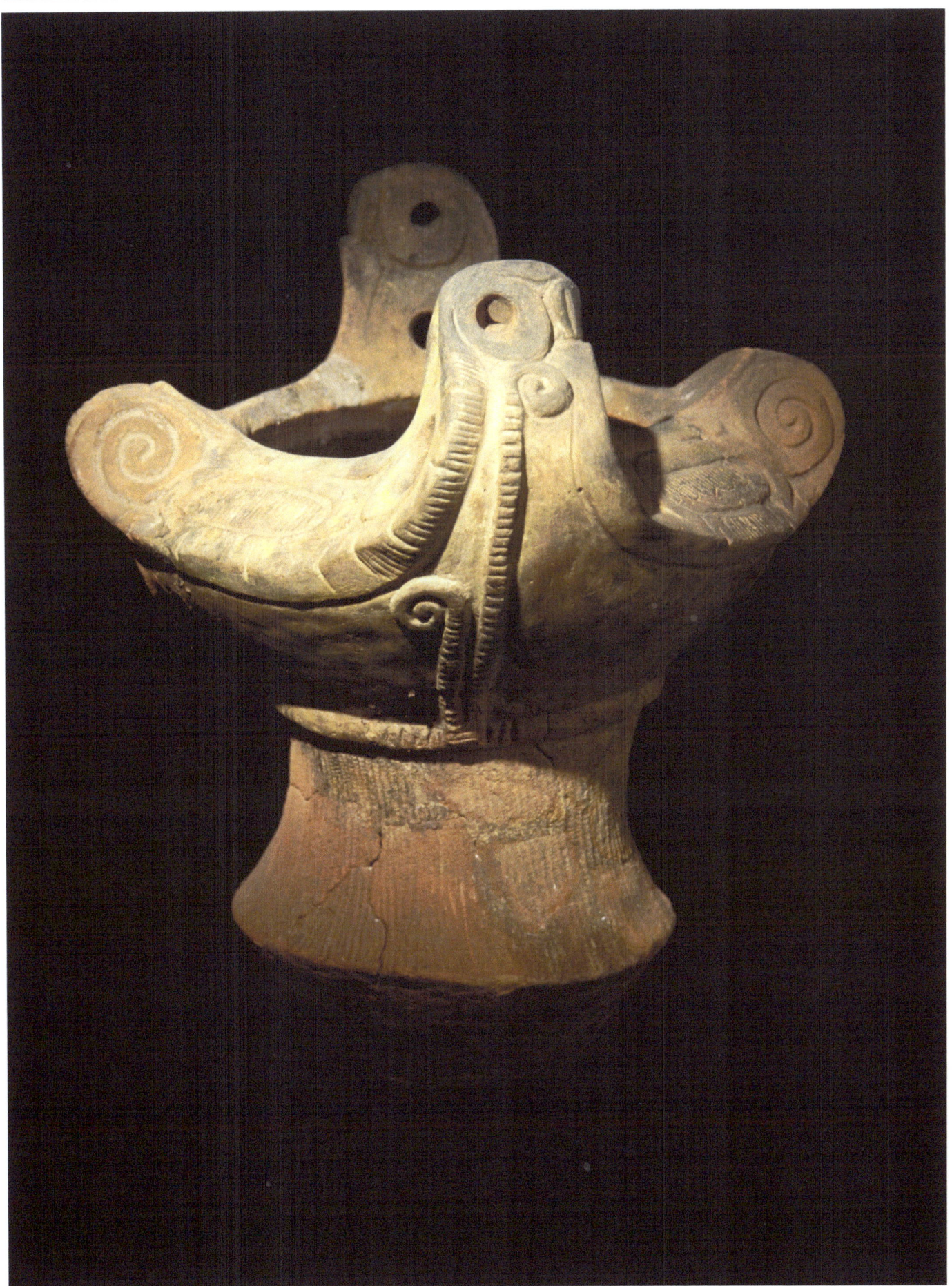

井戸尻の縄文土器　英語版　第 1 巻　藤内遺跡出土土器

編 著：長野県富士見町教育委員会 井戸尻考古館
英 訳：横越 徳男・深沢武雄・Freddy Bellouard
初 版：2015 年 10 月 21 日
印刷製本：CreateSpace, An Amazon.com Company, USA
発行所：株式会社テクネ / 東京都渋谷区宇田川町 2-1　Tel: 81-3-3464-6927　Fax: 81-3-3476-2372
　　　　e-mail:texnai @ texnai.co.jp　http://www.texnai.co.jp/POD/

© Fujimi-cho Board of Education,　Norio Yokogoshi, Takeo Fukazawa, Freddy Bellouard, 2015
ISBN 978-4-907162-96-2

Cover designed by Takeo Fukazawa

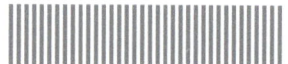 Texnai's On Demand Publishing via Amazon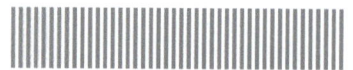

Publishing shortly

Jomon Potteries in Idojiri ②
Sori, Tatsuzawa, Nakahara Ruins
Compiled by Idojiri Archeological Museum
Translated by Norio Yokogoshi, Takeo Fukazawa, Freddy Bellouard

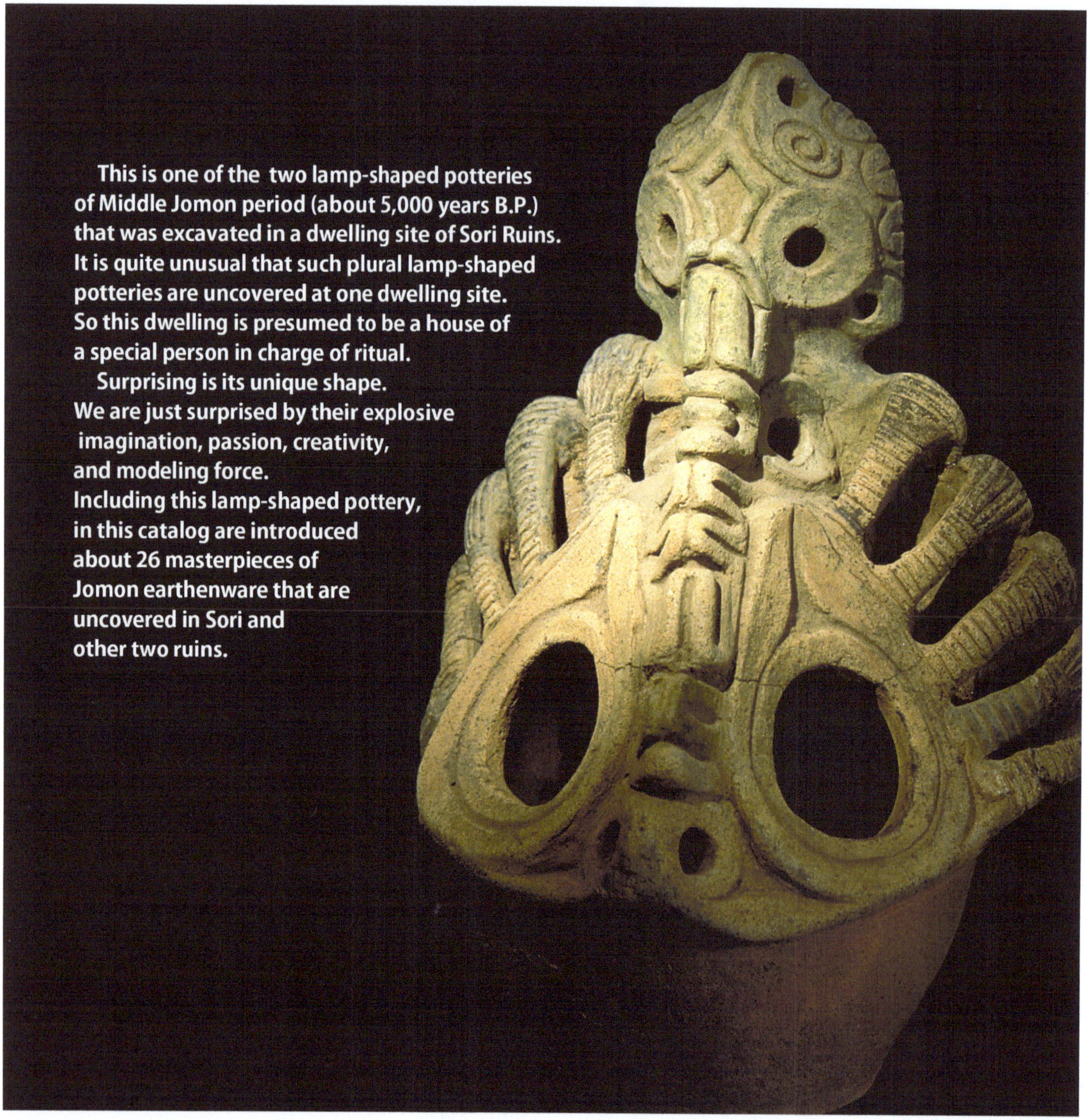

This is one of the two lamp-shaped potteries of Middle Jomon period (about 5,000 years B.P.) that was excavated in a dwelling site of Sori Ruins. It is quite unusual that such plural lamp-shaped potteries are uncovered at one dwelling site. So this dwelling is presumed to be a house of a special person in charge of ritual.

Surprising is its unique shape. We are just surprised by their explosive imagination, passion, creativity, and modeling force. Including this lamp-shaped pottery, in this catalog are introduced about 26 masterpieces of Jomon earthenware that are uncovered in Sori and other two ruins.

Texnai, Inc. / 2-1 Udagawa-cho, Shibuya-ku, Tokyo, Japan   Tel: 81-3-3464-6927   Fax: 81-3-3476-2372   info@texnai.co.jp

Texnai's On Demand Publishing via Amazon

Introduction to Palaeolithic Cave Paintings in Northern Spain

By César González Sainz, Roberto Cacho Toca, Takeo Fukazawa

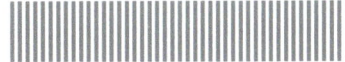

From 1997 to 2004, we executed Photographic VR shooting of Palaeolithic cave paintings in 23 major caves and about 150 Mobile Arts in 5 museums in Northern Spain as a co-project between the University of Cantabria, Spain and Texnai, Inc., Japan and the result was published in Spanish and English in 2003 by GOBIERNO de CANTABRIA as "ARTE PALEOLITICO EN LA REGION CANTABRICA, PALAEOLITHIC ARTS IN NORTHERN SPAIN" with a DVD ROM of the image database.
This book is published based on these book and database.

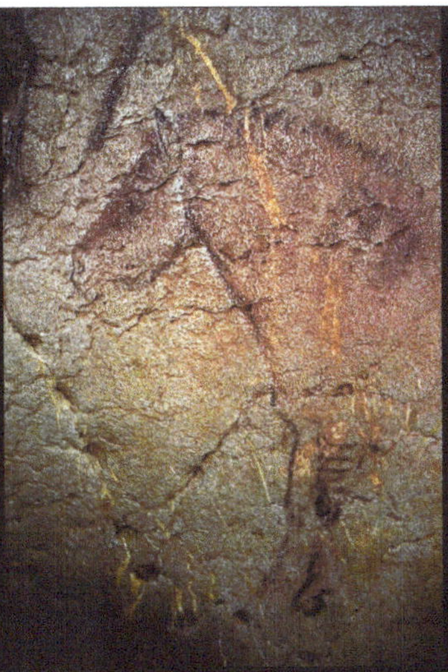

Photo below: Panel of Horses, Ekain Cave, Basque Country
Photo right: One of the most delicate and outstanding cave painting of Palaeolithic period in Europe

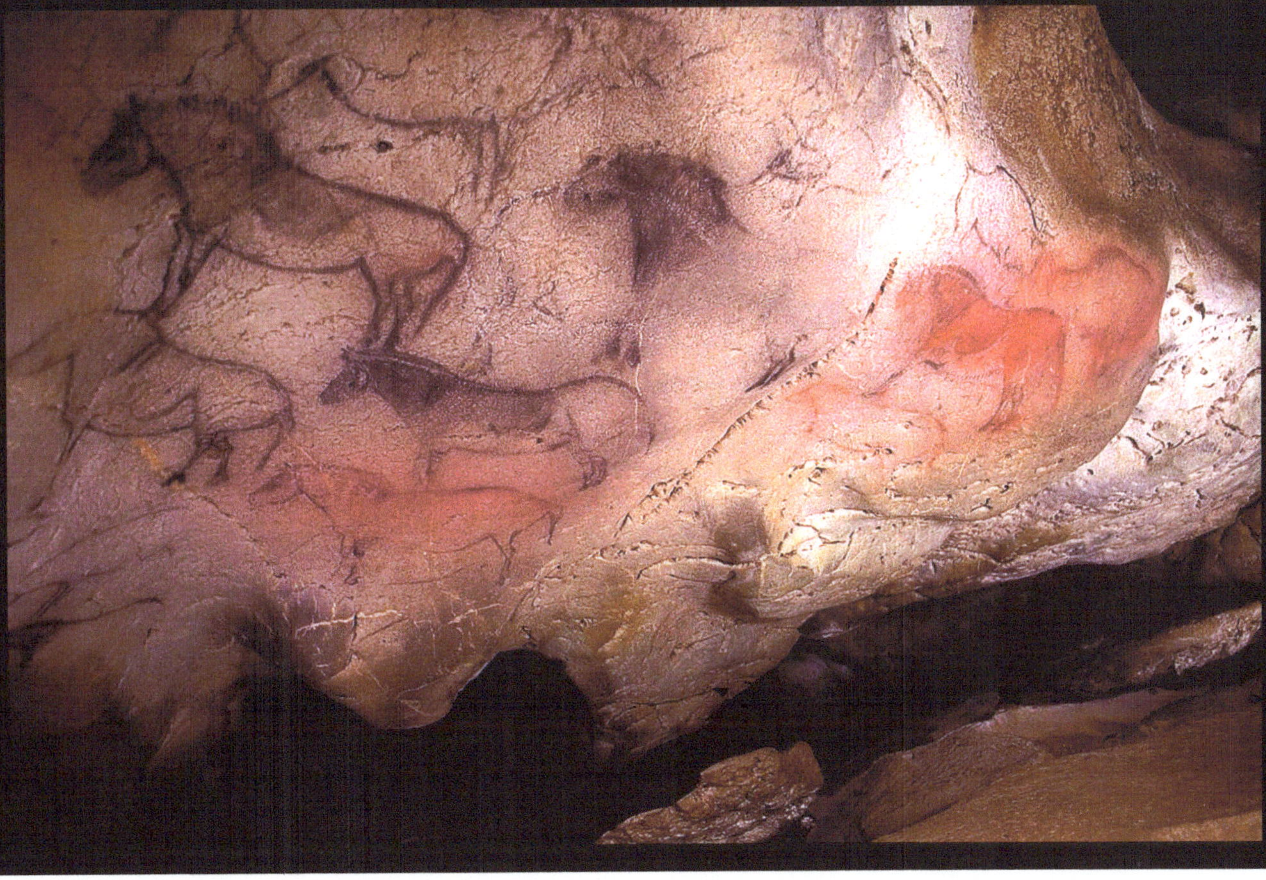

Texnai, Inc. / 2-1 Udagawa-cho, Shibuya-ku, Tokyo, Japan   Tel: 81-3-3464-6927   Fax: 81-3-3476-2372   info@texnai.co.jp

Texnai's On Demand Publishing via Amazon

Valley of the Deer Stones
Jargalantyn Am Site, Arkhangai, Mongolia

By Takeo Fukazawa

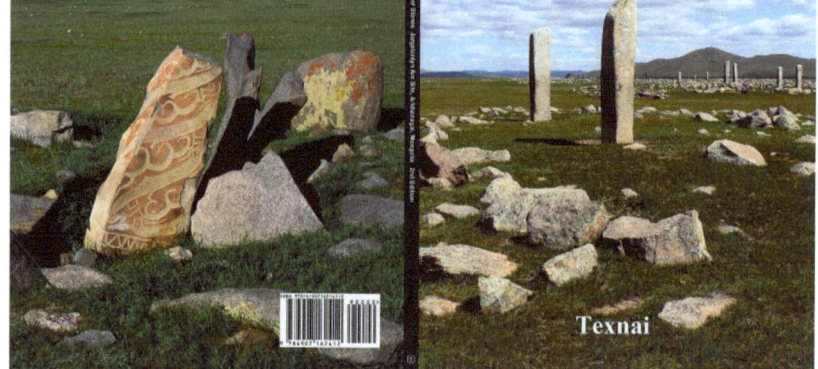

Over 550 monuments of the Bronze age that are called "Deer Stone" have been identified in the steppe of Mongolia.

Among those. it is said that the monuments at the Jargalantyn Am site in Arkhangai province is one of the largest deer stone ritual sites in existence, not only in Mongolia but also in all of Eurasia.

We introduce here almost all the deer stones of the Jargalantyn Am Site as well as those of Erdenetsogt site in Bayankhongor where we encountered with the beauty of the deer stones for the first time in 1996.

The Jargalantyn Am site is located in Jargalantyn Am of Khanui Bag, Arkhangai province. Archeologists first studied these monuments in the 1970's and archeological rearch determined that this is one of the largest deer stone ritual sites in existence, not only in Mongolia but also in all of Eurasia.

In addition to multiple Bronze Age deer stones, the site has approximately 1400 ritual offering structures. Located in the west portion of the site there is a Kheregsuur monument complex flanked to the east by sacrificial mounds and deer stones and to to the north by three square stone structures built by later cultures.

A Mongolian-Soviet Joint Historical and Cultural Expedition first excavated this site from 1989 to 1991, unearthing many important artifacts. It quickly became apparent to the team in 1989 that of the three larger square stone structures that were oriented in a line from east to west, the one to the west had been looted at an earlier period of time. Ten deer stones were found on the top of the ground and around the looted structure. During the 1989 excavation of the adjacent two square stone structures it was also determined that many other deer stones had been reused as building materials for their walls and interior, though these had also been looted at an earlier time. Eighty animal skulls were unearthed at the second square structure while almost 100 animal skulls complete with neck vertebrae were discovered in the third square stone structure. The skulls included five types of livestock (as domesticated dogs were rarely sacrificed) including four horse skulls complete with a pair of bronze bridles with leather pelham. Other artifacts included a cauldron and a spoon with a circular hole.

Based on these artifacts, these later square stone structures were dated between the 8th to 7th cnturies B.C. It is important to understand, however, that the deer stones used in the construction of these monuments date to an period a few hundred years earlier. samples of horse remains from mounds surrounding the deer stones yielded a date of 930-785 B.C.

The Mongolian-Soviet team did not return after 1989-1991 seasons, but the excavations which unearthed numerous deer stones were not refilled. As a result, deer stones were left lying on the ground and in the excavation pits, and they were continuously at risk to damage from weather, animals, vandals, and even theft.

In order to remedy the situation, the Mongolian tangible Heritage Association, through financial support from the United States Ambassador's Fund for Cultural Preservation, came in the summer of 2009 to preserve the deer stones in their original setting and bring awareness to the importance of this site to Mongolian heritage and the study of nomadic cultures.The project was undertaken by special researchers and restoration experts from the Institute of Archeology of Mongolian Academy of Sciences, the National Museum of Mongolia and materials conservator from Queen's University in Canada. The restoration team established the locations for the fallen stones based on the location of 3 deer stones that had survived in their original positions, as well as research on the cultural and religious practices of Bronze Age nomadic peoples. In total 24 deer stones were erected, allowing a glimpse into the landscape of the past (From the information panel).

Language:English; Color: Full Color with Bleed
Page Count:138; Binding Type::US Trade Paper; Trim Size::8.5" x 11"

Texnai, Inc. / 2-1 Udagawa-cho, Shibuya-ku, Tokyo, Japan　　Tel: 81-3-3464-6927　Fax: 81-3-3476-2372　　info@texnai.co.jp

www.ingramcontent.com/pod-product-compliance
Lightning Source LLC
Chambersburg PA
CBHW051148220526
45473CB00003B/703